Developing a New Christology for a Postmodern Culture

Developing a New Christology for a Postmodern Culture

Knowing Christ Today

Donald D. Phillips

LEXINGTON BOOKS/FORTRESS ACADEMIC
Lanham • Boulder • New York • London

Published by Lexington Books/Fortress Academic
Lexington Books is an imprint of The Rowman & Littlefield Publishing Group, Inc.
4501 Forbes Boulevard, Suite 200, Lanham, Maryland 20706
www.rowman.com

86-90 Paul Street, London EC2A 4NE

Copyright © 2025 by The Rowman & Littlefield Publishing Group, Inc.

All rights reserved. No part of this book may be reproduced in any form or by any electronic or mechanical means, including information storage and retrieval systems, without written permission from the publisher, except by a reviewer who may quote passages in a review.

British Library Cataloguing in Publication Information Available

Library of Congress Cataloging-in-Publication Data

Names: Phillips, Donald D., 1954- author.
Title: Developing a new Christology for a postmodern culture : knowing Christ today / Donald D. Phillips.
Description: Lanham : Lexington Books/Fortress Academic, [2025] | Includes bibliographical references and index. |
Summary: "From a semiotic description of secular, postmodern culture, the author distills its primary social values; and using a narrative approach to the Gospel's description of the person and work of Jesus Christ, constructs a Eucharistic Prayer that is accessible to inquirers, and equips church members with the vocabulary needed to share their faith"—Provided by publisher.
Identifiers: LCCN 2024041332 | ISBN 9781978716087 (cloth) | ISBN 9781978716094 (elecronic)
Subjects: LCSH: Christianity—Canada. | Jesus Christ—History and offices.
Classification: LCC BR570.P45 2025 | DDC 232—dc23/eng/20240920
LC record available at https://lccn.loc.gov/2024041332

∞™ The paper used in this publication meets the minimum requirements of American National Standard for Information Sciences—Permanence of Paper for Printed Library Materials, ANSI/NISO Z39.48-1992.

To Nancy
my life partner in the journey

Contents

Acknowledgments		ix
1	The Challenge	1
2	Understanding Local Culture(s)	20
3	Local (Contextual) Theology	33
4	"What about the impact of the Gospel in a local culture?"	46
5	Developing a Contextual Christology in a Postmodern Culture	81
6	Transformative Potential of Inculturated Texts in the Liturgy	116
7	Examining the Christology of Canadian Anglican Contemporary Eucharistic Prayers for Cultural Reflexivity	143
8	Bringing Together Culture and Christology in Proposed Eucharistic Prayer Texts	158
9	The Way Forward	180
Appendix: A New Eucharistic Prayer		187
Bibliography		191
Index		201
About the Author		203

Acknowledgments

I am grateful for all of the support and encouragement I received while writing this book. First, I want to express my gratitude to all those who guided and supported me in my doctoral thesis work which preceded this book: to my thesis advisors while I studied at Durham University, Gerald Loughlin, David Kennedy, and Paul Murray, and to the principal, David Wilkinson, and staff at St. John's College, Durham, as well as for the proofreading assistance given by Jane Barter, University of Winnipeg. I am also grateful for the gracious hospitality and support I received from my friends in Scotland, David and Heather Sceats, Tim and Irene Morris, and Susan Macdonald during my visits to the UK. I am grateful for the helpful information I received from my interviewees, the late William Crockett, and Richard Leggett, of Vancouver. I want to acknowledge Bishop Victoria Matthews (then of Edmonton, Canada) for encouraging me to begin this work, as well as David Widdicombe and my colleagues in the Anglican Diocese of Rupert's Land (Canada). I express my appreciation to Christopher Trott, sometime Warden of St. John's College, Winnipeg, for his encouragement and generous provision of office space during a sabbatical time, along with the assistance I received from St. John's College Library and from Hung-Hsueh Shao, in particular.

Finally, I wish to thank my family and acknowledge the sacrifices, on many levels, that they have made over many years. Without the selfless love, patience, support, and encouragement of my spouse, Nancy, none of this work would have been possible. For this, I am most grateful.

Quotations from the *Book of Alternative Services of The Anglican Church of Canada* and *Eucharistic Prayers, Services of the Word, and Night Prayer* are used with the kind permission of the General Synod of the Anglican Church of Canada.

Chapter 1

The Challenge

BACKGROUND

The motivation behind this work did not begin, initially, as a desire for some kind of academic pursuit. After some twenty-four years in ordained ministry in the Anglican Church of Canada, including five of those serving as the diocesan bishop of a Canadian diocese, it became (painfully) clear that the future, if not the present, state of the church and its membership was in serious difficulty. As I shared these concerns with others over a period of time, I developed a kind of parable—a scenario—that described the concern in concrete terms. This is the parable.

There is a regular member of one of our Christian churches living in one of the newer suburban neighborhoods of a North American city. The neighborhood is quite diverse and is made up of persons from a variety of cultural and religious backgrounds. The fact that this particular person is a committed church member is obvious to his neighbors as they see him and his family leave almost every Sunday morning to attend worship, and through the occasional "over the back fence" conversation, they are aware that he and his family are committed Christians and involved in their church's ministry and mission in the community.

One day, when our church member is working in the garden, one of his neighbors engages him in a more serious conversation. The neighbor admits that he knows almost nothing about the Christian faith or the person of Jesus Christ. He simply knows that the figure of Jesus Christ is central to the whole practice of Christianity. He asks our church member: "So tell me about this Jesus. Who is he and why is he so important? What did he do?" Our church member is caught off guard, but he knows that the question is sincere and that his neighbor has at least some interest in God and in spiritual things. So based on what he has gleaned from his experience of church, he shares these words: "Well—Jesus Christ was a unique individual who lived in Palestine about two thousand years ago. He was born into the Jewish faith but gradually both his Jewish followers and others, called Gentiles, realised that he was sent by God on a special mission for everybody—the whole human race. They realized that Jesus had come from God and eventually became aware that he was actually God in human form. He came and lived among us on the earth to show us what God was like. And then he was arrested, suffered and died for us in a horrible death on a cross so that our sins could be forgiven. God raised him up—brought him back to life—three days later, and now he is in heaven. And he has provided a way for us to live forever with him and with God." The neighbor listens politely but at about the point of the reference to "death on a cross so that our sins could be forgiven," and being "raised up" his eyes begin to glaze over. It is clear that he really has no idea what our church member is talking about and can't begin to see how this Jesus might have any connection to him, or why he should be interested in such.

Given my role in the Church, this seemed a little more like a "nightmare" when I ponder the future of our church. It is clear that, though our church member has a sincere, devout, Spirit-filled faith in Christ, he is not at all equipped to talk intelligently to *someone who has no knowledge or experience of the biblical Christian narrative.* The vast majority of our church membership has been equipped with "insider" language to speak about their faith. They are able to communicate effectively only to those who are already Christians, or at least have had considerable exposure to the salvation history story at some point in their lives. It is the reality of this parable and its implications for the church and the effective proclamation of the Gospel that is the primary motivation for this book. How can church members be equipped to share the Christian faith with persons who don't know "the Story?" In order to do so, they must be equipped with an understanding of the person and work of Jesus Christ—a Christology—that is expressed in contemporary terms. At the same time, they need to be able to speak about Jesus Christ in such a way that the engagement provides an appropriate opportunity for someone to encounter the risen Christ today.

This personal concern is coupled with the fact that the Christian churches in Canada have been in serious decline since the middle of the twentieth century. All of the major Protestant denominations have experienced significant decline as measured in terms of the declared membership of these denominations.[1] The membership of the Anglican Church of Canada in the twentieth century peaked at 1.4 million members in 1961, but had fallen to approximately 850,000 by 1985,[2] and by 2007, there were only 545,957 Anglicans on parish rolls.[3] Church rolls are helpful in determining the number of practicing members, but the Canadian national census, and as of 2011, the National Household Survey (NHS), reveals the number of Canadians who in any way self-identify with a particular religion or denomination, even if they are not active participants. Clarke and Macdonald, in their work published in 2017, showed that "Roman Catholics and Protestants from the country's five largest Protestant churches—Anglican, Presbyterian, United, Baptist, and Lutheran churches—made up over 90% of the Canadian population in the 1961 Census."[4] According to the 2011 NHS, Christians still are the majority in terms of declared religious affiliation, but they now comprise only 67 percent of the Canadian population as compared to 96 percent in 1961. And perhaps even more concerning is the rapid rise of those who declare themselves as having "No religion." This group accounted for less than 1 percent in 1961 and made up almost 25 percent of the Canadian population in 2011.[5]

Brian Clarke, in his follow-up book about the rise of the "No religion" group in Canada, reflects more broadly on the effect that the decline of church affiliates may have on Canadian society.

> Take, for example, the health of Canadian civil society. At this point, it would be helpful to take a step back in time. Historically, churches have functioned as the primary gateways to civil society. In the past, people first learned how to donate as members of church groups for children and youth and as they got older gained their first opportunity to volunteer and learn the skills essential for associational life in church and beyond.[6]

Clarke continues to expound on the various aspects of civil life that depended, either directly or indirectly, on the presence of vital local congregations for their health and well-being.[7]

What about the situation in the United States of America? Early in the last half of the twentieth century, it appeared as though America was not following the trajectory of decline that was beginning in Canada and was already well underway in Europe. Drawing on data from the General Social Survey, George Hawley, in his work on the decline of America's Christian denominations, reported that during the decades of the seventies and eighties, those who claimed a Christian identity remained at around 90 percent of the population.[8] But by the middle of the second decade of the twenty-first century, the situation of Christianity in the United States closely mirrored that in Canada. Using Pew Research Center data, Hawley writes,

> The percentage of Americans who identified as Christian had reached a new low: as of early 2015, barely seventy percent of Americans called themselves Christians. Meanwhile, the number of Americans who identified with no religion reached an all-time high (22.8 percent).[9]

In spite of a perceived difference in religiosity between Canada and the United States in the past, the present decline is affecting both countries in a similar manner.

Reginald Bibby, who has worked for over thirty years in the sociology of religion in Canada (and beyond), published *Fragmented Gods: The Poverty and Potential of Religion in Canada* in 1987. While he did not attempt to analyze the cause of the decline of the churches, he did compile a thorough description based on his research and proposed present and future trends for both Catholic and Protestant churches in Canada as a whole and also in the province of Quebec, which has shown different trends in the past due to its strong French Roman Catholic origins. Of particular interest to this work are Bibby's comments on the place of organized religion, and the Christian churches in particular, with respect to the local Canadian culture. He makes reference to a controversial book by Pierre Berton (a news media personality in Canada in the nineteen-sixties) entitled *The Comfortable Pew*.[10] While the book came out in response to an invitation from a concerned group of Anglican Church members who were aware of the declining influence of the church in society, the book is a scathing critique which highlights the many ways in which the Christian churches have not engaged the relevant issues in the changing culture of the time. Berton writes of his experience of attending a worship service in a Canadian Anglican church in the 1960s: "When one entered that church . . . one fled the contemporary world: most of what was said could just as easily have been said during the previous century."[11] As a result the churches have largely alienated themselves from the pertinent issues affecting the lives of Canadians.[12] One of the chapters of Berton's book is entitled "The Failure to Communicate," in which he makes this unsettling observation:

> It has become a cliché of our age . . . that the Church is no longer able to communicate with the people. If this is true . . . it is because the Church no longer understands either the people or the modern science of communication.[13]

Of particular relevance to this work, Berton makes this observation about the church's liturgical texts: "The Church's outer shell of liturgy . . . has become fossilized . . . When the language is unintelligible, is it any wonder that the Church's attempts to reach the ear of modern man [*sic*] have so often failed?"[14]

Some twenty years later, in response to Berton's critique of the church, Bibby states that "the Church was playing it safe and lagging behind culture . . . The Church of today has largely caught up with culture, but has in no way passed it. *The Comfortable Pew* has become The Cultural Pew."[15] Even though the church appears to have caught up to culture, "religion, Canadian style, is mirroring culture . . . culture leads, religion follows."[16]

It is not surprising then that the decline pertains not only to the number of members within the church itself. The importance of the church in the everyday life of Canadian society has diminished as well. The 1980 *Project Canada* survey asked Canadians how important a number of characteristics were in determining attitude and behavior. "Only 20% said that they thought religion was a very important determinant, compared with almost 50% for education and 30% for occupation."[17] Perhaps even more surprising is the fact that only 29 percent of the religiously committed surveyed thought that religion was an important factor in determining human attitude and behavior.[18] And even of more direct relevance were the responses in a 1985 survey of Anglicans in the Diocese of Toronto. The responses indicated that committed Anglicans viewed the church as important in issues of personal faith and family life, but its influence diminished in other areas of everyday life—"areas such as value formation and the perception of problems, in views of people and in social, economic, and political attitudes."[19] Sadly, at least for those who conceive of the church as being capable of proclaiming a life-transforming Word in and to the world, Bibby's research shows "how little Canadians who go to church differ from those who do not."[20] Even committed church members had low expectations of the impact of their Christian faith, individually and collectively, on much of their day-to-day life.

Both Bibby's research and Berton's critique examine Christianity in light of the Canadian cultural context in which it exists. What characterizes this Canadian culture that seems to have had such a strong impact on Christianity in Canada? Though we share the same continent with the United States of America and are proud of our large, undefended border, which encourages a great deal of interchange between our two countries, the nature of the federalism of these two "close friends and allies" is distinctly different.

> In the United States . . . the issue was how to create a large country without destroying individual liberty and local initiative. In Canada, the problem was different largely because the existence of a Canadian nation could not be taken for granted . . . Canada was to be a nation in which multiple identities and multiple loyalties could flourish within the framework of a common political nationality. Far from presupposing the nation, federalism created it.[21]

Fossum reaches an interesting conclusion about Canadian culture. Because Canada's federalism lacks any strong meta-narrative (except perhaps for an overarching honoring of diversity), he suggests that Canadian culture could be characterized as being "postmodern."[22] Given this identifier, a study of Canadian culture and its impact on the Christian church can be instructive for any Western, contemporary, postmodern context.

The lack of a strong, unifying meta-narrative poses an interesting challenge in trying to characterize Canadian culture. In some sense, it is a culture characterized by its regional diversity, even though this designation is dependent on one's perspective. If one is considering Canada from the viewpoint of an external observer looking at the whole, this would be a fair conclusion to reach. However, if one's vantage point is as an internal member of one of the regions, one might come to a different conclusion—that Canada is a kind of loosely connected confederacy of distinct cultural units. It has even been suggested that the term "nation" is inappropriate in a definition of Canada because of its multiple claims of language, culture, and ethnicity.[23]

Thomsen and Hale propose a similar view of Canada from their observations of Canadian literature and art. They suggest that Canadian society can be compared to a patchwork quilt—"a social space made up of a multiplicity of ethnic, cultural and social segments that collectively constitute the national quilt we may identify as Canada."[24]

In this book, Canadian culture, as an example of a Western postmodern context, will be described in terms of shared social values that have emerged from research surveys administered to samples from the country as a whole. But it is realized that these merely represent a kind of consensus from across the regions of the country rather than a full representation of the diversity present in Canada. In a similar manner, the Anglican Church of Canada, as an example of a mainline Christian denomination, will be treated as a "local culture"—even though it is composed of members in each of the country's "patch quilt-like" regions. This is justified not merely by the fact that these members are part of the same institution. As will be shown through a semiotic description of culture and the language texts that make it up, groups of persons share a common identity and view themselves as a distinct "local" culture because they are shaped by a common set of narrative texts. In the church, many of these narrative texts are liturgical texts used in common worship and, of particular importance, are the Eucharistic liturgies which are common across the Anglican Church of Canada.

However, one of the challenges for religious institutions in today's contemporary culture is something that Bibby refers to (from Charles Taylor) as the "coming of age narrative," where people feel they don't need to look beyond themselves for norms and values.[25]

> Once human beings took their norms, their goods, their standards of ultimate value from an authority outside of themselves; from God, or the gods, or the nature of Being or the cosmos. But then ... they realized that they had to establish their norms and values for themselves, on their own authority.[26]

Hence, it is no longer effective for churches to assume that they will grow in numbers and influence by simply encouraging persons to "join up." Instead, the church needs to be able to engage the individual in a way that directly makes an impact on their life and invites them to engage with the Christian proclamation because *they* have chosen to do so.

Perhaps even more challenging were Bibby's findings that most people who identify with the church have:

> no particular reason to associate what they want and need with what those groups [Catholic and Protestant churches] are doing. That has to change. People have to know what groups . . . are capable of having a positive impact on their lives and the people and issues they care about. Religious groups that can do those kind of things have futures. Those that can't or won't are going to fade away.[27]

This is a particularly discouraging observation for the Christian church. The church's self-understanding and, in fact, quite likely, a basic assumption about itself, is that it should be a resource for wrestling with the profound questions in people's lives. From Bibby's findings many, if not most, people do not make that assumption or have that expectation about the church.

Obviously, with the church's *raison d'être* being to proclaim the Gospel, it is the person of Jesus Christ whom the church has to offer to people. But introducing people to the person of Jesus Christ can even be hampered by the church's own teaching about the person and work of Jesus Christ—its Christology. In describing the Christology of the twentieth-century theologian Karl Barth, for example, Graham Ward highlights how the way in which God and Jesus Christ are perceived can be problematic, even in an otherwise orthodox Christology. In attempting to assert the wholly-otherness of God, even attempting to describe the person of Jesus (as God-incarnate) as being unsubstitutable can cause difficulties in understanding the human nature of Jesus.[28] If the "otherness" of Jesus Christ is over-emphasized, then "the work of Christ cannot be characterised in terms of the ordinary human operations of [the] world—its politics, economics, social and cultural milieu, his friends, his family, his enemies, his admirers." The result is that people are not able to relate their experience of humanity (theirs and others) to what they understand as Jesus' humanity—a connection which is essential to grasp the identity of Jesus Christ, and to lay hold of one's own identity in him. As will be shown, this identification is essential to accessing the saving work of Christ.

The problem here is not the unsubstitutable nature of Jesus Christ. Clearly, God did become incarnate in Jesus Christ in a particular time and place, and with a particular human identity in the midst of a particular *human culture*. Our challenge is to propose a Christology that upholds this orthodox understanding of Jesus Christ and at the same time enables persons to realize the connection between Jesus' humanity and their own.

On a pragmatic level, even if the church is able to proclaim the work and person of Jesus Christ in such a way that persons can make the essential identification with Christ, how is that understanding disseminated? Clearly, it is not sufficient for it to be carefully outlined in a theological journal, or even published in a book on Christology. If one wishes to share this Christological understanding with the church as a whole, one of the most obvious opportunities to come to know the person of Christ is in the context of Christian worship, particularly the Eucharist, in which Jesus promises to be present to those celebrating this sacrament. "The way we conceive of God, the way we understand the nature of the Christian community and the manner in which we engage the world [as Christians] are all shaped by our common liturgical life." Consequently, how we experience and proclaim the Gospel of Jesus Christ is formed by the liturgical texts we use.[29]

One of the contentions of this book is that all proclamations of the Gospel of Jesus Christ, and therefore all liturgical representations of his identity, are described and mediated through a particular culture. Clearly, the more closely the culture of the proclamation of Jesus Christ and the culture of the worshiper are similar, the more likely it will be that the worshiper will indeed come to know the identity of Christ and, thereby, experience the presence of Christ. However, as Bibby's research clearly shows, the church has struggled to even stay abreast of its local culture, let alone be the initiator of culturally sensitive proclamations about the God in Jesus Christ. According to Berton's view, the church has actually resisted engaging the pertinent issues of contemporary culture—at least in the middle of the twentieth century. Perhaps it is this "lack of understanding of what culture is, of what drives it, of what shapes it, and how it relates to our Christian faith,"[30] that continues to weaken and contribute to the decline of the church. It is the contention of this book that the proclamation of the Gospel, the understanding of the work and person of Jesus Christ, can only be proclaimed in and through a cultural context. If the church is not engaging its contemporary culture, then it is proclaiming the Gospel in a previous, or now foreign, cultural context.

Therefore, in this work, I will develop a Christology that will be able to "converse" with its cultural context—hence the term "local Christology." In order to effectively communicate this Christology to the church membership, this local Christology will be employed in forming Eucharistic Prayer texts which would be heard on a regular basis in Sunday worship, in order to enable members of that local culture—in this case, the Anglican Church of Canada—to be embraced by, and to embrace, the identity of Jesus Christ.

OVERVIEW OF THE PROJECT

The notion of and understanding around "culture" has evolved and developed considerably in the past couple of centuries. But the reality of the particularity of context is evident even in the Gospel texts themselves. In the Gospel texts, the person and work of Jesus Christ were manifested in a particular cultural context. Given the relevance of cultural context to the Gospel writings, this book explores the development of the notion of culture by examining its early roots, the impact of anthropology on the understanding of culture in the twentieth century, and the contemporary (postmodern) critique of many of the assumptions of the earlier understandings of culture and their ability to be described and assessed. Utilizing the work of Kathryn Tanner in particular, cultures are shown to be dynamic (constantly evolving) as opposed to static entities—therefore requiring one to come to an understanding of the processes that formed them and continue to reform them. In addition, the notion of cultures being monolithic, internally consistent wholes is challenged. This realization of internal non-consistency leads one away from attempting to produce scientific models for culture and instead to concentrate on ways of describing cultures, as proposed by the work of Clifford Geertz. A semiotic method of description, which views culture as being a network of verbal and nonverbal messages that together create systems of meaning, is proposed based particularly on the work of Robert Schreiter. In a semiotic method of description, the interaction of these signs, groups of signs that mutually define each other, and the "rules" or codes which govern their interaction come together to form a culture. Attention is also drawn to distinguishing between *etic* perspectives (those describing a culture other than their own) and *emic* perspectives (those describing their own culture). The aspects that need to be considered in describing and coming to understand a culture—the location of verbal and nonverbal cultural texts and the rules that influence their interaction—are discussed along with Geertz's approach of "thick description." The goal of this kind of cultural description is to enable one to "converse" about the person and work of Jesus Christ with members of a particular cultural community—particularly through the medium of liturgical texts—so that they become open to the same profound significance that the original witnesses and writers experienced in the biblical texts.

The relationship between culture and theology is then explored, beginning with the contemporary realization that theology itself is actually a form of cultural activity. From this follows the notion that all theology is *contextual*, which is introduced and explored, particularly employing the work of Kathryn Tanner, Robert Schreiter, and Stephen Bevans. Schreiter's approach of all theologies beginning as "local theologies" is discussed and the resulting conclusion that certain tenets of systematic theology, which were thought to be universal and "a-cultural," originated as expressions in a regional culture. The challenges this presents to establishing *catholicity* among local theologies are then explored.

The internal aspects of the Christian Gospel, including the particularity of the incarnation itself; the heavily contextual nature of God's history of salvation as recorded in scripture; the sacramental nature of life including signs and symbols; the climactic example of the incarnation; and the catholicity of the church, all illustrate the validity of a contextual approach. The result of this approach will reveal that the true locus of theology needs to shift. Contextual theology puts the construction of theology into a Christian way of life, and therefore to local cultural communities. Hence, the role of academic theology shifts to reflecting upon and evaluating social practices and the beliefs, symbols, and values that inform them.

It will also be shown that establishing traditional "truth claims" is neither straightforward nor particularly relevant, since in a semiotic understanding of culture, the language that is used to express such claims is part of the sign system of that culture. Therefore, the primary test for "truthfulness" is within the cultural community itself. The notion of whether one can refer to a "Christian culture" when attempting to describe Christian identity proves not to be a helpful construct, and instead, one should describe Christian identity from the ways in which the Christian community uses and understands particular cultural forms.

The relationship between culture and theology is shown to be a reflexive one. *Reflexivity* (the mutual impact of engaged entities upon each other) and its significance on both theology and culture are discussed, with particular attention being paid to the interaction of language (as a cultural sign) within and between cultures. Given this characteristic of reflexivity, the principle of inculturation is discussed based on the question, "How does one genuinely enable a local, indigenous, expression of the Christian faith to take root in another culture?" The importance of inculturation is discussed with particular reference to the work of Aylard Shorter and with respect to inculturation in developing liturgical texts to the work of Anscar Chupungco. True inculturation is shown to involve a reciprocal relationship between the Christian proclamation and the local culture.

The principles and characteristics of the interaction of culture and theology are put into practice. The culture of the Anglican Church of Canada is employed as the "local" culture. A justification for recognizing the Anglican Church of Canada as a distinct cultural entity is presented while recognizing that this is a non-homogeneous culture and that any description of this culture will simply be a statement about only the dominant aspects of this cultural group.

As a historical starting point, the mid-twentieth-century work of H. Richard Niebuhr in *Christ and Culture* and his model of five types of interaction between Christ and Culture is explored. Niebuhr begins by attempting to define "Christ" in this engagement and not merely the Christian religion. He admits that the Gospel accounts, and theological descriptions based on these narratives, are all slightly different portraits but that they clearly describe one and the same person. Niebuhr defines culture in a way that is typical of a later twentieth-century understanding of culture as being non-homogeneous and internally dynamic in nature.

Each of Niebuhr's five types (Christ against culture; Christ of culture; Synthesis of Christ and culture; Christ and culture in paradox; and Christ, the transformer of culture) is discussed. Additionally, some of the critiques of this typology are presented, revealing the limitations of employing the typology in real encounters. In response to some of Niebuhr's critics, the importance of treating Niebuhr's five types as *ideal* types and not accurate descriptions of any particular real historical encounter is emphasized. The conclusion of this discussion is the realization that the fifth type (Christ the Transformer of Culture) is best treated as the culmination of the other four types. The fifth type best represents the actual processes that take place in history as all human cultures are brought into congruence with the reign of God in Christ.

Working from a position of Christ as the transformer of culture, the relationship between the culture of the Anglican Church of Canada and the liturgical texts of its Eucharistic prayers is explored to see whether some of the descriptive characteristics of the church's culture (its values and priorities) are reflected in the texts of the Eucharistic prayers. This is a type of test for inculturation—assessing whether the cultural values of the contemporary church are reflected in its Eucharistic rites. Employing Niebuhr's fifth type (Christ, the transformer of culture) is shown to be particularly appropriate in light of the hope and expectation of the members of the church culture that this engagement would result in the transformation of their lives into greater congruence with Christ. Similarly, the Eucharistic Prayer texts are particularly helpful instruments to present the proclamation of Christ to those gathered in worship.

This exploration begins by examining pertinent aspects of the Anglican Church's history in Canada in order to compile a description of the church's culture. Drawing on the historical development of its internal structures, as well as descriptions offered both by members and researchers from outside the denomination, the conclusion is reached that, for at least the majority of the twentieth century, there is little discernible difference between the culture of the Anglican Church of Canada and that of Canada as a whole. The culture of the Anglican Church of Canada is found to be marked by a concern for *inclusion* (including *feminism*), *tolerance*, *democratic processes, the environment, poverty, racism, war*, and a heightened awareness of *those on the margins* of society.

The Eucharistic Prayers of the Anglican Church of Canada are then examined for signs that contemporary culture is reflected in the prayer texts. Given that cultures can really only be compared and contrasted, the texts of the Eucharistic Prayers of the 1962 and 1985 liturgical rites are compared against the prayer text of the 1918 Rite (which is treated as being a-cultural because of its almost three-hundred-year history and its source being from outside of Canada) for signs of these characteristic emphases, and therefore for evidence of inculturation.

The Eucharistic Prayer of the 1962 rites shows only very marginal evidence of inculturation. In considering the Eucharistic Prayers of the 1985 *Book of Alternative Services*, even the introductory material at the beginning of the Eucharistic rite is evidence of the attempt to make the texts more accessible to members of contemporary culture. Each of the prayers follows what has become a traditional (Antiochene) structure, whose narrative sections provide opportunities to highlight the values of the local culture. Each of the six Eucharistic prayer texts is examined for evidence of the cultural values of the Anglican Church of Canada as observed in the latter half of the twentieth century. These prayers contain texts that allude to the cultural values of inclusion (particularly of women), democratic processes, environmentalism, concern for those in poverty, and awareness of those on the margins of society. This relationship between the church culture and its liturgical texts is further confirmed by examining the official policy and program decisions of the church's senior legislative body, which also reflect these same cultural concerns.

Having determined the presence of a reflexive relationship between the church's liturgical forms and its local culture, the focus shifts to exploring a culturally appropriate expression of Christology and its manifestation in the Eucharistic Prayers of the church. The work of the twentieth-century historical theologian, Hans Frei, with its "call" back to the primacy of the biblical text, and Frei's hermeneutical approach to biblical texts, is employed to formulate a local Christology. Two other twentieth-century theologians had a strong influence on Frei. From Karl Barth, Frei embraced the conviction of the absolute freedom of God in the incarnation of Jesus Christ as well as the unsubstitutable uniqueness of Jesus Christ. The other major influence in Frei's work came from H. Richard Niebuhr, from whom he acquired an interest in human history and, in particular, the details of Jesus's life and the importance of the Gospel narratives. From both of these theologians, Frei developed an appreciation for the integrity of the biblical narratives.

Frei's hermeneutical approach of treating the narrative texts of the Gospels as "realistic narratives" intended to describe the identity of Jesus Christ through what he does and says, and what others do to him and how he responds—formal description—is employed in constructing the Christology.

Frei's insistence on allowing the Gospel narratives to speak for themselves—to provide a description of Jesus Christ—and not to look for or expect any external referent was key to his Christological approach.

In Frei's work, there were three other key hermeneutical pieces. The first of these, as acquired from Barth and the work of Erich Auerbach, was employing figural interpretation to link events within scripture, and especially beyond it, to our individual lives. Frei's purpose here was not so much to try and establish figural linkages between particular scriptural texts, as it was to demonstrate how events within scripture are in a figural relationship with events in history and particularly in our own lives.

The second of these, drawing on the work of Brevard Childs, was giving primacy to the *sensus literalis* interpretation of texts within the community. The primacy of the scriptural story, with its objective representation of the identity of Jesus Christ and its dominant interpretation by the community, actually governs and shapes that community and, in this case, its understanding of Jesus Christ. Frei insisted that the narratives did not refer to anything beyond themselves.

The final hermeneutical principle, based in part on a figural interpretation of scripture and historical events, is the providential ordering of history. Frei was clear that he was not able to prove the providential ordering of history—in part because we are still part of that evolving history and are, therefore, incapable of stepping outside of it. Instead, Frei proposed that, instead of the world of scripture being put to the test to see if it could "fit" into the rational world of modernity, the direction of exchange is trying to see if the individual could fit their lives into the world as revealed in scripture. By reversing the direction of this "operation" Frei is able to root the person and work of Jesus Christ in the history of the world.

Holding to Frei's (and Barth's) conviction of the unsubstitutability of Jesus Christ, the resulting Christology is built on the premise that Christ's identity and presence are given together. Therefore, the particularities of Jesus's life, death, and resurrection are all of key importance in describing his identity (and therefore realizing his presence). Christology is built entirely upon the person who emerges from the Scripture narratives themselves and not from any external referents. It accommodates "the powerlessness of Jesus as God incarnate on the cross" with the omnipotence of God, by showing that Jesus' obedient submission is also a part of the revelation of God's purposes and character. The challenge of the reality of the resurrection is explained by showing that it is inconceivable, given the revelation of Jesus in the narratives, to think of him as not being raised. In addition, the internal evidence of the narratives themselves asking the question, "Did this really happen?" demonstrates that the Christian faith has a historical consciousness of its own.

The critiques of Frei's approach are also discussed. George Hunsinger challenges Frei's claim to a "high" Christology. Hunsinger concludes that it is a relatively "low" Christology—one in which the divinity of Christ is not made as clear as it could be. It is shown that Hunsinger's concern arises more because of his desire to focus on ontological categories arising from traditional Chalcedonian texts and attempting to apply those to Frei's Christology. Frei takes a novel approach in attempting to address the historical reality of the resurrection. It is shown that, in order for Jesus to be fully the person that the Gospel narratives portray him to be, he must be resurrected. The emphasis, as Frei claims, of the Gospel narratives is that the resurrected Christ is one and the same person as the crucified Christ.

This is followed by a discussion of some of the "unresolved issues" in Frei's Christological approach—particularly pertaining to the historicity of the resurrection and the expressed need to be able to make culturally independent truth claims. These are responded to by showing how Frei actually moves inside the narrative text to demonstrate the narrative's concern about historical reality and that this is the only possible approach given the non-referential nature of those narratives. The concern about making culturally independent truth claims is dealt with by recalling that language itself is culturally dependent and, therefore, the only such truth claim that could be made about a non-externally referential event would come from within the particular worldview of the text.

The operation of this Christology is then demonstrated where the individual, in the context of a Christian community, and with the benefit of the sacramental presence of Christ, patterns their life after Christ's. It is made clear that as members of the Christian community focus on the identity of Jesus Christ, they discover, in this "history-like" figure, one whose identity is inseparable from God, and one who stands at the center of human history. Ultimately, the acceptance of this historical claim is a matter of faith. As members of the Christian community are able to see in Jesus both the divine savior and their own humanity, they are able to lay hold of, or receive, their identity in Christ, which is the manifestation of Christ's salvation. Ultimately, what is unique about this among other contemporary Christologies is that it neither begins with soteriology nor is "apologetically driven."

In order to establish the transformative potential of an "inculturated" Christology, the importance and potency of narrative, not only in written texts but in the lives of individuals and the communities of which they are part, are discussed. Building on the transformative potential of the encounter between an individual (and their personal narrative) and the Christian community patterning their lives after Christ and thereby, with the grace of the Holy Spirit, being able to manifest the identity (and presence) of Christ, the challenge of developing liturgical texts to give expression to this task is explored. The intent of these texts is to enable the worshiping community to engage in *anamnesis* of God's saving work in Jesus Christ, as well as in *prolepsis* of the final consummation of that work in the eschaton. And what is referred to as "Guardini's challenge" (from the Roman Catholic theologian, Romano Guardini, to Vatican II's *Constitution on the Liturgy*)—the possibility of this actually taking place in the late twentieth-century worshiping community—is discussed, referring to the approach of David Stosur. Stosur proposes adopting different expectations from liturgical texts in the act of worship. Contrary to the traditional approach of liturgical texts ensuring "uniformity" of worship (and therefore, belief), Stosur proposes a narrative approach to texts with their ability to encompass and even encourage diversity. It is shown that the ability of the liturgical text to interact with the unique perspective of each worshiper, allowing them to locate their narrative in the narratives of the liturgy, actually enables the transformative encounter to take place. Hence, the importance of local Christologies in local cultures being able to be incorporated into local liturgical texts—inculturated—becomes clear. A discussion of the work of the Lutheran World Federation on worship and culture in the closing decade of the twentieth century is presented and parallels are drawn between the findings of these reports and Niebuhr's typology.

In order to appreciate the global nature of this approach to inculturation and liturgical texts, early examples of liturgical inculturation in the Anglican Communion are discussed with reference to the Church of South India and the Church of Kenya in particular. In the discussion of the liturgy of the Church of South India, some of the complexities of the interaction between previous cultural influences and present-day influences are highlighted. Examples of inculturated texts are given for both the Church of South India and the Church of Kenya rites. Eventually, these early experiments permeated the Anglican Communion and some of the responses from around the Anglican Communion are presented.

In addition, the role of Vatican II in catalyzing liturgical revision and a growing awareness of the importance of inculturation is presented along with a discussion of the impact on the revision of the Roman Rite. The impact of Vatican II and the Roman revisions on Eucharistic prayers in the Church of England and the Anglican Church of Canada in the latter part of the twentieth century is also examined. While the prayers of these churches do show significant evidence of inculturation, this inculturation is better understood as being into contemporary "church culture" more than the culture of the societies in which these churches exist. In the case of the Church of England (*Alternative Services Book*) the revisions are shown to be primarily a response to the "theological church culture." In the Anglican Church of Canada (*Book of Alternative Services*) the response is better described as a response to the "liturgical and ecclesiological church culture" of the day.

However, from the final decade of the twentieth century, the liturgies of the Anglican Church in New Zealand, England, and Canada reveal clear evidence of a shift in the focus of this inculturation—showing more awareness of the local culture of the community and not simply the church. In all of these revised liturgies, there is clear evidence of a concern for inculturation in the wider community beyond the church—particularly in the introductory pieces which offer thorough explanations of even why one worships, how best to use the liturgy, and what is the significance of each major piece of the liturgy. In addition, the relevant revisions in both the Eucharistic Prayers of the Church of England's *Common Worship*, and the Canadian Supplementary Eucharistic Prayers are discussed as examples of inculturated texts. For both the *Canadian Book of Alternative Services* (1985) and the Supplementary Eucharistic Prayers (1998), these conclusions are supported by verbatim portions from interviews of persons directly connected with the compilation of these texts. One example of an Anglican Eucharistic Prayer text inculturated from a First Nations (Indigenous) culture in Canada is discussed.

Having explored the cultural impact on Eucharistic Prayer texts, the engagement of the inherent Christologies in the Eucharistic Prayers of the Book of Alternative Services and the three Supplementary Prayers with the local (Canadian) culture is explored. In order to assess the appropriateness of the Christology, the three criteria developed by Roger Haight are used—faithfulness to the tradition, intelligibility in today's world, and empowerment of the Christian life. This third criterion would be measurable only by carrying out a study with a particular Christian community over time, and is, therefore, beyond the scope of this work.

These criteria are amalgamated with the key aspects of the Frei-inspired Christology developed and, together with reference to Niebuhr's typology, the Christologies inherent in the six Eucharistic Prayers of the *Book of Alternative Services* are discussed in detail. It is shown that in all of these Christologies the saving work of Christ is presented not as a forensic transaction but rather as a transformative event. From the work of William Crockett, the three Christological images (vicarious suffering, sin offering, and divine deliverance) that are present in these prayers are discussed, and it is shown that one or more of these images form the soteriological basis in each of the prayers.

Each of the Eucharistic Prayers is briefly examined and its historical development and inherent Christology discussed. The result of this examination reveals that, in a manner similar to the examination of the *Book of Alternative Services* (BAS) Eucharistic Prayers and Canadian culture of the time, the primary motivation behind these revised texts was a response to the "Anglican Church culture" of the day—reflecting the desire to provide a richer biblical and theological "diet" for the worshiping community. An analogous examination of the three Supplementary Eucharistic Prayers, while clearly revealing a greater inculturation of the contemporary social values, results in a similar conclusion to the BAS in regard to the Christologies inherent in them.

Progressing from this exploration, new proposed Eucharistic Prayer texts are then developed. The proposed prayer texts follow an Antiochene structure primarily because of the several opportunities this structure provides to include narrative material describing the creative and redeeming acts of God, the life and ministry of Jesus, and the ongoing work of the Spirit in transforming the world toward the consummation of the reign of God. In order to satisfy Frei's emphasis on an objective presentation of the identity of Jesus Christ, and Haight's "faithfulness to the tradition" criterion, the narrative images are all chosen from scripture. The challenge, then, is to determine appropriate cultural values which are both intelligible to contemporary Canadian culture and faithful to the values of the Gospel, in order to present theology and culture as being in a reflexive relationship. In order to derive these values, two studies in Canadian social values are used and their findings discussed, along with some critique of the work. Both studies generated five appropriate Canadian social values:

- Personal autonomy—particularly as expressed in the freedom to choose communities, associations, and commitments
- Inclusion—particularly as it pertains to women in society
- Tolerance (a natural outcome of personal autonomy and inclusiveness)
- Democratic processes (a natural necessity with personal autonomy and inclusiveness)
- Concern for the environment

These are combined with three additional values that emerged from the culture of the Anglican Church by the close of the twentieth century:

- Poverty
- Racism (may be related to inclusion and tolerance)
- War and peace

These eight values are then interpreted through appropriate scriptural narrative texts and incorporated into the proposed Eucharistic Prayer. The three narrative sections of the Antiochene structure are utilized under their traditional headings:

- Thanksgiving for creation and redemption
- Thanksgiving for the life, ministry, death, and resurrection of Jesus Christ
- Anamnesis and Epiclesis

The proposed prayer is also formatted in such a way as to demonstrate some of these observed social values.

Employing the "Frei-inspired" Christology developed, the proposed prayer is designed in such a way that the worshiper is confronted with the divine love and power of God in the person of Jesus—exemplified in his earthly ministry and especially in his death and resurrection. They receive the truth that this divine love and power have accomplished the necessary transformation of humanity, including their own, and that the Spirit continues to work toward the complete transformation of creation, expressed through the closing supplications of the prayer. This is congruent with the understanding of Niebuhr's Type 5—Christ the transformer of culture. These supplications also use images that are both faithful to the Gospel and reflect the important values of the local culture.

NOTES

1. Reginald W. Bibby, *Fragmented Gods: The Poverty and Potential of Religion in Canada* (Toronto: Irwin Publishing, 1987), 14.
2. Ibid.
3. Anglican Church of Canada, "Number of Canadian Anglicans, Parishes and Congregations," http://www.anglican.ca/help/faq/number-of-anglicans/.
4. Brian Clarke and Stuart Macdonald, *Leaving Christianity: Changing Allegiances in Canada* (Montreal: McGill-Queens University Press, 2017), 4.
5. Ibid., 6.
6. Brian Clarke, "Going, Going, Gone? Canadian Churches and the Rise of Non-Religion," in *Nonreligious Imaginaries of World Repairing*, ed. L.G. Beaman and T. Stacey (Cham: Springer, 2021), 54.
7. Ibid., 55–56.
8. George Hawley, *Demography, Culture, and the Decline of America's Christian Denominations* (Lanham, MD: Lexington Books, 2017), 7.
9. Ibid., xiii.
10. Pierre Berton, *The Comfortable Pew* (Toronto: McLelland and Stewart Ltd., 1965).
11. Ibid., 20.
12. In particular, in a section entitled *The Abdication of Leadership*, Berton examines the church's passivity to the horrors of World War II and in particular the continuing threat of nuclear war and the voices of some who claim that there may be instances where nuclear war is justified. He also looks at the relatively passive response of the church to racism, the ethics of business and industry, and the challenge presented by the sexual revolution, as well as the remarriage of divorced persons.
13. Berton, 104.
14. Ibid., 106.

15. Bibby, 1.
16. Ibid., 233.
17. Ibid., 151.
18. Ibid.
19. Ibid., 152.
20. Kenneth Westhues, "Conrad Grebel Review," in *Fragmented Gods: The Poverty and Potential of Religion in Canada*, ed. Reginald W. Bibby (Toronto: Irwin, 1988).
21. W. LaSelva, *The Moral Foundations of Canadian Federalism: Paradoxes, Achievements, and Tragedies of Nationhood* (Montreal: McGill - Queens University Press, 1996), xi–xii.
22. Robert C. Thomsen and Nanette L. Hale, "Exploring Environments," in *Canadian Environments: Essays in Culture, Politics and History*, ed. Robert C. Thomsen and Nanette L. Hale (PUBLISHER?, 2005), 11–15.
23. Ibid., 15.
24. Ibid., 11.
25. Reginald W. Bibby, *Beyond the Gods and Back: Religion's Demise and Rise and Why It Matters* (Lethbridge, Alberta: Project Canada Books, 2011), 26.
26. Charles Taylor, *A Secular Age* (New York: Belknap Press, 2007), 580.
27. Bibby, *Beyond the Gods and Back: Religion's Demise and Rise and Why It Matters*, 214.
28. Graham Ward, *Christ and Culture* (Oxford: Blackwell Publishing, 2005), 9.
29. David R. Holeton, ed., *Liturgical Inculturation in the Anglican Communion Including the York Statement 'Down to Earth Worship'*, vol. 15, Acluin/Grow Liturgical Study (Bramcote: Grove Books Ltd., 1990), 6.
30. Paul Marshall, "Overview of Christ and Culture," in *Church and Canadian Culture*, ed. Robert E. VanderVennen (Lanham, MD: University Press of America, 1991), 9.

Chapter 2

Understanding Local Culture(s)

DEVELOPMENT AND DESCRIPTION

Before exploring the relationship between culture and theology, one needs to begin by establishing a contemporary understanding of the concept of culture. In this chapter, the notion of culture is explored by examining its early roots, the twentieth-century modern approaches of anthropology, and the subsequent postmodern critique. Attention is paid to the *local* nature of culture—the idea of culture being a local construct or meaning system that functions for an identifiable group. A semiotic approach, which uses meaningful symbols from the local culture, including language and its assigned meanings to establish semiotic domains, is used to describe a culture. The various characteristics that need to be considered in cultural description as well as the perspective from which the description is being constructed are discussed. And since there is no objective, external reference point by which to assess a particular culture, various cultures can only be described by the way in which they are similar to or different from another culture. In addition, the effect of change on the sign, code, and message of a semiotic domain is explored. This lays the groundwork to be able to understand the interaction between local culture and theology, which is explored in the following chapter.

As is clear from the Gospel texts of the New Testament, the person and work of Jesus of Nazareth were experienced in a particular context. His teaching, his own self-description, and the record of others' perceptions of who he was and what he was trying to accomplish are all expressed in the cultural context of first-century Palestine. The Gospel writers themselves all lived and wrote in their own particular context which, as modern critical methods have shown, influenced how they interpreted and described the person and work of Jesus. The later systematic theological statements that came to be made about the Christian faith, such as the historic creeds, referred to the Christian faith as being *incarnational*—meaning that the revelation about God as received in Christianity came through a particular person (i.e., Jesus) living as a human being at a particular time, and in a particular place—a particular language.[1]

The commonly accepted notion of associating particular ways of living (language, group customs, values, and norms) with the word culture is a recent one that only emerged at the beginning of the twentieth century. Equally recent is the notion that human beings develop the character of their own patterns of behavior through living in a group, as opposed to inheriting them from a particular racial ethnicity.

Where does the word "culture" originate? An early use of the term culture shares a similar derivation with the word *agriculture*. Just as agriculture refers to the tilling of the soil (to help it bear fruit), culture refers to the tilling (perfecting) of one's self. This sense of what came to be known as *high culture*—referring to a process of individual education and refinement—had its origins in seventeenth-century Europe.[2] While it was acknowledged that different groups of people would produce different types of culture, there was still a sense of a developmental continuum along which different cultures could be assessed and placed, based upon the intellectual activity or social institutions one found. This was particularly the case in the British colonial empire of the nineteenth century. Since many of those conducting the studies were British, the assumption was that the best of British society would be the standard by which to make assessments of the various global cultures.[3] In Germany, scholars also maintained the sense of culture as a state of greater refinement into which humanity grows, but in addition, they recognized that this state might be manifested differently in the cultures of different peoples.[4] Rather than seeing the entire human race growing in its sense of culture, "each of its peoples was like an individual person, displaying in its intellectual, spiritual and aesthetic achievements a characteristic form."[5] This understanding marks the beginning of the modern ethnographic understanding of culture.

At the beginning of the twentieth century, the emergence of the study of anthropology and the rise of evolutionism had a considerable impact on the notion of culture. Now, the sense of a particular people's culture being viewed as a whole or system—a kind of homogeneous expression of a collective group—began to emerge. The expectation that "the various aspects of a culture should make sense with reference to one another" characterized the emerging approach to exploring cultures.[6] Equally important at the beginning of the twentieth century, however, was the rising concern of historicism and its challenge to the assumption that similar cultural forms in different contexts had necessarily evolved in the same way and represented the same development. Beginning with the work of Franz Boas in the later nineteenth century, it became clear that, when comparing what appeared to be similar aspects of different cultures, "one must distinguish for each group what was original and what was borrowed, both as to customs and folklore as well as language."[7]

The result was the gradual removal of external or evaluative standards by which a particular culture could be measured. There was no external way to evaluate differences in customs and practices. "The specific historical context of a people's practice was itself therefore the primary explanation for differences among peoples' customs, values and worldviews."[8]

What emerges in the twentieth century is what is commonly referred to as a *modern* understanding of culture—heavily dependent upon anthropological studies. The emergence of this understanding gave rise to the realization that one does not study culture as a single entity, but rather as cultures. Culture is "an observable feature of all human groups; the fact of "culture" is common to all; the *particular pattern* of culture differs among all."[9] A cultural form is viewed as belonging to a particular, geographically located group or society with definable boundaries. This cultural form includes the group's entire way of life—its social habits, rituals, beliefs, norms, and values. For that group, their culture was thought of as a kind of "consensus way of living" so that differences are observed between different cultures, not within them.[10] Culture was now seen not as something that a person works at developing within himself or herself but rather viewed as possessing a kind of social determinism, in that a particular culture shaped the lives of its members.[11] As twentieth-century anthropologist Ruth Benedict states, in a way that is analogous to *Gestalt* psychology: "The whole determines its parts, not only their relation but their very nature."[12] Benedict goes on to point out an equally important characteristic: that these whole cultures are incommensurable to one another. "Between two wholes there is a discontinuity in kind, and any understanding must take account of their different natures, over and above the recognition of the similar elements."[13]

To summarize the dominant view of culture that had emerged in the early part of the twentieth century: a culture is a local construct rooted in a historically and/or geographically identifiable group, tribe, society, or nation. It is an internally consistent whole with the expectation that each of the parts makes sense in relation to one another and to the whole. A culture is all-inclusive—touching on every aspect of the social life of that culture's community. Since each culture develops in its own unique historical context, there is no external standard against which it can be measured. It is *only the differences between cultures* that can be observed and described. And because cultures are thought to be internally consistent, change is viewed as coming primarily from external forces as opposed to from within a culture.

However, an important shift takes place throughout the twentieth century that begins to challenge this view of culture and similarly affects how theology interacts with culture. First, just as a historical concern led to the consciousness about a culture being grounded in a historical context, this same dynamic eventually led to questioning about what caused a particular culture to become what it is: What were its origins and what processes are still at work in its present development?[14] It was realized that by not taking a culture's historic and ongoing development seriously, anthropologists were, in fact, freezing in time their present observations and creating an ahistorical construct.

Second, the notion of treating cultures as internally consistent wholes was challenged. It became apparent that a particular culture was experienced as a whole only by the anthropologist and not by the participants in the culture itself.[15] This admission of non-consistency certainly makes the anthropologist's work more difficult,[16] but it was clearly not acceptable for the culture to be described only from the privileged perspective of the external observer. Likewise, if the participants in the culture only experienced parts of the culture, and not in any systematic way, it became clear that scientific models for describing cultures were neither helpful nor accurate. In trying to find an analogy to describe the lack of a clearly defined system for describing cultures, Clifford Geertz, a late twentieth-century anthropologist, compared a culture to an octopus.

> The appropriate image . . . of cultural organization, is neither the spider web nor the pile of sand. It is rather more the octopus, whose tentacles are in large part separately integrated, neurally quite poorly connected with one another . . . and yet who nonetheless manages both to get around and to preserve himself.[17]

Related to the issue of internal consistency was the earlier modern notion that cultures were assumed to be a reflection of a shared consensus among their members. However, this was very difficult to prove. Rather, it was realized that homogeneity was something that was assumed and introduced by the anthropologist. Edmund Leach, another late twentieth-century anthropologist, raised a concern about the practice of trying to develop a general characterization from the observations of small, specific studies.

> It has become increasingly apparent that neighboring small-scale communities, even when they are lumped together under the same "triba" label, are just as likely to be sharply contrasted as they are to be very much the same. The contrast may itself be a significant feature of the overall pattern.[18]

At the same time, the fact that one is able to observe only those aspects of the culture that are publicly on display introduces the question of power: Who is able to contribute to the visible aspects of the culture and who is not?

> Coming at a society as an outsider, the anthropologist is deceived by the surface appearance of consensus. Every member of a society may declare the same beliefs, prominently display in their discourse the same fundamental categories, hold high the same values; it is highly unlikely, however, that they will all mean the same thing by them.[19]

Kathryn Tanner justifies this claim of non-homogeneity within a given culture by using the example of our own Western societies which are clearly made up of many different political persuasions and values. She goes on to make the point that

> shared elements of a culture are prone to be vague and unelaborated in and of themselves, more a matter of form than of substance . . . This very lack of definition is what enables them to be shared, to be the focus of interactions among a whole group of differently situated people.[20]

This lack of definition will prove to be an important element in the consideration of a shared theology (and its representation in liturgy) across a particular cultural entity.

As a result of the above deconstructions of the tenets of a modern understanding of culture, Tanner proposes two additional conditions. In the modern view, cultures were assumed to be static, formed entities. But it has been shown above that they are not internally consistent wholes; neither do they necessarily represent a *consensus* of the participants of the culture. Therefore, it cannot be assumed that cultures are internally stable entities. "The same active processes of social interaction that gave rise to cultural forms and their interconnections remain continuously at work. . . . Cultural forms cannot therefore be artificially frozen."[21] Change in the cultural forms can be generated internally as easily as externally. And, second, given the dynamic and fluid nature of cultural forms, it is no longer appropriate to assume that cultures are sharply bounded, self-contained units. This understanding (part of a *postmodern* understanding of culture) will be particularly helpful when beginning to consider the highly mobile, interconnected nature of today's global societies. Cultural forms become associated with a particular group only after they have been interpreted and integrated into their common life. The same forms can be used differently by other cultural groups.[22] This realization will be important when considering the adaptation of liturgical texts from earlier local cultures and their use in a new cultural context.

DESCRIBING A LOCAL CULTURE

Even though the postmodern understanding of culture arrived at above emerged in the late twentieth century, the work of Johann G. Herder in the latter part of the eighteenth century can be seen as a forerunner of postmodernism's critique of some of the tenets of the Enlightenment project referred to as modernism. Herder challenged the Enlightenment notion of generalization—of trying to take specific local characterizations and fit them into a larger general scheme.

> The universal, philosophical, philanthropic tone of our century readily applies "our own ideal" of virtue and happiness to each distant nation, to each remote period in history. But can one such single ideal be the sole standard for judging, condemning, or praising the customs of other nations or periods?[23]

Herder thought that one could not take an external scheme and impose it upon a particular people. Rather, each people's culture needed to be studied according to its own internal nature and historical development. Herder believed that the real or genuine was found in the particular, not in the universal.[24] Similarly, this study attempts to engage the local culture without imposing an external reference frame, nor with the goal of constructing a general overall scheme for culture.

How does one listen to, begin to understand, and describe a culture? For this work, with its attention to liturgical text and ritual meaning, a semiotic approach has been chosen. Semiotics is the study of signs (from the Greek *semeion* = sign). Robert Schreiter, in his work with local culture and theology, describes a semiotic approach in this way: "It sees culture as a vast communication network whereby both verbal and nonverbal messages are circulated along elaborate, interconnected pathways, which together create systems of meaning."[25] While being cognizant of some of its limitations, this study uses the semiotic approach of Schreiter, which is discussed below.

There are three characteristics that need to be part of the cultural analysis of a community. The approach must be *holistic*—meaning that it cannot preferentially deal with only parts of the experience of the culture. Second, it must be aware of, and include, the dynamics that give rise to the *identity* of the community, or else its labeling as a distinct entity is purely external and lacks credibility with the members of the community itself. Within the characteristic of identity, of particular interest, are two considerations: *group boundary formation* and *worldview*. Group boundaries have to do with deciding the "we/they" question—determining who is part of us and who is not. Worldview has to do with "our collective attitude toward those who are outside of us." The third characteristic of cultural analysis involves the ways in which the community deals with *social change*—especially in light of the dynamic nature of cultural expression.[26]

There are other valid approaches to cultural analysis besides semiotics, and all of them can, in some way, deal with the characteristics listed above. A *functionalist* approach is common in the English-speaking world. As is clear from the label, this approach focuses on the various aspects of a community and how those pieces fit together to form the whole—with particular attention to how those various parts function in order to "get things done." Its strength lies in the requirement of careful empirical observation and description. However, it is less likely to be sensitive to relationships, symbolic and ritualistic gestures, and related behaviors, unless these pieces somehow obviously contribute to the observed "functioning" of the community.[27] But these relationships, behaviors, and symbols may be particularly important in examining the theological understanding and liturgical practice of a community.

Structuralist approaches have also been important in the study of cultures. A structuralist approach attempts to identify unconscious structures that shape and dictate the various patterns of relationship and behavior. These approaches attempt to identify binary oppositions (male vs. female, old vs. young), which result in sets of rules or classifications that govern aspects of the community's life. Their strength lies in their ability to reveal identity structures and the way in which diverse aspects of a culture are held together. But as Schreiter points out, one is still left with the question of whether the binary opposition categories and the way they operate are more a reflection of the intuitions of the researcher than a method that can be repeated by others.[28] Given the fact that this study will concentrate on a community founded on theological belief and practice, and its expression in liturgical language and action, a semiotic approach, which is sensitive to the way language is used and symbols are understood, is most appropriate.

In a semiotic analysis of culture, signs are the bearers of the messages being communicated. Some signs have a natural relationship to the messages they carry, but many have an assigned meaning (a *code*) and the assignment of these meanings centers around three areas: syntactic (definitions of relationships between signs—analogous to grammar for a language), semantic (the content of the message), and pragmatic (governs the range of intelligibility of the message).[29] One has to know these codes and the way in which they operate within the particular local culture in order to understand the signs and the messages they carry. "The interaction of signs, groups of signs that mutually define each other, and these three kinds of rules are a creative collaboration that produces a culture."[30]

As one attempts to describe signs and groups of signs, one needs to be aware of the perspective from which the description is being constructed. Anthropologists have typically referred to *emic* (view from the inside looking out) and *etic* (view from the outside looking in) descriptions.[31] While these categories are helpful in a general way, attempting to differentiate "emic/etic" exclusively as "insider/outsider" descriptions can be problematic.[32] However, it is important to realize the difference in perspective of those describing their own culture versus those describing a culture different from their own.

Both *emic* and *etic* descriptions are important because each tends to emphasize different aspects. *Emic* descriptions are characterized by the use of narrative that employs references that are internal to the community. They tend to reaffirm reality as it is rather than dissect or critique it.[33] They also tend to veil the presence of internal power dynamics. Because this form of description affirms what is, it will tend not to expose power imbalances or offer a challenge to present practices. Marvin Harris cites an example of how a tribe in Brazil indirectly allowed the practice of infanticide but did not label it as such in its own (emic) description.[34] *Etic* descriptions may also use narratives, but they are used as examples and then translated into another discourse or sign system. This is what frequently happens when persons experience a culture different from their own and then describe it in terms of their own cultural system. While it might be held that emic descriptions would always be preferred, in fact etic descriptions are necessary for members of one sign system (culture) to be able to communicate to those of another sign system, because it is through an etic description that one who is outside of the culture being described begins to enter into dialogue with that culture.

A Semiotic Approach to Describing a Culture

This semiotic approach to describing a culture begins with locating culture texts. A culture text may be a single sign, or a series of signs held together by a set of codes or a common message. These "texts" may be verbal, nonverbal, visual, auditory—incorporating any or all of the ways in which members of a community inter-relate.[35] An example in a liturgical setting might be the act of kneeling for certain types of corporate prayer. In traditional Anglican liturgies, this action is often introduced by the verbal cue, "Let us pray." While there is no specific mention of kneeling in the spoken words, in many communities, the act of kneeling to this verbal cue would be part of that culture's worship life. However, more frequently now in contemporary liturgies, the code determining how the verbal cue is understood has changed, such that the cue "Let us pray" may be understood as an invitation to stand. This example emphasizes the importance of knowing how the code applies in a certain local context—even though the content of the verbal text is the same.

For our present interest in local culture and theology, culture texts that describe *identity* and *social change* will be of particular interest. Schreiter outlines in detail the process of engaging in semiotic description of a culture in terms of its identity and the factors affecting social change.[36] The relevant points for this study are summarized below.

Signs, as referred to above, bear *messages* in the semiotic system. The Eucharistic bread and wine are examples of such a sign. And in order to discern the message of the sign(s), *codes* will need to be identified. These codes are like answers to questions such as, "How are things done?" or "How is this to be understood?" Aspects of the way in which the Eucharist is celebrated would be examples of such codes. The interaction of the sign(s) with these codes carries a particular *message*—in this case about the significance of the Eucharist *for this particular community*—and thereby conveys something of its meaning in this culture. As referenced above, particular attention should be paid to the boundaries of such signs and codes. Using the Eucharistic example above: What kind of bread and/or wine can be used for this to still be considered a valid Eucharist by this community? Examples might include whether the bread is leavened or unleavened; whether it needs to be made from wheat or can be gluten-free. What types of prayer and gesture (and by whom?) would be appropriate for this community's Eucharistic celebration? For example, with the implementation of contemporary liturgies in the Anglican Church of Canada in the 1980s and following, congregations underwent a significant cultural change when they were asked to stand for the Eucharistic Prayer rather than kneel. Schreiter makes an important observation that in times of change, one can experience different competing messages about the same meaning topic.[37] This is of particular interest in comparing changes in culture and the impact upon a community's understanding of its theology.

Two other aspects of Schreiter's model are important for this work. The first is *metaphor*. When two distinct signs are compared with one another, a metaphor results. But in this usage, the resulting metaphor also causes associations to be made among all of the aspects of that sign's system. For example, in the twentieth century, when some churches made the decision that women could be ordained as priests, the two signs, woman and priest, were brought together, thus opening up the possibility of new understandings of both womanhood and priesthood. These two signs were placed in a *reflexive* relationship—meaning that each impacts the understanding of the other. The second aspect that needs to be considered is the creation of semiotic domains. "When this complex sign, code, message, and metaphoric process spreads itself over an area of culture and brings it together as a constellation of meaning, it results in a *semiotic domain*."[38] Typically, culture texts that refer to a particular area of activity in a culture (e.g., religious beliefs and practices) make up a semiotic domain and thereby are interdependent with one another. A liturgical example might be bowing or genuflecting toward the altar in a traditional church building. This might also be accompanied by brief silent or spoken prayer, and at another point in the liturgy, might be paired with another action associated with that semiotic domain, such as crossing oneself at certain points in the liturgy. The performance of each of these "texts" is linked to the others in a common domain. In other words, for members of that community, these actions/words "go together."

Finally, one must respond to the question of why one is attempting to describe a particular culture in this way and not by some of the more scientific, modern approaches? As outlined above, postmodern critique has established the fact that there is no external reference frame or universal criteria by which to describe or analyze a cultural context. The only reference point available to us is our own cultural context. Clifford Geertz,[39] a later twentieth-century anthropologist, responded to cultural exploration and description in this way:

> Believing with Max Weber, that man is an animal suspended in webs of significance he himself has spun, I take culture to be those webs, and the analysis of it to be therefore not an experimental science in search of law but an interpretive one in search of meaning.[40]

Geertz borrowed Gilbert Ryle's notion of "thick description" in which one attempts to show the complexity and depth of what is observed in the practices of a culture. The classic example (of Ryle's) Geertz used to illustrate the nature of "thick" versus "thin" description involved the difference in meaning between a twitch of the eye and a wink. A thin description of such a phenomenon would simply describe the physical action itself—the blink of the eye—leaving these two signs indistinguishable. A thick description would attempt to explore not only the meaning that the receiver of the twitch or wink might discern, but also the intentions of the sender, and even whether those intentions were genuine, or whether they were intended to mislead the receiver in the message they received.[41] Geertz's declared purpose for his anthropological study of culture is most helpful in this study.

> We are not . . . seeking either to become natives . . . or to mimic them. . . . We are seeking, in the widened sense of the term in which it encompasses very much more than talk, to *converse*, a matter a great deal more difficult, and not only with strangers, than is commonly recognized.[42]

However, care must be taken in how Geertz's approach is used, and in how far one can go in moving from description to analysis of a culture. Adam Kuper raises this concern in his work on culture. Interestingly, even though it is an anthropological study about culture, he makes this sobering observation in the book's introduction: "The more one considers the best modern work on culture . . . the more advisable it must appear to avoid the hyper-referential word altogether . . . There are fundamental epistemological problems."[43]

Kuper faults Geertz's work ultimately because it does not deliver what he claims Geertz originally intended—a development of social theory. But this should not come as a surprise, because behind Geertz's work lies the (postmodern) assumption that there is no such thing as a universal social theory.[44] However, Geertz's approach will be used modestly here to provide a description of how life is in a particular cultural context and not attempt to draw systematic conclusions about how cultures function. In this study, the goal is to be able to converse about the person and work of Jesus Christ with the members of this cultural community, through the medium of liturgical texts, in such a way that it opens to them the same profound significance that it did for the original witnesses and writers of the biblical texts.

With this understanding of local culture, where does one go in a corresponding local theology? One place to begin, internally, is to investigate metaphors that characterize the reality of the local Christian community or its experience of the saving reality of Christ. But it is equally important to look outward too. "Relating the religious domain to the other semiotic domains of society is equally pressing."[45]

NOTES

1. George W. Stocking, Jr., *Race, Culture and Evolution* (New York: The Free Press, 1968), 205–6.
2. Kathryn Tanner, *Theories of Culture: A New Agenda for Theology* (Minneapolis, MN: Fortress Press, 1997), 4.
3. Tanner, *Theories of Culture: A New Agenda for Theology,* 17.
4. A.L. Kroeber and Clyde Kluckhohn, *Culture: A Critical Review of Concepts and Definitions* (New York: Vintage Books, 1952), 13–14.
5. Kathryn Tanner, *Theories of Culture: A New Agenda for Theology* (Minneapolis, MN: Fortress Press, 1997).
6. Ibid. See also George W. Stocking, Jr, *Victorian Anthropology* (New York: The Free Press, 1987), 174.
7. George W. Stocking, Jr, *Race, Culture and Evolution* (New York: The Free Press, 1968).
8. Tanner.
9. Kroeber and Kluckhohn. Kroeber and Kluckhohn cite the work of Bennett and Tumin. See J. Bennett and M. Tumin, *Social Life* (New York: Alfred A. Knopf, 1948), 209.
10. Tanner.
11. Ibid. See also *Kroeber and Kluckhohn.*
12. Ruth Benedict, *Patterns of Culture* (Cambridge, MA: The Riverside Press, 1934), 52.
13. Ibid.

14. Tanner. For a discussion of this awareness through the work of Renato Rosaldo, see also George E. Marcus, Michael M.J. Fischer, *Anthropology as Cultural Critique* (Chicago: The University of Chicago Press, 1986), 98f.

15. Tanner, *Theories of Culture: A New Agenda for Theology*, 42.

16. Benedict.

17. Clifford Geertz, *The Interpretation of Cultures* (New York: Basic Books, Inc., 1973), 407–8.

18. Edmund Leach, *Social Anthropology* (New York: Oxford University Press, 1982), 142.

19. Tanner.

20. Ibid.

21. Ibid., 51.

22. Ibid., 53.

23. Johann Gottfried Herder, *Against Pure Reason: Writing on Religion, Language and History*, trans. Marcia Bunge (Minneapolis, MN: Augsburg Fortress Press, 1992).

24. Robert J. Schreiter, *Constructing Local Theologies* (Maryknoll, NY: Orbis, 1985), 265–6.

25. Schreiter, *Constructing Local Theologies*, 49.

26. Ibid.

27. Ibid.

28. Ibid., 48–9.

29. Ibid.

30. Ibid., 50.

31. Ibid., 57.

32. Marvin Harris, *Theories of Culture in Postmodern Times* (Walnut Creek: Altamira Press, 1999), 35–6. The definition of "insider" and "outsider" is not always clear. A member of a culture (insider) can still reflect an "outsider" position and one who appears to have joined a culture may still give an "outsider" description.

33. Schreiter, *Constructing Local Theologies*.

34. Marvin Harris, *Theories of Culture in Postmodern Times* (Walnut Creek, CA: Altamira Press, 1999).

35. Schreiter, *Constructing Local Theologies*.

36. Ibid., 63–73.

37. Ibid.

38. Ibid.

39. Clifford Geertz, and particularly his five-point definition of religion, has come under criticism—especially by those seeking to establish universal understandings for how he uses terms such as "symbol" and "conception." Geertz uses the term, "meaning," in a way that is completely internal to the cultural system he is describing. His critics, however, are concerned about meaning in the universal sense, with appropriate truth conditions that govern it. See Nancy K. Frankeberry and Hans H. Penner, "Geertz's Longlasting Moods, Motivations and Metaphysical Conceptions," in *Language, Truth, and Religious Belief*, eds. Nancy K. Frankenberry and Hans H. Penner (Atlanta, Georgia: Scholars Press, 1999). I agree that Frankenberry and

Penner rightly describe the inherent limitation of symbolic models for a non-symbolic system by showing that this approach is a coherence theory of truth, and "there is no way to stave off skeptical worries that the world could be completely different from what we actually believe it to be, or from what the symbolic vehicles represent it as being." (p. 226). This is the case because the external measurement that would be applied to determine such a thing would involve yet another semiotic system. However, for the purposes of this study, we are using Geertz's (and Schreiter's) approach in order to describe and ultimately converse with a particular cultural community, rather than assess its claims to truth as we perceive it in our semiotic system. See also Frankenberry, Nancy K. and Hans H. Penner (eds.), *Language, Truth and Religious Belief* (Atlanta, GA: Scholars Press, 1999) in which the authors raise concern about Geertz's approach as a *correspondence* theory and make the point: "However, there is no vantage point from which the speakers can transcend the symbolic language in which they are embedded in order to judge that the correspondence is indeed 'simulating,' 'imitating' or in any other way representing some non-symbolic reality." (p. 225) But this problem is exactly the one raised by the postmodernist critique: one cannot get outside the system one is trying to measure—except from within one's own (contingent) system.

40. Clifford Geertz, *The Interpretation of Cultures* (New York: Basic Books, Inc., 1973).

41. Ibid.

42. Ibid. Emphasis mine.

43. Adam Kuper, *Culture: The Anthropologists' Account* (Cambridge, MA: Harvard University Press, 1999), x–xi.

44. Kuper, *Culture*, 118.

45. Schreiter, *Constructing Local Theologies*, 74.

Chapter 3

Local (Contextual) Theology

REFLEXIVITY AND INCULTURATION

At the turn of the twenty-first century, Sheila Greeve Daveney remarked on the "widespread move to cultural and social theory on the part of religious studies scholars (in the United States perhaps most notably theologians) and the increasing interpretation . . . of theology as a form of cultural analysis."[1] This is quite remarkable in light of the ambivalent attitude of many theological approaches toward culture only fifty years earlier in the middle of the twentieth century.[2] (This will be discussed more fully in chapter 4.)

Therefore, if theology can be used in cultural analysis, it is clearly a part of culture—a form of cultural activity. "Theology is something that humans produce."[3] It is historically and socially conditioned. However, even among postmodern theologians who hold this view, there is a difference as to how it is understood. Is Christian theology something that takes place within a culture or is it better to assign it in a very general way to culture as being a characteristic of being human? Gordon Kaufman would be a representative of the latter view. For Kaufman, "approaching Christian theology as a part of culture means, then, correlating the Christian message with human universals, with general structures that are at the bedrock of all human knowing and doing."[4] While this understanding of the relationship of Christian theology to culture is attempting to address the universality of the Christian message—that it can become manifested in any and all cultures—the difficulty with this approach to culture and theology is that it runs counter to the very thrust of postmodern anthropology. Kaufman's approach explicitly suggests there are such things as human universals that are common to all cultures, whereas current anthropological studies show that there may be common cultural processes but only particular cultures.[5] Consistent with a postmodern understanding of culture, the former view, that Christian theology is expressed in a particular way within a particular culture, is employed in this work.

This emerging understanding of theology being a part of culture is represented in the discipline of theology referred to as *contextual* theology. The rise of liberation theologies in the latter part of the twentieth century is a key piece in the development of contextual theology. Drawing on the work of Peruvian theologian Gustavo Gutiérrez, Robert Schreiter outlines three recurring concerns that fueled this development.

First, new questions were being asked. Where Western ecclesiastical practices did not make sense in local cultures, "it was becoming increasingly evident that the theologies once thought to have a universal, and even enduring or perennial character . . . were *but regional expressions of certain cultures.*"[6] This realization presents a significant challenge to a traditional approach to Christian theology, which views the core of systematic theology as composed of particular propositional truths that are a-cultural—meaning that they are understood to convey the same meaning and significance regardless of the cultural context.

Second, "old answers were being urged upon cultures and regions presenting new questions."[7] This was particularly true between the older colonizing churches and the newer emerging indigenous churches. Often, the issues of the older churches (i.e., peace and threat of nuclear war) were not front and center with the issues of churches in the developing countries (i.e., hunger and poverty).[8]

Third, "the realities of new questions and old answers pointed to a concern that recurred in churches around the world: *a new kind of Christian identity* was emerging apart from much of the traditional theological reflection of historical Christianity."[9] All of these emerging concerns helped to catalyze the interest in a (local) contextual approach to theology.

Contemporary philosophical thought has also contributed to the development of contextual theology with its shift from

> a perspective which views truths and human knowledge as universal to a perspective which views them as shaped, determined and even validated by specific cultural, social and political contexts. It has also given rise to an explicit critical awareness . . . that Christian theology is and has always been contextual.[10]

This approach to, and understanding of, Christian theology brings to the fore the challenge of attempting to communicate a particular theological meaning from one context to another. However, this contextual understanding of theology has not been without its critics. Some of the challenges it has elicited are discussed below.

There are also aspects of Christian theology itself, which are internal—elements of the Christian Gospel—that point to the importance of the context in which humanity experiences this Gospel. The first of these is the incarnation itself. The central divine act of the Christian faith—the sharing of God's self with humanity as a human being—takes place not only in a specific time and place, but also in a particular context and culture. Jesus of Nazareth lived as a male participant in a particular culture and historical period. Intimately wrapped up in the proclamation of the Gospel of Jesus Christ are the particulars of a context and a culture. God reveals God's self to a particular people, in a particular time and place, through a particular person. If this revelation is to continue, which it clearly has, the work of incarnation has to continue in other times, places, and cultures. "Christianity, if it is to be faithful to its deepest roots and to its most basic insight, must continue God's incarnation in Jesus by becoming contextual."[11] The faithful expressions of this same truth, this same Gospel of God, must emerge and be experienced in other cultural contexts in order for the Gospel's universality, which is part of its proclamation, to be realized.

A second element that arises from within the Christian tradition itself is related to the theology of revelation and, in particular, its view of God's creation. "The Creation does not have a passive and static function in the history of revelation."[12] Rather, the world and its history are the context in which God has revealed, and continues to reveal, God's Self. The entire story of God's revelation in both the Hebrew and Christian scriptures is intimately bound up in context—whether it is Moses and the people of the Exodus meeting God at Mount Sinai,[13] or Jesus climbing a mountain to teach his disciples in Matthew's Sermon on the Mount.[14]

Related to the discussion of revelation above, a third aspect of Christianity that shows the primary role of context is its sacramental view of reality. "The doctrine of the incarnation proclaims that God is revealed not primarily in *ideas* but rather in concrete reality."[15] One encounters God in signs, symbols, and ritualistic actions, all of which gain their meaning in and from a particular context and culture. These might include liturgical celebrations of baptism or Eucharist—both of which are modeled after comparable rituals of nearly two thousand years ago, but which now unfold in ways that are deeply dependent on the present culture. And just as these revelatory actions took place using the everyday language, symbols, and relationships of first-century Palestine, so do they now exercise their revelatory power using the language, symbols, and relationships of twenty-first-century cultural contexts. As Bevans points out, "If the ordinary things of life are so transparent of God's presence, one can speak of culture, human experience, and events in history—in contexts—as truly sacramental and so revelatory."[16] The importance of contextual liturgy and worship is discussed further below.

A fourth aspect of Christian theology, which illustrates the validity of a contextual approach in theology, is the catholicity of the church. Taken from two Greek words, which together mean "according to the whole," catholicity refers to the "all-embracing, all-inclusive, all-accepting nature of the Christian community."[17] This truth of the Christian Gospel can be realized only by embracing each and every expression of the Gospel in the rich diversity of cultural contexts around the globe. However, it is also precisely the preservation of this property of catholicity that has raised concern and challenges to contextual theology as will be explored later in this chapter.

Even the nature and content of the Christian Gospel itself calls for the theological enterprise to be carried out in a contextual way, a method that sees the local cultural context as an indispensable part of the Christian revelation. It is clear that theology has always been contextual—even if pre-modern theologians were not asking questions about context, and modern theologians assumed that their particular context/culture was essentially universal.

Developing a Contextual Approach to Theology

A contextual model for doing theology begins with a consideration of the cultural context rather than the received faith or tradition. Schreiter suggests that there are two types of local or contextual theologies: those concerned with cultural identity (ethnographic approaches) and those concerned with oppression/justice or liberation approaches. He goes on to state that contextual or "local theology begins with the needs of a people in a concrete place, and from there moves to the tradition of faith."[18] It is proposed in this work that local or contextual theology involves beginning with an awareness of how a community in its local cultural context lives, expresses meaning, and communicates its life—to those within and those beyond it. Its theological approach is simply part of the make-up of a given community and not necessarily a response to any particular need, though it may result in new understanding and/or action.

Robert Schreiter opens up both the principal issue and the key challenge of contextual theology in his book, *Constructing Local Theologies,* which begins with a Foreword by the renowned theologian, Edward Schillebeeckx. Schillebeeckx writes,

> Previously, one almost took for granted that the theology of the Western churches was supraregional and was, precisely in its Western form, universal and therefore directly accessible for persons from other cultures. But . . . Western theologians came to the realization . . . that theology, too, is a *local' theology.*[19]

This was the great awareness and challenge that the liberation theologies of the twentieth century brought to bear against traditional (Western) academic theologies as referenced above. Schreiter poses two helpful questions for expressing a contextual theology:

> How is a community to go about bringing to expression its own experience of Christ in its concrete situation? And how is this to be related to a tradition that is often expressed in language and concepts vastly different from anything in the current situation?[20]

It is these two questions that inform this chapter and, in fact, the book as a whole.

One of the first changes a contextual approach to theology brings about is a shift in the understanding of *who* does theology. Contextual Christian theology puts the construction of theology into a cultural context of a Christian way of life and thereby challenges the elite view of academic theology. This is because this cultural context "refers to the whole social practice of meaningful action, and more specifically to the meaning dimension of such action—the beliefs, values and orienting symbols that suffuse a whole way of life."[21] This is not to say that academic theology becomes obsolete or of little use in a contextual approach. Rather, academic theology needs to become more concerned with everyday social practice. Tanner suggests that academic theology has a critical role to play within a contextual approach to theology. Academic theology needs to engage and reflect upon Christian social practices

> in the sense that it asks critical and evaluative questions of them. . . . Academic theology is about everyday Christian practice in that the beliefs, symbols and values that academic theologians work with have their primary locus or circulation there.[22]

This gets directly to the heart (and hope) of this book.

However, other contextual theologians, such as Angela Pears, do not believe that Schreiter goes far enough in describing just how radical contextual theology is. "He [Schreiter] is not willing or prepared it appears, to describe this shift as a generically new way of doing or new awareness of ways of doing theology."[23] She validates the claim of this radical change by making the statement that, "Local theologies are not systematic in the sense of building up a permanent framework,"[24] suggesting that contextual theology represents an even more radical departure from traditional theological approaches. While contextual theologies are clearly not systematic in the way in which traditional approaches would build such a system, they can still result in an internal system. Contextual theologies do not begin with an external reference frame or a preconceived epistemological approach. Rather, they develop their own structure or system based on their meaning for the local culture or community. For example, rather than describing the doctrine of the person of Jesus Christ by expressing it in terms of a divine and human nature immersed in one another (Chalcedon), a local contextual theology might express its understanding of Jesus as being both human and divine using terminology that it finds explains the biblical narratives and the way the local community uses the tradition of the church. This approach may still be systematic—but the structure or system will evolve out of the experience and expression of the community and not be imposed from an external source.

Traditionally, a philosophic approach to theology has been concerned with truth claims. It often reflects on questions about whether the proposed theological idea is verifiable, or whether it reflects truth in some objective fashion. In a contextual approach in a postmodern culture, since the resulting theology emerges from a reflection on, and description of, the (cultural) life of the community, the truth concern becomes moot. If the description is congruent from both emic and etic perspectives, one can be reasonably confident that it reflects reality for the participants of that culture. However, in the case of Christian theology, there is also the concern about whether or not the resulting theology is true to the tradition of the revelation of God in Jesus Christ. This is the other side of the catholicity question. In the discussion above, it was clear that a local, contextual approach to Christian theology assured a kind of internal catholicity because the resulting theology would be an authentic expression of that community's experience of, and understanding of, the Gospel. However, the other aspect of catholicity is concerned with whether or not the local, contextual theology in question is faithful to the tradition of Christian theology over the past two thousand years in its many different cultural expressions. The catholicity concern is not merely an internal one; that is, of judging whether the theology in question is congruent with the tradition of that particular community. Precisely because of the catholicity that the Christian proclamation demands, the real question becomes: "Is the theology developing in this community genuinely reflective of the Gospel, faithful to the Christian tradition?"[25] Schreiter suggests five criteria that help a community to answer this question for itself. The first three have to do with congruence between the new theology or theological practice and the community's existing theological understanding, worship, and discipleship. The last two criteria take the community outside itself—opening itself to the judgment of other communities and also to the challenging of other communities.[26]

But the truth/faithfulness question still remains. How does a Catholic tradition form? Schreiter proposes that this happens on its own in the sense that he suggests viewing "church tradition in a different way, by seeing it as a series of local theologies, closely wedded to and responding to different cultural conditions."[27] However, questions have been raised about whether this interpretation is sufficient—whether it responds to the necessary relationship of contextual theologies to the scriptures and the practice and documents of the church.[28] Sigurd Bergmann also raises concerns about Schreiter's analogy of culture and faith to that of a language system—comparing faith to language competence, theology and expressive tradition to language performance, and the loci of orthodoxy to grammar.[29] Bergmann points out that "the competence of faith includes not only linguistic expressions but also images and other aesthetic ways of expression."[30] However, this concern can be dealt with by taking care of the semiotic description of the theologically relevant signs of the culture. In this analysis, language is treated as a sign, but it stands alongside other signs, especially non-linguistic actions and rituals. Nonetheless, Bergmann does propose an important further development to the foundation that Schreiter has laid. It has to do with tradition being understood as the creation of a socio-cultural memory of past practices and understandings. "Each local theology affects the development of its cultural context as well. . . . Each interpretation of tradition ultimately aims at the shaping of the formation of the future fellowship."[31] Against the common perspective of "looking back" at tradition, this is an important addition—the realization of the role of present contextual theologies in creating the tradition that will help to shape future theologies. This dynamic is validated in Christian theology itself with its concern not only for *anamnesis* but also for *prolepsis* of the coming Kingdom of God.

The discussion around catholicity and tradition ultimately becomes a question about Christian identity. What describes a Christian community? Is there such a thing as a Christian culture? Do Christians

> form their own society set off from others? If so, the difference between what is Christian and what is not, like the difference between distinct cultures, can simply follow a division between social groups. . . . A view like this is defended by the contemporary Christian theologian, John Milbank.[32]

While this approach attempts to utilize postmodern thinking about the incommensurability of cultures—that their forms, values, practices, and meanings are all generated internally, and therefore the description of Christian culture could be generated solely by the Christian community, this distinct division between social groups is difficult to show in reality because Christians participate in many aspects of the wider societies in which they find themselves. This is particularly true in the present Western postmodern culture(s). "Christian social relations extend beyond the activities with other Christians . . . the character of those outside activities also infiltrate it."[33] Therefore trying to answer questions about Christian identity by attempting to look at discrete social groups is not helpful. "One needs to have already determined what makes someone or something (some belief or action) Christian in order for Christians and non-Christians to be seen as forming discrete social groups to begin with."[34] In light of this movement of persons from one cultural context to another, as well as the movement of cultural elements across boundaries between cultures, it is not the cultural elements themselves that distinguish their identity to a particular culture, but rather how those elements are used.[35] Therefore, it is questionable whether one can describe a distinct Christian culture. Instead, one must describe Christian identity from the ways in which the Christian community uses and understands particular cultural forms.

Reflexivity

The nature of the relationship between culture and theology in contextual theology is a *reflexive* one. While reflexivity is yet another characteristic of the relationship between culture and theology and could have been included in the section above, its importance and novelty justify it being treated as a separate dynamic.

The word "reflexive" is from the Medieval Latin (*reflexivus*) meaning turned back or reflected. While he does not use this specific term, Clifford Geertz explores this very dynamic in his discussion of how cultural patterns are constructed from symbolic information that results in models of reality. "Culture patterns have an intrinsic double aspect: they give meaning, that is, objective conceptual form, to social and psychological reality *both by shaping themselves to it and by shaping it to themselves.*"[36] This is an example of reflexivity. He contrasts this dynamic of symbolic information in cultural patterns with non-symbolic information, such as concrete objects and beings that make up the material world, and uses examples from the biological sciences to illustrate the difference. In spite of the dismissive critique of this type of illustration by Frankenberry and Penner,[37] an illustration from physical science will be helpful to demonstrate a reflexive relationship. From the science of astronomy and the study of our solar system, it can easily be shown that if two bodies in a reflexive relationship collide (interact) with one another, they are both changed by the interaction. The velocity and momentum of earth's moon are entirely affected by the gravitational pull of the earth, causing it to orbit around the earth. However, the earth, too, is affected by its interaction with the moon. Earth's oceans are subject to changing water levels because of the gravitational pull of the moon (tides). Both bodies have been altered in their interaction: they are in a reflexive relationship with each other.

Inculturation

Missiologists are keenly aware of how dependent the meaning of a word is to the context of its use. "The meaning that words have within the Christian community arises from the whole lives experience of the community in Christ. It cannot arise from any other source."[38] Words help to describe the culture in which they are employed, and that culture ultimately affects the meaning that the words have in their context. Linguistic expressions and their cultural context are in a reflexive relationship. Narrative theologians, of course, are also deeply conscious of how words, as cultural forms, are entirely in a reflexive relationship with other forms—including theological understanding.

> Meaning is constituted by the uses of a specific language.... Thus the proper way to determine what "God" signifies, for example, is by examining how the word operates within a religion and thereby shapes reality and experience rather than by first establishing its propositional or experiential meaning and reinterpreting or reformulating its uses accordingly.[39]

Attempting to impose a pre-determined definition, understanding or use of a particular word upon a particular context is simply imposing a piece of one culture upon another.

Therefore, the challenge remains: how does one genuinely enable a local, indigenous expression of the Christian faith to take root in another culture? The primary purpose of the proclamation of the Gospel is to enable a person to know the identity and nature of God as revealed in the person of Jesus Christ and to embrace the new gift of life offered in relationship to that revelation. From the earliest times, the proclamation of Jesus Christ as God's saving gift to the world has challenged its human preachers to enable the living Christ to be made real in many diverse contexts. The first recorded example is the inclusion of the Gentiles in the "new Israel" (Christian disciples) as recorded in the Acts of the Apostles.[40] One common term that has come into use since Vatican II to describe this process is "inculturation." The Roman Catholic theologian, Aylward Shorter, has examined this term from both a theological and sociological perspective. He suggests that it is helpful to distinguish the word, inculturation, which is frequently used in theological discourse, from "enculturation"—the term most commonly used in sociological studies. Enculturation is the "cultural learning process of the individual, the process by which a person is inserted into his or her own culture."[41] Shorter sees inculturation from a theological context as having to do with the interaction of faith and culture. It is "the ongoing dialogue between faith and culture and cultures. More fully, it is the creative and dynamic relationship between the Christian message and a culture or cultures."[42] This is a particularly helpful definition because it gives expression to the dynamic, ever-evolving nature of this reflexive relationship.

The other important aspect that Shorter raises is the fact that any Christian message will always be proclaimed from within a culture. In order to better reflect the reflexivity of this relationship, the term "interculturation" is sometimes used.[43] In this work, the term inculturation will be used to refer to this ongoing, reflexive dialogue between the proclamation of Christ (theology) and the local context (culture).[44]

Therefore, by its very nature, inculturation is always a dialogue between two cultures. And what is attempting to be communicated, or made real, "is Christ himself . . . he is the subject of his own message. . . . It can be truthfully said that what is inculturated is Jesus Christ himself."[45] So the primary purpose of the proclamation of the Gospel (enabling a person to know the identity and nature of God as revealed in the person of Jesus Christ) can only be accomplished in contextually specific ways because that proclamation can only occur within a specific culture, and it can only be communicated effectively to its hearers if the proclamation is in a language (including symbol, ritual, etc.) that is meaningful and, ultimately, transformative.

This concern for genuine reflexivity between the Christian proclamation and its local culture is not in any way limited to the rhetoric of propositional truth, or even to its illustration through analogy, metaphor, or symbol. Ultimately, the reception of this revelation results in the creation of a community of disciples who gather to express their relationship with the living Christ through worship. Since the offering of worship is the worshipers' self-offering to God as they adore and rightly recognize God, it is inevitable that authentic worship will involve the cultural lives of the worshipers themselves, including the symbols, meanings, gestures, and rituals that define who they are as God's people and sufficiently express their devotion.

The challenge in sharing the proclamation of the Gospel from one culture to another, however, is to create the kind of interaction that enables a genuine and creative expression of the lives of the worshipers using language, symbol, gesture, and ritual that are authentic to their culture. Much of the Christian church has recognized the validity of the axiom, *lex orandi, lex credendi,* which Stephen Bevans paraphrases as "the way we pray points to the way we believe and vice versa."[46] Schreiter expands further on this and asks three important questions about the interaction of theology and the worshiping community, which of course takes place in a given cultural context: "What happens . . . when the developing theology is brought into the worshipping context? How does it develop in the communal prayer of the Church? What happens to a community which includes such in its prayer?"[47] These questions all probe at the nature of the reflexive relationship between theology and culture as it is expressed through worship and the liturgical forms employed. This gets at the heart of liturgical inculturation.

However, because of the reflexivity that is part of these cultural/theological interactions, every attempt at inculturating the Gospel in a new context has the potential to expand the knowledge and experience of the revelation of God in Christ—not only in the new culture, but also in the culture(s) of those who are offering the proclamation. Therefore, the challenge and work of liturgical inculturation also afford an opportunity to enlarge and enrich the understanding of the Gospel in all of the cultural groups involved.

While the need to translate scripture and liturgical rites into indigenous languages has been addressed since the beginning of the modern colonial period, the importance of inculturating liturgical texts came to the fore in the middle of the twentieth century—particularly with Vatican II. One of the important liturgical theologians of that period was Anscar Chupungco who, being Filipino, was keenly aware of the need for liturgical rites to move beyond European cultural expressions. Chupungco defined liturgical inculturation as:

> [T]he process whereby the texts and rites used in worship by the local church are so inserted in the framework of culture, that they absorb its thought, language, and ritual patterns. Liturgical inculturation operates according to the dynamics of insertion in a given culture and interior assimilation of cultural elements.[48]

While this is a helpful statement, the sense of inserting texts and rites into the framework of a culture, even with the references to absorption and assimilation, still carries the sense that pre-formed texts are being adapted for use in a new context. A stronger definition, and one that includes liturgy within the wider context of the Christian life, is that of M. de C. Azevedo. He defines inculturation as the "dynamic relationship between the Christian message and culture or cultures; an insertion of the Christian life into a culture; an *ongoing* process of reciprocal and critical interaction and assimilation between them."[49] In this work, in keeping with the definition of inculturation above based on Shorter, liturgical inculturation will follow Azevedo's definition, which is congruent with Shorter's understanding of the inculturation of the Christian message.

Given the close relationship between liturgy and theology (*lex orandi, lex credendi*), in chapter 4, the Eucharistic Prayer texts of the Anglican Church of Canada will be examined for evidence of inculturation in twentieth-century Canadian culture, in order to explore this dynamic further.

In conclusion, it is this property of reflexivity that sets contextual theologies apart from all others. Other theologies attempt to account for context and use terms like inculturation, but in all of these instances, a pre-formed piece of theological truth is being translated, adapted, or otherwise fit into a particular cultural situation. While it is the case, as discussed above, that even in a contextual theology framework, previous local theologies play a part: they form a tradition of sorts. Even as such, the meaning and import of those previous theologies may very well be altered in the present day by the cultural context in which they are found. The admission of theology as being in a reflexive relationship within a particular culture transforms a traditional understanding of theological revelation and makes very real and presents the ongoing incarnation of the person and work of Jesus Christ to each succeeding generation and each particular culture. In the next chapter, the discussion will move specifically to the interaction and understanding of Christian theology with Western culture in the twentieth and twenty-first centuries.

NOTES

1. Sheila Greeve Daveney, in *Converging on Culture*, ed. D. Brown, S. G. Daveney, and K. Tanner (New York: Oxford University Press, 2001), 4.
2. See H. Richard Niebuhr, *Christ and Culture* (New York: Harper and Row, 1951).
3. Tanner, 63.
4. Ibid., 65.
5. Ibid., 66.
6. Schreiter, 3. Emphasis mine.
7. Schreiter, *Constructing Local Theologies*, 3. This was particularly the case between the older "colonizing" churches and the newer "colonized" churches.
8. Schreiter, 3.
9. Schreiter, *Constructing Local Theologies*, 3. See also Gustavo Gutiérrez, *A Theology of Liberation* (Maryknoll, NY: Orbis Books, 1973).
10. Angie Pears, *Doing Contextual Theology* (Abingdon: Routledge, 2010), 1.
11. Stephen B. Bevans, *Models of Contextual Theology*, rev. ed. (Maryknoll, NY: Orbis, 2002), 12.
12. Sigurd Bergmann, *God in Context: A Survey of Contextual Theology* (Aldershot: Ashgate, 2003), 15.
13. Exodus, chapters 19 and 20.
14. Gospel of Matthew, chapters 5, 6 and 7.
15. Stephen B. Bevans, *Models of Contextual Theology*, rev. ed. (Maryknoll, NY: Orbis, 2002), 13.
16. Bevans, *Models of Contextual Theology*, 13.
17. Bevans, 14.
18. Schreiter, 13.
19. Schreiter, *Constructing Local Theologies*, ix. Emphasis mine.
20. Schreiter, *Constructing Local Theologies*, xi.
21. Tanner, 70.
22. Ibid., 80.
23. Angie Pears, *Doing Contextual Theology* (Abingdon: Routledge, 2010), 15.
24. Ibid., 17.
25. Schreiter, 117.
26. Schreiter, *Constructing Local Theologies*, 118–120.
27. Schreiter, *Constructing Local Theologies*, 93.
28. Pears, *Doing Contextual Theology*, 19.

29. See Schreiter, 115.
30. Sigurd Bergmann, *God in Context: A Survey of Contextual Theology* (Aldershot: Ashgate, 2003), 55.
31. Ibid., 56.
32. Tanner, 97. See John Milbank, *Theology and Social Theory: Beyond Secular Reason*, 2nd ed. (Oxford: Blackwell Publishing, 2006).
33. Ibid., 98.
34. Kathryn Tanner, "Cultural Theory," in *Systematic Theology*, ed. J. Webster, K. Tanner, and I. Torrance (Oxford: Oxford University Press, 2007), 536.
35. Tanner, "Cultural Theory," 537.
36. Geertz, 93. Emphasis mine.
37. Nancy K. Frankenberry and Hans H. Penner, "Geertz's Longlasting Moods, Motivations, and Metaphysical Conception," in *Language, Truth and Religious Belief*, ed. N. K. Frankenberry and H. H. Penner (Atlanta, GA: Scholars Press, 1999), 221. They write: "Detours into the biological sciences in essays on religion and culture usually signal a profound loss of direction."
38. Lesslie Newbigin, "Christ and the Cultures," *Scottish Journal of Theology* 31, no. 1 (1978): 7.
39. George A. Lindbeck, *The Nature of Doctrine* (Philadelphia: The Westminster Press, 1984), 114.
40. See Acts 10.1–11.18 and 13.1–15.35.
41. Aylward Shorter, *Toward a Theology of Inculturation* (Maryknoll, NY: Orbis Books, 1988), 5.
42. Shorter, *Toward a Theology of Inculturation*, 11.
43. Aylward Shorter, *Toward a Theology of Inculturation* (Maryknoll, NY: Orbis Books, 1988), 13–14.
44. Different terms are preferred by those working in contextual and cultural theology. Stephen Bevans states that the more inclusive term is "contextualization," which he claims includes "indigenization" and "inculturation." See Bevans.
45. Shorter, 60–61.
46. Bevans, 23.
47. Schreiter, 119.
48. Anscar J. Chupungco, *Liturgies of the Future: The Process and Methods of Inculturation* (New York: Paulist Press, 1989), 29. This quote was cited in Phillip Tovey, *Inculturation of Christian Worship: Exploring the Eucharist* (Aldershot: Ashgate, 2004), 1.
49. Marcello de Carvalho Azevedo, *Inculturation and the Challenges of Modernity* (Rome: Gregorian University, 1982), 11. Emphasis mine.

Chapter 4

"What about the impact of the Gospel in a local culture?"

As initially discussed in chapter 1, it is the decline of the Christian church in the latter part of the twentieth century,[1] and its apparent inability to engage the contemporary issues of individual's lives, that is the impetus for this examination. This chapter will consider primarily the Christian church in Canada—with a particular interest in the mainline Protestant churches, of which the Anglican Church of Canada is a part. The chapter will begin by examining some of the issues between theology and a particular local culture, and then consider the Anglican Church of Canada in light of that theology/culture examination.

As a starting point, the mid-twentieth-century work of H. Richard Niebuhr, *Christ and Culture*[2] will be used to examine the various modern approaches to the interaction of theology—more specifically, the proclamation of Christ—and culture. Niebuhr developed five helpful typologies to describe the interaction of Christ and contemporary culture. This exploration includes a critique of Niebuhr's work as well as the impact of what will be termed the emergence of postmodernism[3] in the late twentieth and early twenty-first centuries and its relevance in examining the interaction of theology and a local (Canadian) culture. It will be shown that, even though there are limitations to the ideal constructs of Niebuhr's five types, they provide a helpful exploratory path to understanding the different ways that Christ and culture interact, ultimately proposing Christ as the transformer of culture.

In this study, the Anglican Church of Canada will be chosen as the example of an appropriate local culture, though the steps involved could apply to the exploration of any local culture.

One of the results of the postmodern critique of cultural studies is the realization that members of a given society, in this case Canadian society, belong simultaneously to many cultural communities. In some sense, this actuality is an example of "hybridity"—a term frequently used in Postcolonial studies. "Hybridity commonly refers to the creation of new transcultural forms within a contact zone."[4] The term is principally used to describe the hybridized culture (linguistic, political, racial, etc.) that emerges when two or more cultures interact in a common community or society—particularly in the instance of one culture attempting to colonize another.[5] However, in this exploration of theology and culture in the Anglican Church of Canada, there is no particular sense of the cultural community of one aspect of the lives of members of Canadian society attempting to dominate or transform the essence of another cultural community of which they are a part. Rather, there is simply the realization that any particular local culture that is examined will not be a homogeneous entity. Because of the non-homogeneous (or hybridized) nature of contemporary Canadian culture, it is recognized that the description of the local culture of the Anglican Church of Canada will be represented by only the dominant aspects of this cultural group and will not necessarily apply equally to all of its members. (Or, to put it another way, a Maritime Anglican in Nova Scotia will not practice his or her Anglicanism in exactly the same way as a prairie farmer from Saskatchewan). The choice of this particular cultural locus will be supported by the fact that the members of the Anglican Church of Canada are all formed by, and their identity is informed by, the use of common liturgical texts and, in particular, the Eucharistic Prayer texts. These prayer texts are statements of the theology, in narrative form, which characterize this community's identity and its approach to the context in which its membership lives. The specific examination will include the Eucharistic Prayer of the *Book of Common Prayer* (1959/1962) as an example of a text of the mid-twentieth century, followed by an analysis of the Eucharistic Prayers of the Canadian Anglican *Book of Alternative Services* (1985).

THE INTERACTION OF THEOLOGY AND CULTURE IN NIEBUHR'S FIVE TYPES

Just as this examination was begun in response to an observable concern of the Christian church's place in contemporary society in the mid-twentieth century, it was the concern about effective and faithful methods of evangelism and mission in a pluralistic world that caused the church to take interest in local cultures and contexts. In the middle of the twentieth century, Richard Niebuhr published his seminal work entitled *Christ and Culture*. It has become the basis upon which much reflection and critique has taken place, and subsequent approaches explored. Niebuhr's work begins by drawing a distinction between what we perceive Christ's attitude to culture might be and the attitudes of his Christian followers:

Christ's answer to the problem of human culture is one thing. Christian answers are another ... The belief which lies back of this effort, however, is the conviction that Christ as living Lord is answering the question in the totality of history and life in a fashion which transcends the wisdom of all his interpreters yet employs their partial insights and their necessary conflicts.[6]

With this statement, Niebuhr acknowledges a plurality of approaches to Christ and culture, as well as the *unfinished* nature of the encounter. And by focusing on Christ—as opposed to Christianity or a particular expression of Christianity—Niebuhr is bringing the engagement between the Christian faith and culture into the present. It is an ongoing encounter in which both partners are real and living. However, it is complicated by the fact that the scriptural witness of Jesus of Nazareth in his local culture reveals one who exemplifies "what seems like contempt for present existence with great concern for existing men [*sic*]"[7] Also, the relationship between Christ and culture is not simply a polarity that exists between Christians and non-Christians, for Christians are members of society with its culture. Rather, Christians themselves struggle with this relationship as they attempt to discern how to live as disciples of Christ in the culture of which they are a part. And this has been the case since the beginning of the Christian church.[8]

Even with this caveat, one must still define "Christ." And the challenge of doing this lies in the plurality of interpretations of Christ as exhibited in those who follow him—those who call themselves Christians. However, as Niebuhr points out, this diversity of description does not negate the fundamental unity in the fact that Jesus Christ is "a definite character and person whose teachings, actions, and sufferings are of one piece."[9] Niebuhr defines the present-day Christ, whose authority his disciples live under, as "the Jesus Christ of the New Testament . . . this is a person with definite teachings, a definite character, and a definite fate."[10] Niebuhr recognizes that throughout history, there have been, and continue to be, many pictures of Christ with different emphases depending on the biases of the one doing the description. However, he asserts, "there will always remain the original portraits with which all later pictures may be compared and by which all caricatures may be corrected. And in these original portraits he is recognizably one and the same."[11] And even though each description is made from a relative position, "it can be an interpretation of the objective reality."[12] By taking this approach, Niebuhr affirms that there is only one unique reality called "Christ," and that any scriptural or theological portrait will be limited—bringing some aspects to the fore and pushing others to the background. These portraits are essentially various Christologies expressed throughout history.

How does one define culture? In keeping with the emerging anthropological view of his day, Niebuhr realized that culture involved more than simply the arts or speech of a particular society. Rather, it is the "total process of human activity" and the "total result of such activity . . . It comprises language, habits, ideas, beliefs, customs, social organization, inherited artifacts, technical processes and values."[13] Niebuhr also recognizes the pluralism that is characteristic of all culture. "Societies are always involved in a more or less laborious effort to hold together in tolerable conflict the many efforts of many men [sic] in many groups to achieve and conserve many goods."[14] This realization of the dynamic, non-homogeneous nature of culture is an early example of the ongoing development of an anthropological approach to culture in the latter part of the twentieth century as discussed in chapter 2.

In response to the dynamic nature of culture, Niebuhr acknowledges that in describing the interaction of Christ and culture, "an infinite dialogue must develop in the Christian conscience and the Christian community"[15] in light of the complex realities of Christ and culture. He then proposes five answers or stops in the dialogue and suggests that these are artificial constructs—or types—which help illustrate the major principles at work.[16] Niebuhr is quite clear that these are models constructed to help us understand the various interactions of Christ and culture, rather than attempts to describe particular situations.

The first of these he calls "Christ against culture." This approach "affirms sole authority of Christ over the Christian and resolutely rejects culture's claim to loyalty."[17] It can be found in the New Testament, particularly in the First Epistle of John,[18] in which persons choose Christ and the Christian community over the local society from which they have come.[19] This stance becomes more radical after the second century and particularly in the writings of Tertullian.[20]

> The fundamental conviction . . . was the idea that this new society, race, or people, had been established by Jesus Christ, who was its lawgiver and King. . . . Whatever does not belong to the commonwealth of Christ is under the rule of evil.[21]

While the primary strength of this stance is its prophetic edge—its clarity of putting loyalty to Christ above all else—it also presents difficulties in moving from theory to practice. As Niebuhr points out, even carrying out the command to love one's neighbor becomes problematic because it cannot be carried out except through ways that involve an understanding of the neighbor's nature and culture.[22] There are theological challenges to this approach as well. The understanding of reason versus revelation is problematic.[23] Reason is derived from one's cultural experience and is clearly involved in one's knowledge and understanding of God.[24]

At the other end of the pole, in terms of a stance toward culture, is the second of Niebuhr's types which he calls *the Christ of culture*. This position represents a positive stance toward culture. "In every culture to which the Gospel comes there are men [sic] who hail Jesus as the Messiah of their society, the fulfiller of its hopes and aspirations, the perfecter of its true faith, the source of its holiest spirit."[25] Niebuhr cites the teaching of Gnostics such as Basilides and Valentius,[26] as well as Abélard's moral theory of the atonement,[27] as examples of this position. With this position, there is a complete removal of an over against or critical stance toward the culture. "All conflict between Christ and culture is gone; the tension that exists between church and world is really due, in the estimation of Abélard, to the church's misunderstanding of Christ."[28] However, it is in Enlightenment Protestantism that this position comes to the fore.

> Jesus Christ is the great enlightener, the great teacher, the one who directs all men [sic] in culture to the attainment of wisdom, moral perfection, and peace . . . things for which he stands are fundamentally the same—a peaceful, cooperative society achieved by moral training.[29]

Ritschl is representative of this approach in the nineteenth century. "Christianity itself needed to be regarded as an ellipse with two foci, rather than as a circle with one centre."[30] One focus is justification, the forgiveness of sins; the other focus is ethical striving for the attainment of the perfect society of persons, which Ritschl equated with the Kingdom of God.[31] Ritschl's idea of the Kingdom of God was "the synthesis of the great values esteemed by democratic culture: the freedom and intrinsic worth of individuals, social cooperation, and universal peace."[32] As admirable as this approach may seem, it presents a major theological difficulty in the fact that the Kingdom of God has become a human construct! "Christ is identified with what men conceive to be their finest ideals, their noblest institutions, and their best philosophy."[33]

The remaining three types of Niebuhr's models all attempt to deal with the dialectic between these first two positions. Niebuhr classifies all three models as belonging to "the Church of the centre," in the sense that each "has refused to take either the position of the anticultural radicals or that of the accommodators of Christ and culture."[34] All three of these positions recognize that human beings are obligated to be obedient to God, using their intelligence and will, and therefore their engagement in their culture as part of their discovery of, and obedience to, discipleship in Christ. All three positions agree on the universality of sin and also of the gift of grace at work through them as they carry out works in the life of their culture in obedience to Christ.[35]

The first of these positions is termed the *synthesis of Christ and culture*. This amounts to a both/and approach. An early example of this is the teaching of Clement of Alexandria.[36] It contains lots of practical teaching but is tied in with the revelation of Jesus Christ.[37]

> His Christ is not against culture, but uses its best products as instruments in his work of bestowing on men what they cannot achieve by their own efforts . . . Clement's Christ is both the Christ of culture and the Christ above culture.[38]

Niebuhr uses the term "above" in an eschatological sense, meaning that the end journey of humanity is to a society that is beyond this world. Niebuhr identifies Thomas Aquinas as another great synthesist. In dealing with the understanding of law, Aquinas achieves this synthesis:

> Culture discerns the rules for culture, because culture is the work of God-given reason in God-given nature. Yet, there is another law beside the law rational men discover and apply. The divine law revealed by God through His prophets and above all through His Son is partly coincident with the natural law, and partly transcends it as the law of man's supernatural life.[39]

Niebuhr acknowledges the synthesist approach appears to be the ideal, except that it carries with it the tendency to absolutize what is relative,[40] in the way in which it views the human/cultural contribution, and it likewise tends to underestimate the effect of human sinfulness in that contribution.[41] In other words, any synthesis of the understanding of our own experience, ideas, practices, and values (i.e., our culture) with our limited and constantly evolving understanding of Christ and Christ's call on our lives in our time, will inevitably be, in Niebuhr's words, "subject to continuous and infinite conversion," and "is only provisional and uncertain."[42]

Niebuhr's fourth type is termed *Christ and culture in paradox* or a dualist approach. "The dualist lives in conflict, and in the presence of one great issue. That conflict is between God and man [*sic*]. . . . [T]he issue lies between the righteousness of God and the righteousness of self."[43] The dualist is keenly aware of the inadequacy of all human effort and at the same time the extreme grace of God's forgiveness.[44] This position in no way compromises either the seriousness of human sin or the efficacy of God's grace. "The miracle with which the dualist begins is the miracle of God's grace, which forgives these men without any merit on their part."[45] At the same time, the dualist shares with the radical Christ against culture position, the inherent evil in all human action. "But there is a difference between them: the dualist knows that God indeed sustains him in it, and by it."[46] Hence, this position is paradoxical in nature. Unlike the synthesist position, there is no attempt to reconcile the grace of God with the (corrupt) efforts of human culture. Rather, there is the affirmation that, in an inexplicable manner, God is at work in both. Niebuhr points to the apostle Paul as an example of this type.[47] For Paul, all cultures are under sin, and all cultures are redeemed in Christ.[48] Niebuhr uses Martin Luther as a modern example of a dualist approach.[49] There is an obvious duality in Luther's writings, but "Luther does not, however, divide what he distinguishes. The life of Christ and the life in culture, in the Kingdom of God and the kingdom of the world, are closely related."[50] Christ is constantly at work in this world in and through human structures and relationships. One of the strengths of this approach is the fact that it "mirrors the actual struggles of the Christian who lives 'between the times.'"[51] Two of its weaknesses are the tendency for its followers to discount the importance of the laws of society, seeing them as all under sin and therefore of no consequence; and the other is to lose any expectation that significant spiritual transformation can happen on this side of death.[52]

Niebuhr calls the fifth type of response, *Christ, the transformer of culture*, or the conversionist response. This type is most like the dualist in the sense that there is acknowledgment of both the corruption of humanity and the efficacy of the grace of God in Christ. However, conversionists have a more positive and hopeful attitude toward culture.[53] This is based on three theological convictions: that creation and the ongoing creative activity of God are central—redemption focuses on the incarnation and not just the death and resurrection of Christ; that the Fall is a kind of reversal of creation—the consequence of the Fall being the corruption of man's nature as opposed to its utter destruction; and a view of history "that holds that to God all things are possible in a history that is fundamentally not a course of merely human events but always a dramatic interaction between God and men [*sic*]."[54] Simply stated, "The problem of culture is therefore the problem of its conversion, not of its replacement by a new creation."[55]

Niebuhr sees the elements of a conversionist approach in the Gospel of John, in that Christ is portrayed as the converter and transformer of human actions.[56] But the universal nature of that transformation is lacking in John's Gospel. There is not a sense of "a hope for the conversion of the whole of humanity in all its cultural life."[57] Niebuhr identifies Augustine as the great early medieval theologian of this type[58]—particularly as part of the "great historical movement whereby the society of the Roman Empire is converted from a Caesar-like community into medieval Christendom."[59]

Niebuhr finishes this work by asserting, again, the unfinished nature of the task.

> Yet one is stopped at one point or another from making the attempt to give a final answer . . . [T]he problem of Christ and culture can and must come to an end only in a realm beyond all study in the free decisions of individual believers and responsible communities.[60]

As groundbreaking as Niebuhr's work was in trying to capture the breadth of the interaction of Christ (and Christ's church) with culture, several difficulties became apparent. The first of these is the implicit assumption by Niebuhr that culture is *monolithic*. As Niebuhr explored examples from history for each of the five types, these figures were measured by the consistency of their response in all areas of their world or context. When there were variations, these were explained as places in which the historical example was inconsistent.[61] John Howard Yoder appropriately makes the case, when referring to the Christian's approach to culture, that one "should precisely *not* try to be consistent by affirming all, rejecting all, or paradoxing all, as the Niebuhr outline assumes would be consistent, but to be concretely discriminating, after rejecting any notion of an overall recipe."[62] However, Yoder's criticism is really about the application of Niebuhr's typology and is better interpreted as a limitation of the usefulness of the typology.[63] In the same paper, Yoder adds the critique that in *Christ and Culture*, Niebuhr views culture as being *autonomous*. "It is a necessary presupposition of the entire argument that the value of culture is not derived from Jesus Christ but stands somehow independently of him."[64] It is the case that, at an abstract level (where the models of typology need to be formed), Niebuhr must keep Christ and culture distinct—in order to describe the various ways in which they might interact. However, this is, again, arguing with the application of Niebuhr's models and forcing an interpretation on Niebuhr's use of culture that he does not intend. Yoder does not fully appreciate the strong Trinitarian understanding that undergirds Niebuhr's work—that God the Creator and God in Christ are one. Niebuhr clearly appreciates the role of God the Creator in the formation of human cultures and their rightly ordered relationship.[65]

Paul Marshall, in his essay pertaining to Canadian culture, raises similar concerns to Yoder and empathizes with him about how some denominations are mis-represented in some instances when they are placed into one of Niebuhr's categories. In particular, Marshall comments on how Mennonites are often portrayed as being part of the "Christ against culture" type, primarily because of their refusal to legitimize any kind of violence. This is not an accurate portrayal of Mennonites, and Marshall goes on to show, correctly, how involved Mennonites are in lobbying around issues of global poverty, agricultural policies, and criminal justice systems.[66] Marshall raises the problem of how people categorize others' positions as opposed to how they categorize their own position. "There is an epistemological gap: we do not see ourselves as others see us and we do not see others as they see themselves."[67] This is an example of the issue of *etic* versus *emic* cultural analysis—description from those external to a particular culture as distinct from an internal description by those who are indigenous to a particular culture, which was raised in chapter 2. Marshall also makes the claim that Niebuhr's typology ignores certain important features of the Christ/culture relation. Even if Niebuhr's types are accurate and helpful, they are limited by the fact that they do not account for the distinction between different ways of transforming culture (institutional versus individual), nor do they incorporate ways to distinguish between different aspects of culture—accepting some and challenging others[68]

Another limitation in employing Niebuhr's typology to characterize actual cultures and a Christian response to such lies in the typology's lack of consideration of issues of power. Cyril Powles, also working in a Canadian context, points out that, historically, the *way* cultures have "contacted" Christianity is deeply affected by the power relationships of that encounter—citing Western world endeavors such as the missions to China in the nineteenth century. Powles' point is to show that the encounter of Christ and culture is never a simplistic or ideal one.[69] This is a valid comment, but it will be relevant only when one is trying to make judgments about why a culture has a particular stance toward the Gospel or Christianity. As discussed below, Niebuhr's typologies are intended to be used to aid in description, not in a cause-and-effect analysis.

Another Canadian, John Stackhouse Jr., in his book on culture and Christianity in the twenty-first century, begins the work by re-visiting the Niebuhr typology and suggesting that Niebuhr's Type Four (Christ and culture in paradox) provides the best jumping-off point to describe the contemporary situation. He arrives at this position because he believes that the two most common stances toward culture in the West and particularly North America could be characterized as

> the option of cultural transformation, of totally reshaping society according to Christian values, [and] the response of holy distinctiveness, of a definite Christian community living in contradiction to the rest of society and thus offering the beneficial example and influence of an alternative way of life.[70]

He then proceeds to suggest a third way, which he describes as one of cultural persistence—"even though we know that we will not achieve anything like the ideal."[71] However, I think that Stackhouse is shifting the focus from the interaction of Christ and culture to that of Christians and culture and therefore is more comfortable with the already, but not yet sense of the Christ and culture in paradox—Type Four.[72] On the other hand, Niebuhr is referring, in an idealized way, to how Christ is carrying out the realization of the fullness of God's kingdom in the real world of cultures. While some things may appear paradoxical at any given moment, this is not necessarily the case. The appearance of paradox may simply be our inability to see the whole picture because we are still part of the transformative evolution of that picture.

Some have perceived another limitation to Niebuhr's work, particularly to his climactic fifth type, "Christ the Transformer of Culture." It is the vagueness around his description of what these transformations might look like, as well as his lack of concrete illustrations in history of this type.[73] But there is another way of viewing Niebuhr's approach. Glen Stassen examines both Niebuhr's life and his other writings and comes to the conclusion that Niebuhr was only too aware of the problems of historical relativism. "He was a postmodernist long before the term became fashionable."[74] Niebuhr avoids concrete examples because whatever descriptive transformations might be proposed would be products of their own context and therefore they, too, would be subject to transformation. Such is the nature of the unfinished work of transformation as Niebuhr saw it.

In the section of his book dealing with Niebuhr's typology, Stephen Long makes the statement that Niebuhr's types only work if we accept that Christianity is primarily about a permanent revolution.[75] In other words, this ongoing (or unfinished) transformation is a fundamental piece of the application of Niebuhr's typology. "Christ as the eternal mediates culture through historical, temporal manifestations. But every historical, temporal manifestation of the eternal Christ, including that of Jesus of Nazareth,[76] is inadequate precisely because it is historical and temporal."[77] Therefore, because of this permanent revolution, one cannot ultimately accept any temporal presentation of the eternal Christ. Rather, these presentations will always be subject to transformation according to the culture in which they are presented.

Ultimately, both Niebuhr's work and the response of his critics begin to reveal a more helpful approach to the issues around Christology and culture. Niebuhr's five types (or typologies in general) do not evaluate the different approaches to Christ and culture. They are mental constructs that help us to understand more fully the issues that are part of the discussion. By analogy, they could be thought of as markers on a sports field. They do not necessarily correspond to the location of any one player, but they greatly assist in the description of where the various players are and how the game is proceeding. Niebuhr clearly favors the fifth type, "Christ the Transformer of Culture," and Yoder chides him for not providing concrete criteria for, and examples of, such transformation.[78] But in considering Yoder's argument, it becomes more apparent that there can be no human standard by which, ultimately, one might judge such transformation, because that standard would also be relative and subject to transformation as part of our present culture.

There are other common examples of how typologies are used in order to differentiate one complex manifestation from another. When periods of history are described, they are often labeled with terms like the "Elizabethan Age" or "the Dark Ages."[79] These tags or types are useful to describe certain realities though, for example, there is no concrete, general manifestation of the "Elizabethan Age." The same could be said of the term "postmodernism" and how it is used to differentiate present reality from the previous experience labeled modernism.

There is also theological justification for Niebuhr's approach to his typology underlying *Christ and Culture*. Even before its composition, Niebuhr's theological perspective was grounded in a strong sense of the sovereignty of God. It included three themes: the reality of God's rule in all things, the independence of God from all subjective values and human institutions, and the redemptive manifestation of God in Christ in our historical time.[80] From these three themes, it is readily apparent how Niebuhr could propose Christ, the transformer of culture. This type acknowledges that human life, and therefore culture, is God-given; it avoids attempting to describe in independent terms what might characterize a God-redeemed culture, but it also acknowledges that God is present in the risen Christ, through the Holy Spirit, in history—working to fully effect the redemption of creation.

Given the criticisms of *Christ and Culture*, which, even if not entirely deserved, certainly reveal limitations, and the historical period in which it was written, is it still useful in exploring the interaction of Christian theology and culture? While it may have led some theologians and portions of the church to less-than-helpful positions in the past (see Hauerwas, endnote 63), it may be that Niebuhr's types can become increasingly useful as we attempt to define questions that help us to describe a culture, while being less concerned with trying to evaluate that culture.[81]

It was stated above that Niebuhr does not really offer many concrete examples or substantive critiques of Type Five, Christ, the transformer of culture. Perhaps it is better not to see this fifth type as one option among the other four types, but rather to see it as Niebuhr's end result—the final mature description of this interaction of Christ and culture which, in some sense, includes aspects of all of the other four types in the way it is applied in the real world. It is this fifth type that can serve as the overall principle at work in the interaction of Christ and culture—with every concrete example manifesting aspects of Christ against culture, Christ of culture, Christ above culture, and Christ and culture in paradox. Until the complete transformation of human culture to congruence with the reign of God in Christ, all cultures will be non-homogeneous mixtures of these various approaches—all in processes of transformation.

Therefore, going forward in this work, Type Five (Christ, the transformer of culture) will be used as the most appropriate lens through which to view the interaction of Christ and culture. It is also recognized that Niebuhr's Types Three (Synthesist) and Four (Dualist) are actually static representations of an attempt to hold in tension Types One (Christ against culture) and Two (Christ of culture). Given the fact that the interaction of Christ and culture will be treated as a dynamic activity of transformation, in the concrete examples of liturgies in particular cultural contexts, only the notions of Christ against culture (Type One) and Christ of culture (Type Two), together with Christ, the transformer of culture (Type Five) will be used, with the understanding that together they contribute to Christ's active transformation of culture.

THE EMERGING CULTURE OF THE ANGLICAN CHURCH OF CANADA

In this section, the interaction of Christ and culture is explored assuming the overall principle of Niebuhr's fifth type—Christ the Transformer of Culture—as referred to above. In addition to the rationale stated above, this fifth type is particularly well suited to the local culture being considered. Those gathering in worship and using the liturgical texts of the Anglican Church of Canada are, in fact, gathering in order to experience the transforming power of Christ. Worship, and Eucharistic worship in particular, involves persons coming together as a Christian community to offer themselves[82]—all of the aspects of their lives—to God, in order to receive God's grace (particularly through the sacraments)[83] to be transformed more closely into the likeness of Christ. Ideally, those who gather to celebrate the Eucharist (this church's central act of sacramental worship) receive and participate in a proclamation of the Christian faith in a way that affirms their common identity as members of the same culture. The Eucharistic Prayers, in particular, are the primary texts that accomplish this proclamation.

> In the Eucharistic rite, the primary focus for the proclamation of Trinitarian faith is found in the Eucharistic prayer, the Great Thanksgiving. Within its single encompassing form, the common faith is proclaimed before the assembly of those baptized into that faith.[84]

When these liturgical texts are shaped from within a local culture, incorporating its semiotic signs (language, symbol, ritual, and gesture), it can be said these texts are inculturated.[85] When particular liturgical texts inform the theological understanding of a culture and, in turn, theological understanding is being informed through the life experience of a people (i.e., culture), then culture and theology are in a reflexive relationship as discussed in chapter 2.

This reflexive intermingling of theological understanding communicated through local cultural signs goes back to the very beginnings of Eucharistic practice. In a manner that combines both Niebuhr's Type One (Christ against culture) and Type Two (Christ of culture), the Eucharist was made out of cultural material, yet that material "is also criticized, reoriented, sifted, seen as insufficient and equivocal."[86] Lathrop summarizes how content and practice were received from ancient Greek culture, transformed by Hellenistic-Jewish meal practice to serve a biblical faith, and was incorporated into the early

Christian practice. "But faithful Christian meal practice also *resisted* the cultural power of the banquet, in both its Greek and its Hellenistic Jewish forms."[87] Rather, the early Christians sought to enact openness and grace. "They . . . build a critique of the closed meal-society into their tradition: the bread and cup were for 'the many.' They accentuated the bread and wine while giving the rest of the food away."[88]

As one considers specifically the Eucharistic texts of the Anglican Church of Canada, one is faced with the question: "In what way can that church be described as a single local culture?" As discussed in chapter 2, participants in contemporary societies belong, in fact, to many cultures. Hence, the Anglican Church of Canada cannot claim to be the sole cultural identity for its members. Also, as discussed in chapter 2, cultural analysis must be holistic, include the dynamics that give rise to the identity of the community (group boundary formation and world view), and must include the ways in which the community deals with social change. The Anglican Church of Canada does engage all aspects of at least the religious life of its members. This would obviously include the use of common liturgical texts that shape the theological formation of its membership, but it also involves a common constitutional framework (Canons of General Synod, Provincial Synod, and local Diocesan Synods) and, within that, formal patterns of decision-making in local congregations, as well as common patterns of leadership such as the election and appointment of two senior lay offices (churchwardens). These same cultural patterns are involved in identity formation—those faith communities who organize themselves differently are viewed as different from ourselves. And these patterns would also, to some degree, determine the worldview of this cultural community in the sense that the Anglican Church would more easily cooperate and collaborate with churches that it recognizes as more similar to itself, such as other episcopally led denominations (Lutheran, Roman Catholic, Orthodox)[89] and less so with more congregationally organized churches such as Baptist or Pentecostal. In addition, there are distinct and describable ways in which the Anglican Church of Canada deals with social change. In the twentieth century, the decision-making structures of the church debated and made authoritative decisions about matters of social change such as the remarriage of divorced persons and the admission of women to the ordained ministries of the church. Therefore, it is reasonable to assume that the Anglican Church of Canada can be described as a distinct cultural entity.

In order to explore the interaction of theology, specifically Christology, and a given local culture, one must be able to describe that culture. However, how does one discover the nature of the Anglican Church of Canada (or any particular denomination) and describe it as a local culture? David Lyon poses the problem in the introduction to a collection of essays reflecting on twenty-first-century religion in Canada, where he asks, "Why is more not known about the contemporary religious cultures of Canada and their social significance?"[90] In order to probe more deeply into this question, one must explore both the origins of the Anglican Church in Canada as well as the evolution of the country of Canada in which this church developed.

The Anglican Church of Canada traces its roots back to the Church of England in Canada, which followed the settlement patterns of British immigrants to North America. As was the case in its motherland, Anglicanism began in Upper and Lower Canada as the officially established religion in 1791. Even though its establishment status was gradually eroded in the first part of the nineteenth century and legally ended in 1854, the Church of England in Canada continued to be an important force in the development of Canadian society.[91] But the Church of England in Canada, along with the (Presbyterian) Church of Scotland (in Canada), saw themselves, and were viewed by others, as still having strong ties to their mother churches in Great Britain, rather than being expressions of an emerging Canadian religion.

> The Churches of England and Scotland, as institutional projections of established churches in Britain, were slow to accept Canadianization because their mission status involved such strong physical, financial and ideological dependence on the mother churches that the umbilical cord seemed almost to be made of iron.[92]

That being said, the Christian church in the latter part of the nineteenth century had a major impact on the emerging state of Canada.

> In the broadest sense, the vitality of Victorian Christianity has profoundly shaped the character or identity of the nation. Thus, many features of modern Canadian life, including the political party system, the welfare state, foreign policy goals and a distinct "law and order" bias arguably originate, at least in part, in religious ideas, attitudes and structures.[93]

This is in contrast to its neighbor to the south—the United States. Because of the history of its citizens intentionally dissenting from European religious control, as well as its official constitutional stance of the separation of church and state, the religious landscape of the United States favored the development of the sect—an independent religious expression gathered around similar theological and ecclesiological preferences. "In contrast, Canadian religion boasts manifestly establishment roots . . . it has been large churches with strong links to powerful political, business and cultural elites which have dominated Canadian religious experience since their importation."[94]

Even though none of the churches in Canada possessed establishment status in the twentieth century, with the merger of most of the Methodist, many of the Presbyterian, as well as the Congregational churches to form the United Church of Canada in 1925, the majority of Canadians belonged to one of only a few denominations. John Moir contrasts this development with what took place in the United States: "Interestingly, when the American constitution was written in 1789 only ten per cent of Americans were church members. In Canada at Confederation [1867] only the unconverted natives [*sic*] were reported as non-church members."[95] Even though the Canadian census lists at least one hundred denominations active in Canada, almost 90 percent of the population belonged to one of only six churches.[96] Moir goes on to point out that "the Big Three" (Roman Catholic at 50 percent, United Church of Canada and the Anglican Church of Canada each at nearly 20 percent) accounted for almost all of that 90 percent. "The country's official adoption of the ideas of multiculturalism and religious pluralism cannot hide evidence of that tendency toward majority religious conformity."[97] Looking at the influence on Canadian society in the twentieth century and mainline denomination affiliation and influence, Roger O'Toole comments, "Whoever else is incorporated . . . Roman Catholics, Anglicans and United Church of Canada are undoubtedly the dominant components."[98]

Even though the Anglican Church was among the lesser of the Big Three in the early part of the twentieth century,

> Anglicans could boast among their membership 25 percent of the economic elite, though the entire church membership represented only 14 percent of the general population . . . The particular nature of Canadian capitalism, overwhelmingly mercantile rather than industrial, gave to Canadian society a cautious and legalistic tone which was reproduced among Anglicans.[99]

Powles closes his essay with this telling comment about the role of "activists" in the Anglican Church of Canada: "Their action in turn has led to a fresh impact of the church on the society *within which* it exercises its mission."[100]

The primary purpose of this exploration into the emerging influence of the Anglican Church of Canada on Canadian society in the twentieth century is to show how closely the members of this church saw themselves immersed in, influencing, and creating a Canadian culture. In fact, the large Protestant and Roman Catholic denominations in Canada viewed themselves, in the early twentieth century, as being about "the social project of building Canadian society."[101] In (English-speaking) Canada, the developing denominations

> cultivated a much closer relation (than in the United States) to the gradually forming Canadian state. . . . Rather than becoming spheres with different missions and different cultural roles, the Canadian state and churches came to see themselves as largely cooperating in the same enterprise of building a *Christian*

society in *British* North America. . . . The denominations that came to dominate the Canadian scene by the end of the nineteenth century were those that identified with this project.[102]

This reality lends support to the notion that the membership of the Anglican Church of Canada views itself as a good representation of Canadian culture, though obviously only one manifestation of that culture. While it may be, at times, critical of aspects of Canadian culture, Anglicanism has not viewed itself as separate from or necessarily against the state. Rather, the church "was thought to infuse the whole of society, acting as the soul, or conscience, of the state."[103] This unfettered identification of Anglicanism (or any of the major Christian denominations in the twentieth century) with a strand of Canadian culture is made possible because of a unique characteristic of religion in Canada as opposed to the United States. "The contrast between U.S. and Canadian religious life is nowhere more apparent than in the realm of civil religion, for Canada has been singularly unsuccessful in forging an emotionally charged and binding national ideology."[104] In the United States, this emergence of civil or culture-religion has a long history. "It occurs because religion has become intertwined with culture, or the 'American way of life,' which defines religion as desirable."[105] As opposed to the heightened religiosity of the United States, Canada seems almost unconsciously religious.

Given the description above of the Anglican Church of Canada in the later nineteenth and early twentieth centuries, it is predominantly an example of Niebuhr's Type Two, Christ of culture, including some of Niebuhr's Type Three, synthesis of Christ and culture. The Anglican Church of Canada clearly embraced much of the existing local culture (Type Two) and at the same time saw its role as trying to build (synthesize) a more completely Christian (Anglican) culture in emerging Canadian society (Type Three). This is particularly the case with its self-description of helping to build Canadian society. Wainwright aptly raises a concern about this perception of the relationship between Christ and the local (Canadian) culture. The "Christ of culture" "risks reducing Christ to a culture-hero. A chameleon Christ cannot criticize an idealized culture with which he has been too closely identified."[106] However, with the Anglican Church of Canada's self-perception of acting as the soul or conscience of the state (as discussed above), it would be accurate to claim (as above) that it is also an example of Niebuhr's Type Three, the synthesis of Christ and culture. As presented later in this thesis, the Anglican Church of Canada increasingly focused on issues of social justice in Canadian society in the latter half of the twentieth century, attempting to synthesize or perfect the existing culture—taking some of its emerging values (inclusion, anti-poverty, anti-racism, etc.) and attempting to implant them more extensively and effectively in Canadian culture.

Given this strong sense of immersion into, and ability to influence Canadian culture, what specifically characterizes the culture of the Anglican Church of Canada? One of the earlier defining characteristics that emerged in the Canadian expression of Anglicanism in the latter part of the nineteenth century was a democratizing tendency, which manifested itself in the calling of synods involving laypeople (and not just clergy) as well as the election of bishops by clergy and lay members as opposed to their appointment by senior church leaders, as was the case in the Church of England at the time.[107] In the latter part of the twentieth century, in trying to respond to the changing cultural make-up of Canada, the Anglican Church has attempted to become more multicultural in its character as it seeks to embrace non-British immigrant communities. It has also become known for its emphasis on social justice. The Anglican Church of Canada

> defines the major emphasis of its ministry in terms of *social concern* . . . *Tolerant, democratic and open to compromise* . . . the Anglican community accommodates within its ranks a range of theological opinion. . . . Its prevailing ideology, however, is a somewhat indistinct fusion of *liberal theology and progressive politics.*[108]

In part, this social justice emphasis is expressed in its overarching concern for inclusion. "Its quest for *inclusion* is further enhanced by a growing involvement in emergent movements for *social change* and greater public identification with those *inhabiting the margins of society.*"[109] In an accompanying footnote on the same page, O'Toole identifies Anglicans being involved in emerging social movements such as feminism, environmentalism, anti-poverty, anti-racism, and anti-war alliances. Evidence of this emphasis in official church policy will be shown below in the discussion of Eucharistic prayer texts.

Therefore, one would expect the culture of the Anglican Church of Canada to be marked by a concern for inclusion (including feminism), tolerance, democratic processes, the environment, poverty, racism, war, and a heightened awareness of those on the margins of society. However, from the exploration above into the development of the Anglican Church in Canada, with its close identification with the culture of Canadian society, it is clear that one cannot easily distinguish between a description of Canadian culture and a description of a unique Anglican Church of Canada culture—particularly in the first century of the country's existence.

Geoffrey Wainwright, in his book *Doxology*, uses Niebuhrian typology in his discussion of the interaction of (Christian) faith and culture. In particular, he focuses the discussion on "the liturgy as a meeting-place between faith and culture."[110] This is a particularly helpful understanding because it helps to define liturgy as a faith community's best attempt at both discovering, and being discovered by, the identity and nature of God as revealed in Jesus Christ.

As shown above, in the nineteenth and early twentieth centuries, the culture of the large denominations in Canada clearly had an impact on the evolving nature of the emerging culture of Canada. But was this "church culture" reflected in the church's liturgical texts as Wainwright suggests it could be?

LITURGICAL INCULTURATION: EUCHARISTIC PRAYERS OF THE ANGLICAN CHURCH OF CANADA

For the balance of this chapter, the focus will be on determining whether the texts of the Eucharistic Prayers, as primary liturgical texts, reflect the cultural values of the Anglican Church of Canada as noted above, and therefore show evidence of inculturation. As Meyers states, an inculturated liturgy "will reflect a dynamic relationship between the culture and the Gospel, a relationship in which there is an ongoing dialogue between Christian faith and culture."[111] To explore this issue, the texts of Eucharistic Prayers from the 1918, 1962, and 1985 liturgies of the Anglican Church of Canada will be examined for evidence of these concerns and values and compared to other policy decisions or statements of the Anglican Church of Canada during the same period of history.

The first Canadian *Book of Common Prayer* was published in 1918. This book was a Canadian adaptation of the Church of England's *Book of Common Prayer* of 1662. While there were some modifications in the Canadian liturgy, the single Eucharistic Prayer in the 1918 book is an exact replication of the Eucharistic Prayer of 1662. Therefore, this prayer would not represent an inculturated liturgical text for the Anglican Church of Canada since it was compiled over two hundred years earlier (with much of the material from three hundred years earlier) and in a completely different context. The Eucharistic Prayer of the Canadian 1918 liturgy will serve as an a-cultural base line against which the Eucharistic Prayer of the Canadian 1962 liturgy can be compared to see if the modifications that occurred by the mid-twentieth century reflect the emerging cultural values of the Anglican Church of Canada throughout the twentieth century. Finally, the six Eucharistic Prayers of the Canadian *Book of Alternative Services*, published in 1985, will also be explored for evidence of these same emerging cultural values. (The Christologies expressed in these Eucharistic Prayers and their relationship to their present, postmodern cultural context will be explored in chapter 5.) It should be noted that obvious theological justification may also be presented for the changes that occur in these liturgical texts. However, if these texts are in a reflexive relationship with the culture in which they are being used, the attempt to distinguish a theological versus cultural motivation for altering a text is almost moot, since each will impact the other and are ultimately dependent on one another.

After the opening versicles and responses of the *Sursum Corda* of the Eucharistic Prayer, the 1962 version adds a descriptive phrase to the acclamation about God in the 1918 version. Both prayers begin with:

> It is very meet, right, and our bounden duty, that we should at all times, and in all places, give thanks unto thee, O Lord, Holy Father, Almighty, Everlasting God,

However, the 1962 Prayer adds at the end of this sentence these words:

> Creator and Preserver of all things.[112]

This addition obviously affirms that God has created everything and continues to sustain all things of this world and, therefore, could simply be a theologically motivated addition in order to bring a stronger creation emphasis to the prayer. However, it also alludes to the created order and could be interpreted as responding to a heightened awareness for the world in which we live—that is, the environment; which is one of the emerging characteristics of the twentieth-century culture of the Anglican Church of Canada. The 1969 meeting of the Anglican Church of Canada's top legislative body—the General Synod—passed a resolution on pollution, referencing that "increased attention to problems of human environment is essential for sound worldwide economic and social development," and expressing "strong hope that countries will co-operate internationally to share knowledge on environmental pollution as well as the responsibility for its control."[113] It contained a multi-point directive to all levels of government and the local community about changes needed to protect the environment. However, given that there is no direct reference to the theological notion that it is our responsibility to the Creator to be good stewards of creation, it is unlikely that the reference to God as Creator was consciously added to express a concern for the environment.

Following the Preface (and Proper Preface if used) and the Sanctus, all of which remain unchanged from the 1918 to 1962 versions, there follows what both Prayer Books refer to as "the Prayer of Consecration." The 1962 version begins with an added exclamation of thanksgiving: "Blessing and glory and thanksgiving be unto thee,"[114] which serves to bring the structure of the prayer more into line with a typical Antiochene anaphora from the liturgies of the early church.[115] While this addition may not directly reflect one of the cultural values above, it is evidence of a church willing to change its traditionally received liturgical texts (from the Church of England) to reflect the priorities of the Canadian liturgical theologians of the day—and thereby express some sense of local context in the text. Immediately following this addition, both prayers continue with:

> Almighty God, our heavenly Father, who of thy tender mercy didst give thine only Son Jesus Christ.

But the 1962 Prayer adds these words:

> to take our nature upon him, and[116]

before continuing with the phrase:

> to suffer death upon the Cross for our redemption;

which is common to both prayers. While this obviously serves to affirm the full humanity of Jesus, it also is an inclusive statement, bringing the efficacy of a past event into the present. This would seem to be an example of the Anglican Church of Canada's concern for inclusion. Later in this same section of the prayer, the 1962 version replaces the word memory with the word memorial. Again, while this serves to give a richer theological expression of the anamnesis of Christ's death and resurrection which is at the heart of this prayer, it also provides a sense of inclusiveness—the present-day worshipers are engaging in an act of anamnesis and not merely a cognitive recalling of Christ's salvific event.

The 1918 prayer concludes after the words of institution: "Do this as oft as ye shall drink it, in remembrance of me." After the congregation has received Communion and the Lord's Prayer has been recited, the rite continues with this prayer:

> O Lord and heavenly Father, we thy humble servants entirely desire thy fatherly goodness mercifully to accept this our sacrifice of praise and thanksgiving.

However, the 1962 Prayer restores this portion back into the Prayer of Consecration where it appeared in the first English *Book of Common Prayer* of 1549. After the words of institution, the 1962 Prayer continues:

> Wherefore, O Father, Lord of heaven and earth, we thy humble servants,

and then adds this section:

> with all thy holy Church, remembering the precious death of thy beloved Son, his mighty resurrection, and glorious ascension, and looking for his coming again in glory, do make before thee, in this sacrament of the holy Bread of eternal life and Cup of everlasting salvation, the memorial which he hath commanded.[117]

And it concludes with a modified epiclesis and doxology, which are absent in the 1918 version of both the Prayer of Consecration and the prayer said after Communion.

> And we pray that by the power of thy Holy Spirit, all we who are partakers of this holy Communion may be fulfilled with thy grace and heavenly benediction; through Jesus Christ our Lord, by whom and with whom, in the unity of the Holy Spirit, all honour and glory be unto thee, O Father Almighty, world without end.[118]

While this serves to bring the prayer more into line with the ancient anaphoras that are characterized by moving from thanksgiving and remembrance (anamnesis) to supplication, including an epiclesis, it also highlights the concern for inclusion—that this action is taking place in the present, and that it is part of the worship of whole church.[119]

While the 1962 version of the Eucharistic Prayer shows only minimal evidence of the emerging twentieth-century cultural values of the Anglican Church of Canada, it does provide evidence that this church was becoming aware of the need to reform its received liturgical texts and begin forming them according to the theological priorities of that present-day Canadian Church and, therefore, its local culture. In light of the little evidence of interaction with the wider Canadian culture, assessing the text in light of Niebuhr's Types is not particularly relevant.

After a twenty-year period of liturgical experimentation, the Canadian *Book of Alternative Services* was published and authorized for use in 1985. In the several pages that precede the (contemporary) Eucharistic rite, there is a rationale of the order presented, and in particular, a section on the Great Thanksgiving and each of the six Eucharistic Prayers. The section on the Great Thanksgiving reads:

> The Eucharistic prayer is the great prayer of blessing said over the bread and the cup on the model of the Jewish table prayers of blessing. It is a prayer of faith addressed to God the Father, an act of praise and thanksgiving for the whole work of creation and redemption. The prayer is a unity from the opening dialogue to the final doxology and Amen. In the Eucharistic prayer the Church expresses the meaning of the whole Eucharistic action in which the memorial of

redemption is made, and the Church is united with Christ in offering and communion through the sanctifying power of the Holy Spirit.[120]

Even the inclusion of this explanatory rationale section could be interpreted as an attempt to make the Eucharistic Prayers more accessible to all—an indication of a desire for democracy (the prayers do not belong only to the ordained and liturgically educated), as well as inclusiveness.

William Crockett states in his paper on the theology of the Eucharistic Prayers in the *Book of Alternative Services*, the predominant pattern that emerged in all later developed (eastern) anaphoras was:

"Thanksgiving for creation and redemption
Institution Narrative and Anamnesis
Epiclesis and Doxology.

The prayer is, therefore, primarily a recital of the mighty acts of God. It is theology as doxology."[121] All six Eucharistic Prayers in the BAS have this Antiochene (West Syrian) shape.[122] Crockett's reference to theology as doxology is particularly noteworthy as contemporary Orthodox West Syrians still speak of the foundation of their Eucharistic theology in this way.

> The word *orthodoxy* has the double meaning of "right faith" and "right glory" (or 'right worship'). Thus this word . . . implies inseparability of doctrine and doxology. Right doctrine is the articulation of the right vision of God (*theoria*) received by minds purified through prayer and lived as members of the Body of Christ.[123]

Clearly the intent of the theology and structure of these six prayers is to immerse the worshiping assembly in one of the oldest Eucharistic traditions of the Christian church. These prayers have been constructed in such a way as to express faithfully the received theological and liturgical Christian tradition in the contemporary culture.

Do the texts of these Eucharistic Prayers express the cultural values and concerns of the Anglican Church of Canada in the latter part of the twentieth century? In his ThD thesis, Boyd Morgan describes the *Book of Alternative Services* of the Anglican Church of Canada as

> a major event in the church's life and it represents a new self-understanding for the Anglican Church of Canada at the close of the twentieth century. . . . This dissertation considers the revised liturgical texts within the *Book of Alternative Services* as *primary sources generated within a sociological and ecclesiological context.*[124]

In this same work, Morgan interviewed the late Dr. George Black, a Canadian liturgical scholar, concerning the role of God as Creator and the sacredness of creation in the BAS Eucharistic Prayers. He quotes Black's statement, "Issues of the integrity of creation and concept of God as creator are important for Canadians. Creation language, ecology, environmental implications were considered images to be expressed within Eucharistic praying."[125]

Each of the prayers will be examined for evidence of the expressed cultural values and concerns of the Anglican Church of Canada in the latter part of the twentieth century as described above. For the sake of brevity, only the pertinent sections of the six Eucharistic Prayers are included below, and the text of particular interest appears in italics.

Eucharistic Prayer 1

This prayer[126] is a new composition formed out of the Eucharistic Prayer in the *Apostolic Constitutions* thought to be from the later fourth century.[127] After the opening *Sursum Corda*, the fixed Preface begins with these words:

> It is indeed right that we should praise you, gracious God, for you created all things. You formed us in your own image: *male and female you created us.*
> When we turned away from you in sin, you did not cease to care for us, *but opened a path of salvation for all people.*
> You made a covenant with Israel, and *through your servants Abraham and Sarah* gave the promise of a blessing to all nations.
> Through Moses *you led your people from bondage into freedom;*
> through the prophets you renewed your promise of salvation.

"Male and female you created us." The intentional reference to women is new to Canadian Anglican Eucharistic Prayers and is indicative of a concern for inclusion. "But opened a path of salvation for all people." Again, this terminology reflects a concern for inclusion and does so in a democratizing sense—that everyone, regardless of social status, race, gender, etc., is offered salvation by God. "Through your servants Abraham and Sarah," once again intentionally refers to the place of women in God's plan of salvation. "You led your people from bondage into freedom" expresses a kind of solidarity with the oppressed peoples of the world—that God delivers from bondage. The Anglican Church of Canada's cultural values of inclusion (particularly of women), democratic processes, and awareness of those on the margins of society appear to be present in these texts.

Following the Sanctus, Prayer #1 continues with:

> He healed the sick and *ate and drank with outcasts* and sinners;
> he opened the eyes of the blind and *proclaimed the good news of your kingdom to the poor and to those in need.*

Unlike the earlier Canadian Eucharistic Prayers from the Cranmerian tradition, the Eucharistic Prayers of the *Book of Alternative Services* include descriptive narrative about the earthly life of Jesus and the way in which he demonstrated the truth of the Gospel in his words and actions. In the above texts, the reference that he "ate and drank with outcasts" as well as that he "proclaimed the good news of your kingdom to the poor and to those in need" are an obvious reflection of the cultural values of inclusion, with a particular concern for those in poverty.

Eucharistic Prayer 2

Eucharistic Prayer 2[128] is adapted from the Eucharistic Prayer in the *Apostolic Tradition* of Hippolytus.[129] Because this prayer is basically a contemporary adaptation of an ancient text, evidence of the above cultural values is more limited. In the opening Preface of praise and thanksgiving, the following description of the work of Christ appears:

he took flesh of the Virgin Mary *and shared our human nature.*
He lived and died as one of us, to reconcile us to you, the God and Father of all.

This text attempts to bring the contemporary worshiper much closer to the saving act of God (with references to "our human nature" and "us") and thereby honors the cultural value of *inclusion*. The Preface continues with more descriptive narrative about Jesus' saving actions:

In fulfilment of your will he stretched out his hands in suffering, *to bring release to those who place their hope in you*; and so he won for you a holy people.
 He chose to bear our griefs and sorrows, and to give up his life on the cross, *that he might shatter the chains of evil and death,*

While there is an obvious reflection of the Suffering Servant motif from Isaiah, this text also resonates with the cultural concern for the oppressed and those on the margins of society. In the prior decade, the General Synod passed a resolution dealing with poverty and social injustice,[130] which demonstrates that this text also reflects a value of Anglican Church of Canada culture.

Eucharistic Prayer 3

This prayer[131] also rooted in the Hippolytean prayer, though less closely than Prayer 2.[132] This prayer uses a variable Preface, which highlights particular attributes and/or actions of God through Jesus Christ as relevant to the given occasion. (Only the prefaces that show evidence of displaying the cultural values highlighted above are referenced here.)

who for our sins was lifted high upon the cross,
that *he might draw the whole world to himself.*

This Preface for Holy Week is another example of the value of inclusion—that it is God's intention to offer salvation to all. In the Preface for the last Sunday after Pentecost (Reign of Christ), the following text appears:

You exalted him as Lord of all creation that he might present to you
an eternal and universal kingdom:
a kingdom of truth and life,
a kingdom of holiness and grace,
a kingdom of justice, love, and peace.

Note again the reference to a theme of justice that can be related to the concern for inclusion of all, particularly those in poverty and on the margins of society. In the concluding portion of the prayer, the following petition appears:

> In the fullness of time, *reconcile all things in Christ*, and make them new, and bring us to that city of light *where you dwell with all your sons and daughters;*

While these references are less direct, they still resonate with a sense of justice and inclusion of all.

Eucharistic Prayer 4

The model for this prayer[133] is Prayer C in the Episcopal Prayer Book (1979) of the United States. Its language of praise for creation and salvation, using contemporary imagery, has made it one of the most popular of the new Eucharistic Prayers in the Episcopal Church.[134] As is presented below, this prayer (which uses a people's response throughout) includes a descriptive cosmology—highlighting the whole universe as God's creation.

> *Celebrant* At your command all things came to be:
>
> the vast expanse of interstellar space, galaxies, suns, the planets in their courses, and *this fragile earth, our island home*; by your will they were created and have their being.
>
> *People* Glory to you for ever and ever.

Celebrant From the primal elements you brought forth the human race,

and blessed us with memory, reason, and skill;

you made us the stewards of creation.

People Glory to you for ever and ever.

Included in the strong presentation of God as Creator, the references to fragile earth, our island home, and you made us stewards of creation are an obvious reference to the cultural concern of environmentalism. In 1989, the General Synod passed a resolution calling on the provincial and federal governments to help fund and carry out an environmental impact study on a proposed gold mine in British Columbia.[135]

Later, in the fixed Preface, this text appears:

In the fullness of time you sent your Son, *born of a woman*, to be our Saviour.

Earlier Canadian Anglican Eucharistic Prayers made no mention of Jesus' human lineage. A reference to the Virgin Mary might not necessarily be interpreted as showing awareness of women, but choosing to use the expression "a woman" clearly shows an attempt to identify with women in general and therefore represents that cultural value.

The concluding epiclesis contains material from one of the oldest sources of Eucharistic material, the *Didache*, and yet also expresses a modern cultural value.

Pour out your Spirit upon the whole earth and make it your new creation.
Gather your Church together from the ends of the earth into your kingdom,
where peace and justice are revealed, that we, with all your people,
of every language, race, and nation, may share the banquet you have promised.

These words reflect a strong commitment to social justice and bring to mind those in poverty,[136] affected by racism, or otherwise on the margins of society.

Eucharistic Prayer 5

The introduction to the Eucharistic Prayers[137] in the *Book of Alternative Services* includes this comment: "This prayer is a new composition. Its language is simple and direct. It was written for use as a sung text with a common refrain and with celebrations with children in mind."[138] Even the motivation behind the awareness of children being present, in and of itself, shows a concern for *inclusion* in the Eucharistic liturgy as illustrated in this text which appears near the beginning of the fixed Preface:

In Jesus, your Son, you bring healing to our world
and *gather us into one great family.*

Following the Sanctus, in the section praising the Father for the life and work of Jesus, the following statements are made:

He cares for the poor and the hungry. He suffers with the sick and the rejected.

These are obvious statements of the cultural values of concern for poverty as well as those on the margins of society. Like Eucharistic Prayer 4, this prayer also concludes with an expression of an eschatological hope in the concluding doxology.

Father, you call us to be your servants; fill us with the courage and love of Jesus, *that all the world may gather in joy at the table of your kingdom.*

Like the preceding prayer, the value of inclusion is clearly expressed in this petition.

Eucharistic Prayer 6

Prayer 6[139] is unique in this collection because of its strong dependence on the Eastern Eucharistic Prayer of St. Basil of Caesarea.[140] As such, the prayer exalts a lofty vision of "the God in heaven." Even so, immediately following the Sanctus, in the initial praise and thanksgiving of God the Creator, the following text appears:

You formed us in your own image, *giving the whole world into our care,*
so that, in obedience to you, our creator, *we might rule and serve all your creatures.*

These words highlight the stewardship role that humans have for the earth and, therefore, reflect the cultural value of environmentalism.[141] Later in this same section, these words are used to describe part of Jesus' earthly ministry:

To the poor he proclaimed the good news of salvation;
to prisoners, freedom; to the sorrowful, joy.

While these texts are clearly inspired by Jesus' own self-definition of his mission in the fourth chapter of Luke's Gospel, they also exemplify the cultural values of concern for poverty and for those on the margins of society.

From the above investigation of the six Eucharistic Prayers of the Canadian (Anglican) Book of Alternative Services, it is obvious that each prayer includes material that directly expresses the values of the culture of the Anglican Church of Canada in the mid to late twentieth century.

However, the evidence of at least some type of reflexive relationship between the Anglican Church of Canada's expressed culture and its Eucharistic prayer texts in the latter part of the twentieth century needs to be examined critically. As discussed in chapter 2, cultures are neither static, monolithic, nor homogeneous. To state that the culture of the Anglican Church of Canada has certain values and characteristics in the latter part of the twentieth century is merely to state that those who voiced these values were empowered to do so, and that in some way they formed the dominant face of that local culture. This is a particularly relevant issue when dealing with an institutional church. It seems straightforward to deduce the value system, and therefore culture, of a particular church body by simply exploring its official statements and, in the case of the Anglican Church of Canada, by examining its liturgical texts as expressions of its theological understanding of the Christian Gospel. However, this makes the assumption that these formal statements represent the actual values and convictions of the members in their day-to-day lives—where they actually interact with other cultures in society. Paul Marshall, writing in a Canadian context, discusses this concern of the problem of over-identification of the practical understanding of Christian living with the organized church. "When this happens, the relation of Christ and culture is treated as the relation of the church and culture."[142] He reminds the reader that the greatest impact and experience of the Christian faith in the lives of the church's members take place in the everyday lives and encounters of those members—outside of the gathered church. Analysis of individual Christian responses requires a subtle sociological examination of how Christians respond differently—if they do—to major currents of our culture, and how they are shaped by and in turn shape that culture,[143] as they are in a reflexive relationship with many cultures in and through their daily lives. This fact does not change the validity of the claims above concerning cultural expression in liturgical texts. Rather, it simply places a limit on their application. The description of the culture of the latter twentieth-century Anglican Church of Canada given above is simply one description of that culture.

In this chapter, the interaction between the theological understanding of the Anglican Church of Canada, as expressed in its Eucharistic Prayer texts in the mid- and late twentieth century, and that church's expressed culture of the same period has been explored. Given the priority that this church has given to expressing some social issues of its contemporary context and its desire to make those issues a part of its theological concern, it is fair to conclude that the Anglican Church of Canada views the focus of its faith—Jesus Christ—as being involved in that culture and working to transform it. Therefore, this particular expression of the Anglican Church of Canada does follow the pattern of Niebuhr's fifth type, Christ, the transformer of culture.

It is one thing to claim that the Anglican Church of Canada in the late twentieth century showed evidence of enabling its contemporary cultural concerns to influence the liturgical expression of its theology. But this is true only for its existing membership and, in this case, it is true only for the membership that identifies with this particular expression of the church's culture. The purpose of the Christian church, and therefore of the Anglican Church of Canada, is to be able to communicate the reality of the person and work of Jesus Christ (its Christology) in a way that profoundly impacts both its own members and the other members of the communities in which they live. Christopher Wade expresses this always-contemporary concern:

> In his study of images of Christ through the ages, Jaroslav Pelikan observes that every generation of Christians wrestles with this question—*Who do you say that I am?*, restating who Christ is *for* them as they seek to be faithful to Peter's profession while yet responding to changing human realities.[144]

This is the challenge for the Anglican Church of Canada—or for any Christian church for that matter. Precisely because of the reflexive relationship between the theology of the Gospel and the culture in which Christ is to be experienced, the church must discover a faithful Christological expression from within the cultures in which people live and with which they identify. "As language and cultures change over time and in different places, Christian worship must continue to find new ways of articulating the mystery of God who is revealed in the person and work of Jesus."[145]

It is this Christological task that shall be explored in the next chapter.

NOTES

1. Bibby, *Fragmented Gods: The Poverty and Potential of Religion in Canada*, 118. Bibby states that in 1946 roughly two-thirds of adults in Canada attended worship on Sundays. By 1986, that number had dropped to one-third.

2. H. Richard Niebuhr, *Christ and Culture* (New York: Harper & Row, 1951).

3. It is recognized that there is no exact definition of the sociological designation commonly referred to as postmodernism. Rather, as the modifying title suggests, it is referred to more as a breakdown of commonly held assumptions of modernism. In this work, it will be used as a collective term that refers to the critique offered to these assumptions (sociological and anthropological) that characterize modernity.

4. Bill Ashcroft, Gareth Griffiths, and Helen Tiffin, *Post-Colonial Studies: The Key Concepts* (New York: Routledge, 2000), 118.

5. Ibid., 118–21.

6. Niebuhr, 2.
7. Ibid., 6.
8. Ibid., 4–11. Niebuhr discusses examples of this interaction from the period of Graeco-Roman civilization through to the communistic and democratic societies of the twentieth century.
9. Ibid., 12.
10. Ibid.
11. Ibid., 13.
12. Ibid., 14.
13. Ibid., 32.
14. Ibid., 38.
15. Ibid., 39.
16. Ibid., 44.
17. Ibid., 45.
18. 1 John 2:3–11; 3:4–10.
19. Niebuhr, 47.
20. Tertullian, "The Apology," in *The Ante-Nicene Fathers: Translations of the Writings of the Fathers Down to A.D. 325*, ed. Alexander Roberts and James Donaldson (Buffalo, NY: The Christian Literature Publishing Company, 1885). See particularly Chapters xxi and xlii.
21. Niebuhr, 50.
22. Ibid., 71.
23. Ibid., 76.
24. An example would be Paul's argument in Chapter 2 of the Epistle to the Romans around Jewish and Gentile approaches to the law.
25. Niebuhr, 83.
26. Ibid., 86. See F.C. Burkitt, *Church and Gnosis: A Study of Christian Thought and speculation in the Second Century* (Cambridge: Cambridge University Press, 1932), 86–89.
27. Ibid., 89. See McCallum, J. Ramsay, *Abelard's Christian Theology* (Merrick, NY: Richwood Pub. Co., 1976), 83–85.
28. Ibid., 90–91.
29. Ibid., 92.
30. Ibid., 97.
31. Ibid., 98. See A. Ritschl, *The Christian Doctrine of Justification and Reconciliation* (Clifton, NY: Reference Book Publishers, Inc., 1966), 284.
32. Ibid., 99.
33. Ibid., 103.
34. Ibid., 117.
35. Ibid., 118–19.
36. Alexandria Clement of, "The Instructor," in *The Ante-Nicene Fathers: Translations of the Writings of the Fathers Down to A.D. 325*, ed. Alexander Roberts and James Donaldson (Buffalo, NY: The Christian Literature Publishing Company, 1885), 271–98.
37. Niebuhr, 126.
38. Ibid., 128.

39. Ibid., 135. See Thomas Aquinas, *Summa Theologica,* trans. Fathers of the English Dominicans Province (New York: Benziger Brothers, 1912–25), especially Ques. i – v.

40. Ibid., 145.

41. Ibid., 146–48.

42. Ibid., 146.

43. Ibid., 150.

44. Ibid.

45. Ibid., 151.

46. Ibid., 156.

47. Ibid., 165. See Galatians 5.19–21 and Romans 13.4 as examples of the two sides of the duality.

48. Ibid.

49. Ibid., 170. See Martin Luther, *Works of Martin Luther: With Introductions and Notes*, trans. Henry Eyster Jacobs (Philadelphia: Muhlenberg Press, 1930), vol. II, 338 and vol. IV, 251.

50. Ibid., 172.

51. Ibid., 185.

52. Ibid., 189.

53. Ibid., 191.

54. Ibid., 194.

55. Ibid.

56. Ibid., 203. See John 1.29 and 3.16.

57. Ibid., 206.

58. A. Augustine, Bishop of Hippo, *City of God*, trans. John Healey, vol. 2 (London: J. M. Dent, 1945). See Books fifteen to nineteen where, even though the 'Two Cities' are proposed, appearing to be dualist, ultimately those of the City of God are transformed during their life journey in the Earthly City; ibid.

59. Niebuhr, 209.

60. Ibid., 233.

61. John Howard Yoder, "How H. Richard Niebuhr Reasoned: A Critique of *Christ and Culture*," in *Authentic Transformation: A New Vision of Christ and Culture*, ed. D. M. Yeager and John Howard Yoder, Glen H. Stassen (Nashville, TN: Abingdon Press, 1996), 54. Yoder explains Niebuhr's use of Tertullian as an example of Type One—Christ Against Culture, after which Niebuhr gives instances where Tertullian does not fit that type.

62. Ibid., 85.

63. See also Hauerwas and Willimon in Stanley Hauerwas, *Resident Aliens: Life in the Christian Colony* (Nashville, TN: Abingdon, 1989), 40.

> We have come to believe that few books have been a greater hindrance to an accurate assessment of our situation than *Christ and Culture*. Niebuhr rightly saw that our politics determines our theology. He was right that Christians cannot reject "culture." But his call to Christians to accept "culture" . . . and politics in the name of the unity of God's creating and redeeming activity had the effect of endorsing a Constantinian social strategy.

Note that their issue is with how Niebuhr was interpreted.

64. Yoder, 55.

65. Glen H. Stassen, "Concrete Christological Norms for Transformation," ibid., 141–42. See also H. Richard Niebuhr, *Theology, History, and Culture: Major Unpublished Writings*, ed. William Stacy Johnson (New Haven, CT: Yale University Press, 1996), xxx.

66. Marshall, 2.

67. Ibid., 1–2.

68. Ibid., 3.

69. Cyril Powles, "The Anglican Church in Canadian Culture," ibid., 12. Powles cites the work of Raymond Whitehead in "Christ and Cultural Imperialism," in *Justice as Mission: An Agenda for the Church*, ed. Christopher Lind and Terry Brown (Burlington: Trinity Press, 1985), 26.

70. John G. Stackhouse, Jr., *Making the Best of It: Following Christ in the Real World* (New York: Oxford University Press, 2008), 5–6.

71. Ibid., 7.

72. Ibid., see discussion of paradox on p. 27.

73. John Howard Yoder in Stassen, 40.

74. Ibid., 128.

75. D. Stephen Long, *Theology and Culture: A Guide to the Discussion* (Eugene, OR: Cascade Books, 2008), 69.

76. Even if Long is not clear about what is meant by this statement, the author of this thesis is affirming that it is the received record of the manifestation of Jesus of Nazareth that may be limited or inadequate. To claim that the actual person of Jesus of Nazareth as a historical manifestation of the eternal Christ was inadequate would be antithetical to the whole purpose of the incarnation.

77. Long, 69.

78. Yoder.

79. Donald W. Jr. Shriver, *H. Richard Niebuhr* (Nashville, TN: Abingdon Press, 2009), 41.

80. Stassen, 131.

81. D. M. Yeager, "The View from Somewhere: The Meaning of Method in *Christ and Culture*," *Journal of the Society of Christian Ethics* 23, no. 1 (2003): 117. Yeager makes a helpful distinction between Typologies and Taxonomies (which Yoder's understanding of Niebuhr's types appears to be closer to)—the former being ideal constructs and the latter pertaining to generalized classifications from observed data.

82. Anglican Church of Canada, *The Book of Alternative Services of the Anglican Church of Canada* (Toronto: Anglican Book Centre, 1985), 177. "The preparation of the gifts of bread and wine is essentially functional, but together with the offering of money and other gifts, *it does also symbolize the offering of ourselves and of the whole creation to God*." [emphasis mine.]

83. Ibid., 178.

> In the eucharistic prayer the Church expresses the meaning of the whole eucharistic action in which the memorial of redemption is made, and *the Church is united with Christ in*

offering and communion through the sanctifying power of the Holy Spirit. [emphasis mine.]

84. Louis Weil, "Proclamation of Faith in the Eucharist," in *Time and Community: In Honor of Thomas Julian Talley*, ed. J. Neil Alexander (Washington, DC: The Pastoral Press, 1990), 282.

85. Ruth A. Meyers, "One Bread, One Body: Ritual, Language and Symbolism in the Eucharist," in *Our Thanks and Praise: The Eucharist in Anglicanism Today*, ed. David R. Holeton (Toronto: Anglican Book Centre, 1998), 95. Inculturation is discussed more fully later in this chapter and in chapter 5.

86. Gordon W. Lathrop, "Eucharist in the New Testament and Its Cultural Settings," in *Worship and Culture in Dialogue: Reports of International Consultations, Cartigny Switzerland, 1993, Hong Kong, 1994*, ed. S. Anita Stauffer (Geneva: Department for Theology and Studies, LWF, 1994), 80.

87. Ibid.

88. Ibid.

89. The (international) Anglican Communion has well-established ongoing dialogues with Lutheran, Roman Catholic, and Orthodox Churches, and some national Anglican and Lutheran Churches have full-communion agreements. See the Anglican Communion website: http://www.anglicancommunion.org/ministry/ecumenical/dialogues/.

90. David Lyon, "Introduction," in *Rethinking Church, State, and Modernity*, ed. David Lyon and Marguerite Van Die (Toronto: University of Toronto Press, 2000), 8.

91. Roger O'Toole, "Religion in Canada: Its Development and Contemporary Situation," in *Religion and Canadian Society*, ed. Lori G. Beaman (Toronto: Canadian Scholars Press, Inc., 2006), 12–13.

92. John S. Moir, "The Canadianization of the Protestant Churches," in *Christianity in Canada: Historical Essays*, ed. Paul Laverdure (Yorkton: Redeemer's Voice Press, 2002), 39.

93. O'Toole, 8–9.

94. Ibid., 9.

95. Moir, *The Americanization of Religion in Canada*, 151.

96. *Canadian Religious Historiography: An Overview*, 137.

97. Ibid. Moir cites the work of Robert Handy: Robert T. Handy, *A History of the Churches in the United States and Canada* (Oxford: Clarendon Press, 1976), vii.

98. O'Toole, 10.

99. Powles, 19.

100. Ibid., 24. Emphasis mine.

101. Peter Beyer, "Religious Vitality in Canada: The Complementarity of Religious Market and Secularization Perspectives," in *Religion and Canadian Society*, ed. Lori Beaman (Toronto: Canadian Scholars Press, Inc., 2006), 73.

102. "Modern Forms of the Religious Life: Denomination, Church, and Invisible Religion in Canada, the United States and Europe," in *Rethinking Church, State, and Modernity*, ed. David Lyon and Marguerite Van Die (Toronto: University of Toronto Press, 2000), 207.

103. Powles, 15.

104. O'Toole, 19.
105. Samuel H. Reimer, *A Look at Cultural Effects on Religiosity: A Comparison between the United States and Canada,* ibid., 55.
106. Geoffrey Wainwright, *Doxology: The Praise of God in Worship, Doctrine and Life: A Systematic Theology* (New York: Oxford University Press, 1980), 390.
107. Powles, 17.
108. O'Toole, 13.
109. *Anglicanism in Canada: A Sociological Sketch*, ed. M. Darol Bryant, Canadian Anglicanism at the Dawn of a New Century (Lewiston, NY: E. Mellen Press, 2001), 39. Emphasis mine.
110. Wainwright, 389.
111. Meyers, 93.
112. Anglican Church of Canada, *The Book of Common Prayer* (Cambridge: University Press, 1959), 78.
113. "Official Statements of the Anglican Church of Canada—General Synod Resolution Re: Pollution," http://qumran.national.anglican.ca/ics-wpd/Textbases/search/official/search.aspx.
114. *The Book of Common Prayer*, 82.
115. William R. Crockett, *Eucharist: Symbol of Transformation* (New York: Pueblo Publishing, 1989), 50.
116. Anglican Church of Canada, *The Book of Common Prayer*, 82.
117. Ibid., 82–83.
118. Ibid., 83.
119. "Official Statements of the Anglican Church of Canada—General Synod Resolution Re: Human Rights," http://qumran.national.anglican.ca/ics-wpd/Textbases/search/official/search.aspx. The 1969 meeting of the General Synod adopted a resolution on human rights, which directed the federal government to become more involved with the concerns of developing nations and with immigration from these countries and directed Anglicans to reach out to their francophone Canadians (in the height of Quebec separatist concerns). While this resolution does not specifically name inclusion, it clearly demonstrates this sensitivity.
120. *The Book of Alternative Services of the Anglican Church of Canada*, 178.
121. William R. Crockett, "The Theology of the Eucharistic Prayers in the Book of Alternative Services of the Anglican Church of Canada," *Toronto Journal of Theology* 3, no. 1 (1987): 101.
122. David J. Kennedy, *Eucharistic Sacramentality in an Ecumenical Context: The Anglican Epiclesis* (Aldershot: Ashgate, 2008), 185.
123. Varghese Baby, "Some Aspects of West Syrian Liturgical Theology," *Studia Liturgica* 31, no. 2 (2001): 177.
124. Boyd Morgan, "An Historical and Ecclesiological Study of the Book of Alternative Services (1985) of the Anglican Church of Canada" (ThD. thesis, Boston University, 2001), 3–4. Emphasis mine.
125. Ibid., Footnote #136, p. 239.
126. Anglican Church of Canada, *The Book of Alternative Services* (Toronto: Anglican Book Centre, 1985), 193–95.

127. Crockett, "The Theology of the Eucharistic Prayers in the Book of Alternative Services of the Anglican Church of Canada," 102.

128. Anglican Church of Canada, *The Book of Alternative Services of the Anglican Church of Canada*, 196–97.

129. Ibid., 179.

130. "Official Statements of the Anglican Church of Canada—General Synod Resolution Re: Social Action Concerns," http://qumran.national.anglican.ca/ics-wpd/Textbases/search/official/search.aspx.

> That this General Synod being keenly aware of many injustices arising from present social structures and standards, request the Program Committee to initiate a study of our nation's economic structures and processes, with a view to devising policies that our Church may support for the elimination of poverty and social injustice and the establishing of criteria for desirable social development.

131. *The Book of Alternative Services of the Anglican Church of Canada*, 198–200.

132. Crockett, "The Theology of the Eucharistic Prayers in the Book of Alternative Services of the Anglican Church of Canada," 105.

133. Anglican Church of Canada, *The Book of Alternative Services of the Anglican Church of Canada*, 201.

134. Ibid., 180.

135. "Official Statements of the Anglican Church of Canada—General Synod Resolution Re: Cinola Gold Project," http://qumran.national.anglican.ca/ics-wpd/Textbases/search/official/search.aspx.

136. "Official Statements of the Anglican Church of Canada—General Synod Resolution Re: Poverty in Canada," http://qumran.national.anglican.ca/ics-wpd/Textbases/search/official/search.aspx.

> That this General Synod urge the House of Bishops to convey our deep concern about poverty in this land to appropriate levels of government, to the dioceses, and to the parishes of The Anglican Church of Canada, emphasizing especially the need,

which was followed by multi-point, concrete recommendations.

137. *The Book of Alternative Services of the Anglican Church of Canada*, 204–06.

138. Ibid., 180.

139. Ibid., 207–10.

140. Crockett, "The Theology of the Eucharistic Prayers in the Book of Alternative Services of the Anglican Church of Canada," 107.

141. Also see Stephen Reynolds, "Bas Evaluation: Some Theological Questions Responses'," in *Thinking About the Book of Alternative Services: A Discussion Primer* (Toronto: The Anglican Church of Canada, 1993), 42–43.

142. Marshall, 3.

143. Ibid., 4.

144. Christopher Wade, "'To Reveal the Riches of Your Grace': Examining the Authorized Eucharistic Christologies of the Episcopal Church with Implications" (Graduate Theological Union, 2009), 32–33.

145. Meyers, 97.

Chapter 5

Developing a Contextual Christology in a Postmodern Culture

POSTMODERN CHRISTOLOGY: THE PRIMACY OF THE TEXT

The previous chapters have presented a discussion of how the understanding of culture has evolved, and how a contemporary understanding, influenced by what might be called a postmodern critique, has shown that local cultures cannot be evaluated, per se, by any objective criteria, but rather are to be described. It has been shown that Christian theology within a particular local culture is in a reflexive relationship with the other parts of that culture and is expressed through that culture's signs and symbols of meaning. Consequently, there is no single a-cultural expression of Christian theology and, therefore, of the Gospel of Jesus Christ. At the same time, it is realized that "all theology and Christology are culturally situated."[1] This means that the great classical expressions of Christology from the fourth and fifth centuries (Nicaea and Chalcedon), while clearly providing authoritative statements about the person and work of Jesus Christ, are also products of the Greek-influenced philosophy and culture of that time.

This chapter will discuss the work of the twentieth-century historical theologian, Hans Frei, and explore how and why the hermeneutical approach he applied to biblical texts (particularly the Gospel narratives) might be fertile ground for building a local Christology in the twenty-first century. It will examine some of the challenges to this approach to building a Christology and attempt to compare and contrast the resulting Christology with some recent Christological approaches. Finally, it will begin to discuss why such a narrative-based Christology is well suited to being employed in a Eucharistic prayer.

Introduction to the Work of Hans Frei

Hans Frei was a German-born American theologian whose writing spanned a thirty-year period in the latter half of the twentieth century. During this span, he produced three longer works: *The Identity of Jesus Christ*, *The Eclipse of Biblical Narrative*, and *Types of Christian Theology*—this final work was published posthumously due to his untimely death in 1988. However, his impact on theology in the closing decades of the last century and into the present has been enormous.[2] And his insistence on calling the Christian theological enterprise back to the primacy of the biblical text, in particular the narratives of the four Gospels, has opened the way for fresh explorations into understanding these texts in the postmodern world at the beginning of the twenty-first century.

Frei wrote his PhD thesis on Karl Barth at Yale under the supervision of H. Richard Niebuhr. He subsequently became an Episcopalian, was ordained a priest in 1952, completed his thesis on Karl Barth in 1956, and joined the faculty at Yale.[3]

Both Barth and (H. Richard) Niebuhr had a profound influence on the thinking of Hans Frei. Frei embraced Barth's insistence on the absolute freedom of God and God's approach to the world and the salvation of humankind, "that the possibility and even the necessity for God's assuming man unto himself by incarnation himself may be affirmed and explored *because he did so* and only for that reason."[4] This approach, along with Barth's, represented a major shift from many other Christologies of the time because it was not apologetically driven and did not begin from a soteriological starting point. This conviction of beginning with God's freedom in acting in Jesus Christ allowed Frei to step back from much of the nineteenth- and twentieth-century traditional thinking around Christologies (i.e., Christology "from below") and develop a different approach.[5]

Frei was also convinced of Christ's uniqueness—his "own singular, unsubstitutable, and self-focused being."[6] This conviction was in keeping with Barth's turning away from so much of modern theology's anthropological starting point.[7] For example, Schleiermacher, and those who would follow, developed their theology by beginning with humanity's subjective experiences.

> Ordinary or objectifying talk is the kind of talk appropriate to outer, objective history. . . . Religious discourse on the other hand seeks its sources elsewhere, in the realm of *inner history*—an inner history which is to some extent independent of outer history, and which can still serve as the site of divine manifestation.[8]

Schleiermacher's strategy was an attempt to circumvent the result of historical criticism of the biblical texts, which had called into question the historicity of these texts—particularly the Gospel accounts of the life of Jesus. Schleiermacher's resultant Christology proposed that the possibility for connection with the divine was inherently a part of what it meant to be human.

> He argued for an unprecedented development of inwardness in Jesus of Nazareth which constituted, not an absolute rupture of the laws of development and contingency, but a relative miracle: the emergence of something new at the beginning of a fresh stage of human subjective development.'[9]

This is an example of what came to be known as a "Christology from below"—in that it begins with the human experience. On the one hand, it emphasized the humanity of Jesus, but a major difficulty in this approach, as raised by D. F. Strauss and subsequently by Frei, was that it paid little or no attention to *the particularities* of the human life of Jesus of Nazareth.[10] As will be shown below, Frei would approach the problem of the world of historical criticism, not by struggling to fit the Gospel witness of the Christian faith into it, but rather by revealing how the historical world could be located within the Christian faith.[11]

While Frei shared Barth's concern about the need to ensure God's absolute freedom in relation to the created order, Frei was also concerned to preserve a place for human freedom and for an account of its historical development.[12] Consequently, an aspect of Frei's Christology developed against Barth. Frei had trouble with Barth's "inability to speak positively of a human freedom for revelation based on divine freedom for humanity. . . . He [Barth] did not know how to pay attention to that humanity as humanity." [13] Therefore, Frei viewed Barth as guilty of epistemological monophysitism.[14] "Frei found in Barth's account too little attention to the details of Christ's humanity, too little attention to the contingent course of wider history."[15] It will be shown below that paying attention to the particularities of Jesus' humanity is critical to establishing his identity, and hence developing an effective Christology. Frei highlighted the fact that the Gospel narratives do exactly that.

One of the influences for Frei that fostered a concern for the attention to human history and, in particular, to the details of Jesus' life, was that of H. Richard Niebuhr. Rather than trying to reconstruct a picture of the historical Jesus based on the findings of historical criticism, Niebuhr instead begins with the understanding that, while the Gospels each yield a somewhat different description of Jesus of Nazareth, one can begin to

> see the unity in the variety of Christianity by referring all of it to the New Testament portrait, not to a historical reconstruction of the portrait. . . . Niebuhr grants that every description is an interpretation but is confident that it can be "an interpretation for the objective reality."[16]

Frei was impressed by Niebuhr's unwillingness to separate the narrative story from its theological purpose. Frei writes:

> Niebuhr was, despite his own denial, a man of powerful metaphysical vision. This vision, however, was not a shape to be separated out from the narrative shape in which we experience and retell the appropriation of any tradition. . . . The two—the time-filled story, and its mysterious, overarching metaphysical or reality affirmation—are given together. Story images and general concepts are united but *never* convertible into each other.[17]

From both Barth and Niebuhr, this sense of honoring the integrity of the biblical text would lead Frei to explore alternate ways of considering the narrative texts.

During these early years at Yale, Frei was introduced to the concept of *figura* in Barth's interpretation of scripture, in which a particular biblical incident or character "is itself and yet points beyond itself to something else that it prefigures."[18] This interest in the figural interpretation of texts led Frei to the works of Erich Auerbach. From his work on Western literature, and in particular on Tertullian and the church Fathers, Auerbach defined *figura* as "something real and historical which announces something else that is also real and historical. The relation between the two events is revealed by an accord or similarity."[19] For the church Fathers, in addition to determining the literal sense of the texts, the aim was to show that "the persons and events of the Old Testament were preconfigurations of the New Testament and its history of salvation."[20] However, in order to ensure the authenticity of each event on its own, Auerbach was careful to point out that in his figural interpretation, Tertullian always saw both events as real and historical. "Real historical figures are to be interpreted spiritually . . . but that interpretation points to a carnal, hence historical fulfillment."[21] The Protestant Reformers such as Luther and Calvin, along with holding to a grammatical (literal) sense of biblical texts, also employed figural, or typological, interpretation, which helped to undergird their understanding of the Bible as a unified canon.[22] "Figural interpretation, then, sets forth the unity of the canon as a single cumulative and complex pattern of meaning."[23] This approach of seeing biblical events as being providentially ordered as part of a single whole became an important foundation for Frei's understanding of how our historical reality could be contained within God's providential ordering of all of history as revealed in scripture.

The work of Auerbach also impressed upon Frei the idea of "realistic narrative"[24] which became the primary way in which Frei treated the Gospel narratives. Frei used the argument that "realistic narrative was . . . the dominant way of reading scripture throughout the first seventeen hundred years or so of the Christian tradition."[25] Frei's treatment of Gospel texts as realistic narratives will be expanded below.

The other influence on Frei's approach was the work of Gilbert Ryle. At a time when much of current theological thinking was looking for the true essence of selfhood (and in the development of Christologies, the true essence of Jesus' person) behind or under what was outwardly observable in the texts, Ryle gave Frei another way of thinking about personal identity.[26] From Ryle's work, Frei was able to conclude that "the human self is not some unknowable inner entity, whose nature may or may not be revealed by the words and bodily actions so mysteriously related to it. Rather, my words and actions constitute my identity."[27] In other words, narratives help us know who a person really is.

In summary, Frei wrote of Karl Barth, "Barth turned his back on by far the largest part of the modern theological tradition with its anthropological starting point and logic."[28] And, as Frei began to emerge as a historical theologian, he, too, turned away from much of the liberal Protestant theological enterprise of his day, particularly as exemplified in the work of Schleiermacher. In these contemporary approaches to Christology, "he found three 'errors of faith': first, that the starting point of theology is anthropology; second, the belief that the proper mode of anthropology was to analyze man as self-consciousness, and, third, that out of this one could derive a Christology."[29]

In his work entitled *The Identity of Jesus Christ*, Frei also expressed the importance of keeping the work of interpretation in theology separate from apologetic—something that he thought much of modern systematic theology did not do.

> I remain convinced that a sound basis for good dogmatic theology demands that a sharp distinction be observed between dogmatic theology and apologetics. With few exceptions, the theologians . . . have been preoccupied ever since the beginning of the eighteenth century with showing the credibility or . . . "meaningfulness" of Christianity to their skeptical or confused contemporaries.[30]

Frei traces this gradually increasing emphasis on apologetics in biblical hermeneutics in his largest single work.

Frei's Typology of Christian Theology

Frei proposed two essential ways of looking at Christian theology. Christian theology could be viewed as one example of a theology—a kind of specialized subset of a larger and more general discipline. Or rather, theology could be defined as an aspect of Christianity and would therefore be "defined by its relation to the cultural or semiotic system that constitutes that religion. . . . In this view theology is explained by the character of Christianity rather than vice versa."[31] Frei then went on to propose five types of Christian theology, with these two approaches representing the two types at either pole along with three intermediate types that spanned a continuum between them. Each type "described . . . differing substantive theological and philosophical commitments."[32] Briefly, he described the five types as:

Type 1—"Theology is a philosophical discipline within the academy."[33]
Type 2—like #1 except "it seeks to correlate specifically Christian with general Cultural meaning structures such as natural science or the 'spirit' of a cultural era."[34]
Type 3—also correlates theology as "a procedure subject to formal, universal and transcendental criteria for valid thinking, with theology as specific and second-order Christian self-description" but does not impose a comprehensive structure for integrating them.[35]
Type 4—"argues that Christian theology is a non-systematic combination of normed Christian self-description and method founded on general theory." It is similar to Type 3 but now self-description and general criteria are no longer "equals." "The practical discipline of Christian self-description governs and limits the applicability of general criteria of meaning in theology."[36]
Type 5—"Christian theology is exclusively a matter of Christian self-description . . . Christian theology is strictly the grammar of the faith, a procedure in self-description for which there is no external correlative."[37]

Frei clearly situated himself in Type Four where "philosophy will be Christian self-description's handmaid . . . because that is the task for which philosophy, properly understood, is itself properly fitted."[38] Types One through Three become problematic because, in varying degrees, they each assume that Christian theology is expected to fit within a larger, and universal, reference frame for rational thought. However, as has been shown in preceding chapters, with the critique of postmodern thinking, such a universal, metanarrative frame does not exist. The difficulty with Type Five is that it is an entirely closed and exclusive approach to Christian theology, which leaves it with no correlative with which to relate to any rational thought beyond itself—and thereby make itself understood to those beyond its cohort.

USING FREI'S "HERMENEUTICAL PRINCIPLES"

Utilizing Frei's approach to the person and work of Jesus Christ, where does one begin to build a contemporary Christology? What kind of hermeneutics will be used to interpret the scriptural texts upon which this Christology is built? Frei's helpful definition of hermeneutics, "the rules and principles for determining the sense of written texts, or the rules and principles governing exegesis,"[39] will be employed. The key thrust of Frei's approach is to bring the focus of biblical interpretation on the person and work of Jesus Christ back to the narrative texts of the Gospels themselves. Frei insisted that the purpose and meaning of these texts was first and foremost descriptive—letting the text speak for itself and keeping it as independent as possible from apologetic concerns or truth claims. Therefore, rather than beginning with questions or concerns about historicity or theological truth—both of which would unhelpfully load the interpretation of the texts with preconceived concerns, the way into this approach is to ask formal questions of the narrative texts—which Frei defined as being questions that do not materially influence the answer.[40] Because Frei held firmly to the unsubstitutable identity of Jesus Christ, he insisted that the Gospel narratives could not refer to anything external to themselves—only internally to the identity of Jesus Christ. As mentioned above, any attempt to go behind the text and use it to refer to, or construct, an independent and larger picture of salvation, or of a savior, was a distortion of Christian theology.

There are four key features of Frei's hermeneutical approach which are used in the construction of this Christology:

- treating the Gospel texts as *realistic narrative*
- employing *figural interpretation* to link together the rest of the biblical texts and, in fact, to the events in our lives
- giving primacy to the *sensus literalis* interpretation of those texts and
- accepting a *providential view of history* in order to root the person and work of Jesus Christ in the history of the world.

Each of these is developed below.

Realistic narrative

In the preface to his work, *The Identity of Jesus Christ,* Frei writes:

> The aim of an exegesis which simply looks for the sense of a story (but does not identify sense with religious significance for the reader) is in the final analysis that of reading the story itself. We ask if we agree on what we find there, and we discover its patterns to one another. And therefore the theoretical devices we use to make our reading more alert, appropriate, and intelligent ought to be designed to leave the story itself as unencumbered as possible. This is additionally true because realistic stories . . . are directly accessible. . . . [T]hey mean what they say, and that fact enables them to render depictively to the reader their

own public world, which is the world he needs to understand them, even if he decides that it is not his own real world.[41]

This is how Hans Frei began to examine narrative texts in a way that set him apart from the dominant approach of modern theology in the earlier part of the twentieth century. The hermeneutical position that Frei worked from was one in which the narrative's meaning was caught up in its structure. In adopting this approach, Frei was stating that the text's meaning would not be found, at least in a primary sense, in the author's intention, philosophical or theological anthropology, religious or moral impact, or even its historicity. Frei defended this approach by comparing the Gospel narratives to the genre of realistic fiction in which there is "the close interaction of character and incident."[42]

Frei began from the observation that "a realistic or history-like (though not necessarily historical) element is a feature, as obvious as it is important, of many of the biblical narratives that went into the making of Christian belief."[43] Frei then examined historical narrative and fictional narratives and realized that "what they have in common is their insistence that the direct interaction of character and circumstance not be abstracted from each other."[44] Therefore, the theme emerges from the interaction of characters and their circumstance. Frei concluded, "It is my conviction that the interaction of character and circumstance, subject and object, inner and outer human being cannot be *explained*. . . . But it *can* be *described*."[45]

With this approach, Frei begins to ask questions of the narrative texts of the Gospels—in particular, as to the identity of their main character, Jesus. Frei is quick to point out that one cannot inquire, of the New Testament record, into the actual life of Jesus. This makes sense because to do so is to imply that there is a source of extra-biblical material by which to judge critically the accuracy of the biblical texts. As discussed above, all that one could bring to these texts are pre-determined reference frames that attempt to correlate the meaning of the texts to other more general criteria. Ultimately this exercise would not be fruitful if one accepts that the primary purpose of the Gospel texts is to reveal the identity of Jesus, and if one holds to the unsubstitutable nature of Jesus Christ. Rather, following Frei, "Our task is . . . to observe the story itself—its structure, the shape of its movement, and its crucial transitions."[46] Frei was guided by three points: "The identity of the Christian saviour is revealed completely by the story of Jesus in the Gospels and by none other"; "knowing the identity of any person involves describing the continuity of the person who is acted upon through a stretch of time"; and the determination of an individual's identity by asking "two formal questions: 'Who is he?' and 'What is he like?'"[47] As described above, the formal nature of the questions is key. If the question asked materially influences the answer, then the question is not a formal one. "The *question* rather than the story becomes the governing context with which the person is identified."[48]

Frei expands on the question "Who is he?" by stating that it is answered through the subject's self-manifestations—in word and deed. One needs to examine instances when one's actions are so central and significant that they actually constitute who one is. "A person *is* what he *does* centrally and most significantly."[49] In treating the question "What is he like?" Frei considers that person's interaction with others and what happens to them as a result. In referring to the person of Jesus, Frei states,

> The identity of Jesus . . . is not given simply in his inner intention . . . [but] rather in the enactment of his intentions . . . [and] in the mysterious coincidence of his intentional action with circumstances partly initiated by him, partly devolving upon him.[50]

Frei points out that this understanding of self (and in particular of Jesus' self) stands in contrast with modern philosophers and theologians who put a distance between true selfhood and its manifestation—proposing that in some sense human manifestations "are distorted manifestations of the true subject-self."[51] The problem with this approach is that it has allowed the formal categories of description, discussed above, to take over the actual person or story being analyzed.[52] Following Frei, the use of realistic narrative to describe the identity of Jesus Christ, and thereby begin to construct a Christology, will be developed below.

Figural Interpretation

As discussed above, Frei embraced the potential of figural interpretation through the work of Erich Auerbach and through its use by Karl Barth. Auerbach defined figural interpretation in this way:

> Figural interpretation establishes a connection between two events or persons, the first of which signifies not only itself but also the second, while the second encompasses or fulfills the first. The two poles of the figure are separate in time, but both, being real events or figures, are within time, within the stream of historical life. Only the understanding of the two persons or events is a spiritual act, but this spiritual act deals with concrete events whether past, present or future, and not with concepts or abstractions.[53]

Here, Auerbach contrasts the realism of figural interpretation with the abstraction of allegory, which deals primarily at the level of concepts. Auerbach illustrates the powerful use of the figural interpretation of reality through the rise of the medieval mystery plays that grew out of the liturgy of the day. He describes how scenes from everyday life were woven into a biblical and world-historical frame. In a figural interpretation of history, "*every occurrence, in all its everyday reality, is simultaneously a part in a world-historical context through which each part is related to every other, and thus is likewise to be regarded as being of all times or above all time.*"[54] Auerbach draws attention to the theological possibilities of this approach, in which characters in a mystery play might be aware of an event still in the future to which their present situation has a figural relationship.[55] He points out that in God there is no distinction in time since all of history is continuously present. He cautions,

> One must, then, be very much on one's guard against taking such violations of chronology, where the future seems to reach back into the present, as nothing more than evidence of a kind of medieval naïveté. Naturally, such an interpretation is not wrong, for what these violations of chronology afford is in fact . . . the expression of a unique, exalted, and hidden truth, the very truth of the figural structure of universal history.[56]

As stated above, even though figural interpretation was part of the interpretation of scripture until the modern era, it starts to collapse at the onset of the modern era beginning with a distinction being made between the stories and the reality they depict.[57] However, Frei attempts to reclaim figural interpretation by starting from the assumed ordering of history as part of God's providence and accepting that a figural reading of scripture reveals this providential ordering of historical events.[58]

It is important to note that this reclamation of the validity of figural interpretation is not a lapsing back into a pre-critical naïveté. A figural reading of scripture is more about a way of seeing God at work in history—providence—than it is about a relationship between particular texts. The texts appear to have a figural connection because the incidents, events, and persons they describe are in a figural relationship. As Auerbach opened up in his work, the sense of temporal sequence was important: "God's providence was an unfolding, cumulative ordering which joined the distinct phases or stages of history, and still looked forward to a final consummation."[59] Figural reading was the primary way that the church read scripture up until the modern era. It enabled a linking of Old Testament and New Testament texts—evidence of which is in the scriptures themselves.[60] But the importance of a figural approach is not only internal to the Bible. Rather, a figural reading "permits . . . the relation of . . . biblical and extrabiblical stories, *including one's own.*"[61] In *Telling God's Story*, Loughlin shares an example in which the text of Philippians 2, describing the humility of Christ, is paraphrased and used to explain the same approach to life as witnessed in Saint Francis of

Assisi.[62] While this approach at first appears to involve a re-emergence of an older Christian meta-narrative, it is not. One needs to take a more complex view of this apparent overarching meta-narrative.

> In Frei's account, the overarching narrative into which figural interpretation links individual stories is not one which emerges fully to view, nor a story that exists in only one version . . . it is seen to be a very simple structure—a sparse scaffolding into which a bewildering diversity of particular narratives can be fitted.[63]

The way in which the notion of providence and a figural reading of scripture attempts to ground a Christocentric theology in history (or rather history in a Christocentric theology) will be discussed below.

Sensus Literalis—the Interpretation of the Texts

Frei uses this term, *sensus literalis*, to describe the dominant way in which the Christian community has interpreted the meaning of the narrative texts in different times and places. He defends the authority and integrity of such an approach, at least in a partial way, by reflecting back upon the work of both Karl Barth and Friedrich Schleiermacher, who agreed that "Christianity, precisely as a community, is language forming, not purely . . . but sufficiently so that that language as embodied in its institutions, practises, doctrines, and so on, is a distinctive and irreducible social fact."[64]

Drawing on the work of Brevard S. Childs in "The Sensus Literalis of Scripture,"[65] Frei identifies three senses. The first of these is the author's intention. If the author is human, the determination of that intention must include the original audience's understanding of the text. If the author is construed as divine, this sense could be derived from a figural approach, but determining the author's intention has caused problems, particularly with the temptation to be influenced by apologetic considerations in determining that intention.[66]

The second sense

> refers to the descriptive fit between *verbum* and *res*, sense and reference, signifier and signified. . . . Centrally, in the Christian interpretive tradition of its sacred text, the signifier of the New Testament narrative was taken to be the sequence of the story itself, and what was signified by it was the identity of the agent cumulatively depicted by it.[67]

In the instance of a Gospel, the signifier would be the events, teachings, and account of Jesus' life, and the signified would be the person of Jesus.

The third sense, the

> *sensus literalis*, is the way the text has generally been used in the community. It is the sense of the text in its sociolinguistic context—liturgical, pedagogical, polemical, and so on. . . . The *sensus literalis* therefore is that which functions in the context of the Christian life.[68]

Frei claims that this approach to interpretation has always been part of the Christian interpretive tradition. "The *sensus literalis* . . . is deeply embedded in the Christian interpretive tradition of its sacred text, and in that way embedded in the self-description of the Christian religion as a social complex."[69] Frei remarks on the replacement of *halakhah* (interpretation of law) with *haggadah* (non-legal narrative) in Christian interpretation.

> Thus the parables of the Kingdom of God, whatever their original intent, were soon used as figurations of Jesus that substantiated his messianic identity as enacted in his story . . . Jesus, proclaiming, describing, and proleptically presencing the Kingdom of God was himself the subject of what he said in the use of the parables in the interpretive tradition.[70]

On the one hand, Frei states that the literal sense is an example of what Paul Ricoeur has called the "hermeneutics of restoration"[71] (as opposed to suspicion), but Frei is quick to add that he is not arguing for a general anthropology. Frei is insistent that the narrative text only refers within itself.

> For the *sensus literalis*, however, the *descriptive* function of language and its conceptual adequacy are shown forth precisely in the kind of story that does not refer beyond itself for its meaning. . . . The meaning of the gospel story for the *sensus literalis* is, then, that it is *this* story about *this* person as agent and patient, about its surface description and plot.[72]

Frei's "hermeneutic" for the *sensus literalis* might be summarized as:

> We can and do read together in the Christian linguistic community and that the text governs us all—in that context. In interpreting conceptually and existentially, we are governed first by the story and, in the second place, by the way it functions in the Christian religion.[73]

Frei proposed three rules for working with the literal sense of the text. As mentioned above, the "first sense of the literal reading stems from the use of the text in the Church."[74] The second rule accepts the fact that "the author said what he or she was trying to say."[75] The third rule has to do with the descriptive fit between the words and the subject matter, referring to the work of Paul Ricoeur and the sense of achieving harmony between the *what* and the *about what* of the text.[76] Pertaining to the Gospel narratives, Frei came to refer to the third rule as "a use which consistently identified Jesus of Nazareth as the primary subject of these texts ('ascriptive literalism')."[77]

Hans Frei defended this more "flexible" approach to the literal reading of biblical narrative in an essay entitled "The 'Literal Reading' of Biblical Narrative in the Christian Tradition: Does It Stretch or Will It Break?" Frei pointed out that if the priority of literal reading was based on some theory about the interpretation of narratives, then it would be vulnerable to such theories being challenged. "But the informal rules that have traditionally guided the Christian community in its reading of those texts will 'stretch' to accommodate a wide range of theories about narrative texts, history, and human persons"[78] and will therefore accommodate different languages and cultures.

Given how language and texts (both written and verbal) have been shown to be semiotic domains that come together and can be described as local cultures, employing the *sensus literalis* interpretation of scriptural texts is a powerful tool in enabling such texts to continue to live into the contemporary world. While a modern or rational approach might view this dependence on a (linguistic) community for determining the meaning of a text as introducing an unhelpful subjectivity or the potential for multiple (or untruthful?) interpretations, it is in this dependence that this form of interpretation has its strength. Any attempt to claim an objective interpretation that is free from a particular community is simply a pretense—as though such a thing were possible. From the work of Derrida, we discover that

> we never get beyond the realm of interpretation to some kind of kingdom or pure reading.... Text and language are not something that we get through to a world without language or a state of nature where interpretation is not necessary.[79]

And this is not limited to a religious community, such as the church. In fact, "we can't interpret a text, thing, or event without the conventions and rules of an interpretive community; indeed language itself is inherently communal and intersubjective."[80]

At the same time, though Frei relies on the local Christian community to generate the *sensus literalis* in its own context, he never loses sight of the primacy of the text itself. The submission of the Christian community to the text and an interpretation that provides a faithful rendering of the person of Jesus of Nazareth is an important safeguard. It prevents the interpretive community from allowing the needs of its own particular context to distort the meaning of the text. "The meaning of the text remains the same no matter what the perspectives of succeeding generations of interpreters may be. In other words, the constancy of the meaning of the text is the text and not the similarity of its *effect* on the life perspectives of succeeding generations."[81]

Frei is concerned, however, about the usage of the text in the Christian community. As Higton states, Frei speaks of "the kinds of practice which allow Christians to make some kinds of stable reference to and identification of Jesus by means of the Gospels. It is this stable identification of Jesus which remains central."[82] This insistence on use that continues to provide for the identification of Jesus in the Gospels also allows for these texts to stand over against the Christian community itself.[83] But ultimately, this approach to the *sensus literalis* of the Gospel narratives is rooted in something deeper than just the consensus of the Christian community. It is rooted in the Christian doctrine of the incarnation.[84] If the whole purpose of the scriptural witness of the Christian community is to reveal the identity, and therefore the presence, of Jesus Christ as the living Word of God, then "the Christian 'use' of the Bible does not assume that Christians hand themselves over to the text, . . . but rather that they find themselves handed over to the texts' witness to and repetition of the Word of God."[85]

Providential Ordering of History

In order to root the person and work of Jesus Christ in human history, Frei proposed that all of history is providentially ordered by God. Frei suggested that this could not be proven, since we, ourselves, are still part of that ongoing providential ordering of history. In other words, we are still inside this continuously evolving system, so it is impossible for us to attempt to prove it from an external perspective. Rather, it could only be shown by example, and in order to do this, Frei made use of a figural approach to scripture and history—following the example of Erich Auerbach and Karl Barth—as discussed above. "Figural interpretation takes two apparently separate incidents or characters from biblical history, and claims that one is a "type" or "figure" of the other."[86] Frei is very clear, however, not to confuse *figural* with a *figurative* interpretation. Using an Old Testament example, it is not that the story of Moses in Exodus appears to be about this leader of Israelite slaves but is really about Jesus. Rather, the account in the Old Testament is an event in its own right, as is the story of Jesus.[87] However, the narratives are in a figural relationship because together they are comparable examples of God's providential ordering of the history of the world. For Frei, the sense of temporal sequence was important. "God's providence was an unfolding, cumulative ordering which joined the distinct phases or stages of history, and still looked forward to a final consummation."[88] And it is this unfinished character of God's providence in history (awaiting the eschaton) that limits one's ability to apprehend the whole, and instead to see only diverse narratives in history in which some figural relationships can be discerned.[89]

Until the past three centuries, the biblical reader, in trying to apply scriptural truth, expected to fit his or her life into the biblical story. Right from New Testament times, there has been a need for biblical interpretation, "but its direction was that of incorporating extra-biblical thought, experience, and reality into the one real world detailed and made accessible by the biblical story—not the reverse."[90] One would attempt to extrapolate from similar events and situations in the scriptures to discern how God might be operative in the present day. However, this mode of interpretation breaks down with the advent of modernity. Now the question is asked in reverse: "Do the stories and whatever concepts may be drawn from them describe what we apprehend as the real world? Do they fit a more general framework of meaning than that of a single story?"[91] The result is that the meaning of the story becomes separable from the actual story itself.[92] Frei identifies the work of Benedict of Spinoza in the seventeenth century as heralding this focus on the religious meaning of the scripture rather than the truth of the passages themselves. With the thrust of Spinoza's work, a new direction in biblical interpretation emerges, in which "the real subject matter of the biblical narratives is not the events they narrate but the quite separable religious lessons they convey."[93] In one sense this provides a way around the increasing pressure of scientific rationalism that was calling into question the historicity of the biblical texts and thereby challenging their truthfulness. But it also begins to separate the meaning of the text from its historical referent.[94] The biblical story begins to be examined, scrutinized, and ordered by an independent view of the history of humankind.[95] In his work, *The Eclipse of Biblical Narrative*, Frei lays out how the growth of historical criticism, the emergence of hermeneutical theory with its general rules for the interpretation of texts, and the rising need for apologetics in an increasingly rationalistic world gave rise to the movement away from the narrative text and, instead, to look for meaning in ways that both preserved religious conviction and responded to the sensibility of rationalism. The assumption (perhaps implicit) behind this approach is that one can step outside of scriptural revelation and evaluate it—taking what would be an *etic* position to describe such revelation.

Frei believed that this challenge from historical criticism prompted theological scholars to begin publishing lives of the historical Jesus—all in a desperate attempt to establish a relationship between faith and history.[96] One such *Life of Jesus* was published by D. F. Strauss in 1835, and it represented a climax in this attempt to relate faith and history.[97] Strauss did not believe that the historical origin of the Gospel stories could be ascertained from trying to determine if the stories were true. Rather, he thought that the meaning of the stories was to be found in the authors' consciousness, which was historically conditioned. For Strauss, the Gospel writers' intention was literal, but the intention had to be understood historically—within the context of their time. "Even where the narrative contains some factual echoes . . . that is not its meaning. Its meaning is the time-conditioned consciousness from which it was written and which it expresses."[98] Strauss reached the conclusion that the way to assess the factual value and historical reliability of the Gospel story "is the mythical outlook which the authors shared with their time and culture in the Near East."[99] Strauss equated myth with miracle: "He specified as myth any narrative which tells 'in history-like fashion either absolutely inexperienceable matters, such as facts of the supernatural world, or relatively inexperienceable ones, where due to circumstances no one could have been a witness.'"[100] In one sense, Strauss was attempting to keep the reader in the story but did so by trying to connect the contemporary reader to the author and the author's intentions, rather than being connected to what the author was attempting to describe. Frei questioned whether these "narratives of doubtful ostensive value but realistic or history-like form . . . can be unlocked by the identical interpretive device—that of myth and, more broadly, any category separating the meaning from the depictive shape."[101] Frei proposed the possibility that no single interpretive device would be sufficient in dealing with these history-like narratives, and instead, that each might have its own special hermeneutic.

In order to construct the hermeneutic, Frei referred back to the eighteenth-century work of Johann Ernesti who, against Johann Semler and others who held that both the literary and the interpretive work must be historical, "insisted that general hermeneutics reached no further than the words of the texts."[102] For Ernesti and his followers, determining the subject matter was a theological, not a hermeneutical task. Referring back to the work of Ernesti, Frei proposed that "the narrative itself is the meaning of the text, that it refers to no other "subject matter," and that the meaning, to the extent that one does think of it as at all distinct from the text, emerges cumulatively from the text itself."[103] Again, recalling Ernesti's point, Frei stated,

> "If one cannot argue that the author's intention is identical with the words or descriptive shape of the narrative . . . one had best leave the question of the author's intention aside altogether in figuring out the sense of a narrative text."[104]

What Frei was objecting to was a kind of deconstruction/reconstruction of the text. Through a historically-oriented, general hermeneutic (such as the mythical interpretation proposed by Strauss) the text of the narrative was not taken to be the subject. Rather, the subject was determined through historical criticism and the text then reconstructed and interpreted through this subject matter. Explanation of the subject matter, determined separately from the text as noted above, took precedence over exegesis of the narrative itself. The main problem Frei had with this approach is that it violated the nature of the narrative writing—a form he referred to as "history-like."

> Now when the subject (no matter what it is defined as being) and the words are first severed, in order to be joined again thereafter interpreting the words through the subject, . . . it will be very difficult indeed to do justice to that form of writing in which the verbal form coheres with the meaning.[105]

Agreeing with Barth, Frei believed that it was not the purpose of Christian theology to argue for the possibility or the actuality of that truth. "The meaningfulness of Christian belief is not something independent of its truth, but can only be known and understood on the basis of that truth. The business of Christian theology is thus descriptive rather than explanatory."[106]

What Frei wanted to do was to start with the narratives of the synoptic Gospels and to explore the texts themselves without any prior commitment to their historicity or meaning. "Frei opted for an interpretive procedure which he wanted to be as formal and unencumbered by prior commitments about meaningfulness as possible."[107]

SKETCHING OUT A "FREI-INSPIRED" CHRISTOLOGY

Equipped with Frei's special hermeneutics (special to the interpretation of Gospel narratives about the person and work of Jesus Christ), what does the emerging Christology look like?

Following Frei's approach, this work begins with the notion that Christ's identity and presence are given to us together. "We cannot know *who* he is without having him present."[108] When referring to Christ's *presence*, Frei states his basic assumption: *"To have Christ present is to know who he is and to be persuaded that he lives."*[109] At first, this assumption can appear to be limiting. However, because Frei is treating Christ as a "real person," he is simply applying the same criteria that might be applied concerning any other individual person. It is impossible to contemplate someone being present unless one believes that someone actually exists. Frei also confronts the problem of how we might think of Christ by stating that "we cannot even think of Christ without his being present and enabling us to do so."[110] This makes sense because of the unsubstitutability of the person of Jesus Christ,[111] even though in some way one can think of any other human being without them being present—by using their memory and imagination—this is not so with Jesus.[112]

As will become clear later in this chapter, it is important to pay attention to the specifics of Jesus' humanity. Therefore, following Frei, one begins by focusing on the Gospels and the details of their portrayal of Jesus of Nazareth, and then asks the question: "What kind of Christology would fit with those texts?" For Frei, the work of Jesus is bound up in who he is. "The story told in the Gospels is indeed told as the story of salvation, but this story is identical with the story of one particular human being."[113]

Consequently, one begins by exploring the *identity* of Christ as the one who is present. This identity is defined as

> the specific uniqueness of a person, what really counts about him.... A person's identity is the total of all his physical and personality characteristics referred neither to other persons for comparison or contrast to a common ideal type called human, but to *himself*.[114]

The description of a person can be categorized in two ways. The first, called "intention-action" involves the particular actions a person takes in a certain circumstance. The second involves the continuing identity of a person over time and circumstance, including what they declare about themselves, and this is termed "self-manifestation."[115] Frei begins with the understanding that "[t]he concept of identity will involve . . . an affirmation that the singular and true identity of a person is mysteriously and yet significantly manifest and therefore accessible, rather than being a remote and ineffable, unknown quantity"[116] and that, for Jesus of Nazareth, this is most fully accessible in the passion–resurrection sequence.

Frei concludes that the New Testament story of Jesus portrays his perfect obedience to God and that this obedience "characterized him by making the purpose of God who sent him the very aim of his being."[117] Frei discusses the exchange between power and helplessness in Jesus' life, and how Jesus' decision to "not save himself" actually enables him to save others.

> Jesus has . . . a clearly personal center, a self-focussed identity. It is he who makes the pattern of coexistence [power and helplessness] . . . flow together in their complex harmony. . . . They become efficacious for salvation because they are *his* and because he holds them together in the enactment of his obedience to God.[118]

Therefore, rather than power and helplessness being portrayed as a mysterious paradox in the story of Jesus' life[119] and the story of salvation, they are actually part of a transition and exchange which is congruent with who Jesus is, and in particular, in his obedience to God. To illustrate this, Frei shows how, as the story of the passion and crucifixion unfolds, there is an increasing sense of others having power over Jesus (soldiers, Pilate)—all of which is sanctioned by God. "It is God who allows and even initiates all the circumstances that overtake Jesus."[120] And yet, Jesus' identity is never lost. "On the cross the intention and action of Jesus are fully superseded by God's and what emerges is a motif of supplantation and yet identification."[121] As Higton observes, "we find that we are forced to consider the irreducibly complex relationship between Jesus and the one he called Father . . . all these questions come to us (unavoidably) at the cross."[122] In the resurrection the Gospels start to provide answers—not how this has taken place but definitely what has happened. It is abundantly clear that this now powerful, risen Messiah is the same Jesus who went to the cross. It is also interesting how it is God who acts in the resurrection but it is Jesus who appears.

> It is in the resurrection accounts that the final, decisive complexity is added to the Gospels' account of the relationship between Jesus and the one he calls Father . . . The Father is, curiously, left somewhat in the background in the resurrection narratives: God acts, but Jesus appears. It is in *this* reversal that the story of salvation and the story of Jesus are fused into one.[123]

In other words, since obedience to God the Father is the defining characteristic of Jesus, then the complete weakness of his death on the cross is not at odds with his identity. He is simply living out the fullness of who he is. One of the strengths of this understanding is that it avoids a common conundrum of trying to reconcile the omnipotence of God in Christ with Christ's helplessness on the cross. An analogy for this congruence of power, obedience, and helplessness is the position of a woman in childbirth. The ability to create life and give it birth is a glorious power which many women embrace. However, as her pregnancy progresses, the expectant mother has increasingly less control over the life that is growing within her, and ultimately she must completely submit to the pain and helplessness of labor if she is to live out her identity as a mother who has given birth to a child.

George Hunsinger, in an essay in *Theology and Narrative*, comments that Frei claims that his exegesis of the Gospels results in a "high Christology"—that the action of the divine is obviously, and objectively, present in the saving work of Jesus Christ.[124] In examining Frei's treatment of the work of Jesus Christ and this pattern of exchange, Hunsinger finds it insufficient. "Yet much of Frei's account remains murky at best. . . . I am suggesting that Frei is more convincing about Jesus' powerlessness than he is about Jesus' power."[125] And in examining Frei's treatment of the person of Jesus, and his insistence on the unsubstitutability but still full humanness of Jesus, Hunsinger asks the question, "Does Jesus also have an identity which is fully divine?"[126] Hunsinger reaches the conclusion that Frei has actually proposed a relatively "low Christology" for the person of Jesus Christ. "God never seems in any sense to be the ascriptive subject of Jesus' intentions and actions, to say nothing of Jesus' passion and death, as would be the case if the union were personal rather than moral."[127] The problem with Hunsinger's critique is that he is assessing Frei's Christological conclusions using ontological categories that are themselves born out of previous Christological frameworks. He is attempting to assess Frei's "Jesus" on the basis of traditional two-natures-in-one Christology. However, Frei has stepped outside of any particular Christological framework and is attempting to deduce Christological insights directly and formally from the narratives themselves. That said, Hunsinger's critique does raise an interesting observation. Frei's claim that his exegesis of the Gospels results in a high doctrine of the work and person of Jesus Christ reveals that he, too, is implicitly using the language of two-nature (Chalcedonian) Christology which would equate Jesus' divinity with omnipotence. Instead, Frei's Christology invites a different understanding in which the omnipotent will of God manifests itself in the self-sacrificing death of God's Son. It is not helpful to attempt to describe this Christology with terms such as "high" or "low."

The manner in which Frei has chosen to let the Gospel narratives speak of the identity of Jesus (intention-action and self-manifestation) also enlightens about how to accommodate Jesus' helplessness as Savior in this Christology.

> Jesus' followers in the early church did not doubt that the work of saving men was the work of omnipotence. But it is equally true and far more easily forgotten that they believed this power to be mysteriously congruent with Jesus' all too human helplessness and lack of power in the face of the terrible chain of events leading to his death. . . . We find these two apparently contradictory tendencies converging in the gospel narrative.[128]

But they are not present merely as a paradox of contrasting qualities. Frei reminds us that, "A man's being is the unique and peculiar way in which he himself holds together the qualities which he embodies—or rather, the qualities which he *is*."[129] Frei also cautions about speaking too easily about Jesus' changing situation from power to powerlessness. He shows that both are actually in the service of the love of humanity in obedience to God.

> The coexistence as well as the transition between power and powerlessness . . . are ordered by the single-minded intention of Jesus to enact the good of men [*sic*] on their behalf in obedience to God. . . . In short, he makes his power and his powerlessness congruent to each other.[130]

It is interesting to note that Frei has set up an amalgam of power and powerlessness in a way similar to the Chalcedonian coming together of two natures.

Frei now confronts the puzzling portions of the New Testament report of Jesus—his resurrection. "The redeemer himself . . . now stands in need of redemption. Indeed it is by fitting his intention to such a radical participation in this our need that he is said to save us."[131] Using the formal elements of identity as previously defined, and building on the understanding that

> when a person's intentions and actions are most nearly conformed to each other—and ... is of crucial importance, involving his full power in a task—then a person gains his identity. A person's identity is constituted (not simply illustrated) by that intention which he carries into action.[132]

Frei then turns to the resurrection narratives and examines how they complete the narratives of Jesus' life, passion, and crucifixion. Using the similarities between good fiction and good biography in dealing with the narratives of the passion–resurrection, Frei states,

> The narration is at once intensely serious and historical in intent and fictional in form, the common strand between them being the identification of the individual in his circumstances. Our argument is that to grasp what this identity, Jesus of Nazareth ... is, is to believe that he has been, *in fact*, raised from the dead.[133]

Jesus' full identity was established both on the cross (by what he did) and in the resurrection (who he shows himself to be). "In both one may say, 'here he was most of all himself' and mean by this expression ... the specific man named Jesus of Nazareth."[134]

In summary, Frei's argument is that, according to the Gospel narratives, the person they portray is one and the same Jesus of Nazareth and the risen Messiah. Jesus cannot be who the narratives portray him to be if he is not risen.[135] This conclusion is supported by some of the resurrection commentary in the Gospels. In Luke's Gospel, Jesus appears to the disciples after his resurrection and challenges their initial reaction of fear and doubt. "He [Jesus] said to them, 'Why are you frightened, and why do doubts arise in your hearts? Look at my hands and my feet; [for the marks of crucifixion] see that it is I myself.'"[136] In Matthew and Mark's Gospels, it is the speech of angelic messengers that makes the direct connection between the one who was crucified and the one who was raised.

> Do not be afraid; I know you are looking for Jesus who was crucified. He is not here, for he has been raised, as he said. Come see the place where he lay. Then go quickly and tell his disciples, "He has been raised from the dead and indeed he is going ahead of you to Galilee; there you will see him." This is my message for you.[137]

It is clear that all four Gospels make the connection that "the one who is the risen Lord is also the crucified savior, and that the abiding identity of each is held in one by the unity of him who is both in the transition of the circumstances."[138] From a modern perspective, it is tempting to see, in the resurrection accounts, an attempt to provide rational, biological proof that Jesus of Nazareth is now alive again. However, this does not seem to be the primary concern.[139] Rather, the concern that the biblical narrative texts seem to focus on is not whether bodily resurrection is possible; but rather, that the particular, resurrected person is one and the same as the crucified Jesus of Nazareth. It is modern apologetics that have fixed on the empty tomb as evidence that a bodily resurrection has occurred. The biblical texts make it clear not just that the tomb of an executed human being is empty but rather that the tomb of the particular crucified Jesus is empty and that he is one and the same as the resurrected Son of God they are now, or about to, encounter. For Frei, the resurrection narratives need to be "understood primarily as the adequate testimony to, rather than an accurate report of, the reality."[140]

It is important to note that in the transition from the crucified Jesus to the risen Jesus, there is no loss of identity of Jesus of Nazareth.

> Just at the point where the divine activity reaches its climax in God's resurrecting action it is Jesus and not God who is manifest as the presence of God. It is a complex sequence, but nonetheless a sequence in unity. The unity is the sequence of Jesus' identification. In the resurrection he is most nearly himself as a person who is an individual in his own right. . . . For it is he and none other, Jesus the Son of God, who is the representative man, the second Adam, representative of human identity. . . . Because he has an identity, mankind has identity, each man in his particularity as the adopted brother of Jesus.[141]

It is precisely because of the unsubstitutable particularity of Jesus' humanity that the particular identity of every human being is preserved in Jesus' work of salvation on behalf of every human being.

Frei does not shy away from the obvious question that emerges about the resurrection of the crucified Jesus. He points out that an alternative way that one could interpret the passion–resurrection story is as myth, but other factors mitigate against that conclusion. With myth, the question is not "did this happen? but rather, what elemental truth or experience does it represent?"[142] But the resurrection story, with its exclusivity and particularity, brings the question, "Did this actually take place?" And "Did it actually occur?" focuses it at the point where his identity (intention-action and self-manifestation) is most emphasized, and this is in the passion–resurrection narrative. "What the authors [gospel writers] are in effect saying . . . is that the being and identity of Jesus in the resurrection are such that his nonresurrection is inconceivable."[143]

It is clear in this treatment of biblical narratives that they are being seen as texts in their own right and not merely stories that refer beyond themselves to a more subtle religious meaning.[144] There is also broad agreement among literary critics that "a narrative text is its own world, whether it 'refers' in some way or not, and that it should therefore be *read* as a text."[145] Frei has laid out a very elegant argument based, at least to some degree, on what might be termed the literary integrity of the Gospel narratives about Jesus of Nazareth as the crucified and resurrected Savior. But this literary approach has also drawn criticism. Ben Fulford[146] introduces the arguments from the detractors and their challenges to Frei's approach. In his work, Brevard Childs gives an overview of current models for biblical theology and deals with literary approaches to biblical theology. While he affirms the way in which these approaches have caught the imagination of many contemporary scholars, he also states, "For many, narrative theology seemed to provide a way of construing the Bible religiously without concern for ideas of revelation or ontology."[147] Childs is concerned about the effect of reading the Bible merely as literature.

> Therefore even from a non-theological analysis of the literature's genre, the category of fiction appears strangely inappropriate when applied to the Bible. . . .
> It is one thing to suggest that biblical scholars have not adequately resolved the problem of biblical referentiality; it is quite another to suggest that it is a non-issue.[148]

While this concern is understandable, it represents a misunderstanding of Frei's approach. What Frei does is initially set aside the concern about reference in order to unencumber the narrative text and let it speak for itself. In other words, Frei unloads the theological freight initially so that we can fully grasp and appreciate what the text is saying. The only referent that emerges from Frei's approach would be the unsubstitutable identity of Jesus of Nazareth as the Son of God.

Along a similar line, Mark Wallace, in his work on Barth and truth in theological language, engages George Lindbeck's claim that the Bible is to absorb reality and, referring to Frei's approach, questions whether theological discourse is something more than the literary interpretation of biblical stories. Wallace describes Frei as stating that "to ask the question of reality-reference of the Gospels obscures the central purpose of the stories, which is to narrate the literary identity of Jesus, not to refer to actual historical events." In the case of the resurrection accounts, the question is the resurrection's status, which is not that of "reference to occurrence but simply the affirmation that Jesus' self-manifestation is in fact the self-manifestation of God," which Wallace quotes from Frei's major work on biblical narrative.[149] Wallace claims that Frei's approach results in the fact that "a theological statement is true not because of a correspondence between words and things but because the statement coheres with the literary world of Scripture."[150] It seems that

Wallace struggles with not being able to make first-order statements about God and the world and "second order clarifications of these assertions in the form of doctrines."[151] Wallace is convinced that one can (and should) make "cross-cultural, context-independent truth claims about the world per se."[152] The problem with Wallace's approach is that there is no ultimately objective language in which to make those statements. All language is rooted in a context. Therefore, it is in no way diminishing the truth of a claim by stating that it coheres within a certain worldview.

Francis Watson, while agreeing with Frei's observation in *Eclipse* that the fundamental problem began when a text's meaning was identified with its reference, summarized Frei's approach as,

> the central thesis of his study is that "a realistic narrative" or history-like (though not necessarily historical) element is a feature, as obvious as it is important, of many of the biblical narratives that went into the making of Christian belief.[153]

Watson discusses Frei's use of Erich Auerbach and a figural interpretation of the Bible. Watson continues the discussion with reference to how Frei uses the concept of identity. "Presence implies both the bodiliness of the object of presence and the knowledge of his or her identity."[154] He accurately states that in Frei's approach the narrative texts cannot be reduced. He sums up Frei's approach as, "Faith, seeking understanding . . . by way of a literary detour."[155] For Watson, Frei never really answers the concern about truth. Watson insists that, in order for Frei's approach to be integrated into reality, there needs to be "the concept of the *structured, differentiated interrelatedness* of humankind, according to which individual human history is constituted within and not in isolation from its communal or social matrix."[156] Watson's critique raises a key point, except that one can still ask, "Whose reality is he referring to?" because there is not one, accessible, universal reality. And with respect to his desire for human history to be constituted within rather than in isolation from its communal or social matrix, this work is showing precisely that individual human history is being constituted within the communal or social matrix of the followers of Jesus Christ.

Fulford provides a concise description of this narrative approach to the biblical texts:

> The depiction of characters and circumstances by their mutual interactions through chronological sequence renders a world that resembles the historical world of which we have become aware, with its interweaving of actions and events in a complex, continuous web of contingencies.[157]

But does Frei pay enough attention to history, and how the person and work of Jesus Christ are, in some sense, historical? It would be fair to state that Frei was less concerned with debating the historicity of theological claims and more concerned with how the reality of the person and work of Jesus Christ impacted the actual history we live. "Frei became increasingly convinced that the proper relation of faith and history was something which needed to be *shown* rather than *stated*."[158] For Frei, all of history is now reinterpreted through the reality of Jesus Christ. He justifies this profound connection between faith and history in three ways. As has been shown above, Frei argues that the form of the Gospel narratives is historical as opposed to mythical or legendary. Second, the narratives themselves entertain the question of historical reference, internally, in the sense that within the story itself the question is asked, "Did it really happen this way?" And third, the Gospels tell a "historical" story of Jesus of Nazareth and do so in a way that places the story's significance (salvation) in a solidly historical context. Therefore, while Frei does not attempt to prove the historicity, for reasons stated above, he roots his whole understanding of God's actions in and through Jesus Christ within the historical world of the text. Ultimately this results in "the claim that the Christian faith has an historical consciousness of its own."[159]

As has been raised above by critiques of this approach to Christology, "What about the place of 'truth' in narrative theology?" In Hunsinger's "reconsideration" of the debate between Carl Henry and Hans Frei, he raises one of Henry's primary issues, coming from a concern about scriptural authority that "the lack of hermeneutical consensus in narrative theology indicates that it has 'no' objective criterion for distinguishing truth from error and fact from fiction."[160] He continues in the same vein, "When Henry reads Frei what he finds missing is a concern for . . . objective truth. What he finds instead is simply a set of ungrounded assertions, however commendable some of them may be."[161] But, as Hunsinger shows, Frei "does not share the view that cognitive truth is necessarily propositional in form," and Hunsinger refers to further work by Henry where this is Henry's expectation. Hunsinger more accurately states that "Frei does not think that . . . propositions are the only *proper* form of cognitive truth."[162] Gerard Loughlin, in his work *Telling God's Story*, examines the same issue but recognizes that the linguistic understanding of terms like truth is not universal, but rather is dependent upon the reference frame within which they are used.

> Thus, while we may, perhaps, understand how biblical narratives may be both fictive and historical, and how their meaning and truth may be one; that they really are faithful narratives or true stories is a judgement that can be made only from inside the community that takes them to be so.[163]

This is entirely congruent with Frei's idea of the *sensus literalis* for the Christian community.

On the other hand, Loughlin, while being accepting of the literal sense of scripture, raises a challenge to Frei's work. He accepts Frei's analysis of the split in the modern period between the written (or "letteral") and the historical understanding of the literal sense, and Frei's approach to seeking the meaning within the world of the narrative. However, Loughlin points out that Frei "fails to overcome the modern diremption of the literal, simply choosing the letteral in opposition to the historical, which is in danger of becoming merely putative or optional on his account."[164] It is true that Frei's proposal for the *sensus literalis* does not provide a bridge for one holding on to a position grounded in a concern for the historicity of the text to also embrace this approach to building a Christology. But as discussed above, the primary concern of this Christology is to reveal the identity of Jesus Christ in the historical world of the text and to then invite the reader to locate the world of which they have become familiar within the historical world of the biblical text.

How Does This Christology "Work"?

As stated above, because Jesus has a particular identity, humanity has an identity—each human being in his or her particularity as one adopted by Jesus. As discussed above, our identity is constituted by things that we intentionally do, as well as things that happen to us and our response to them. Given that identity is a way of describing and making present those so described, this identity in Christ would be manifest in the context of the history of a community as its members work at conforming their lives to the pattern of Jesus' identity.

"In part this conformity would take place in their own intentional actions and in part it would take place through receipt of some measure of the divine deliverance and justification enjoyed by Jesus in what happens to them."[165] In other words, members of the community, in obedience to God (following Jesus' example), pattern their lives after Jesus' identity. Likewise, the risen Christ acts in their lives to bring about their ongoing transformation and establishes their identity as children of God.

Of course, this requires the ongoing presence of the Risen Jesus to the community. Christ's presence is now indirect—referred to in terms of "Holy Spirit." "Christian believers use the language of the Spirit to refer to Christ's presence as indirect: he is present by way of a spatiotemporal basis yet without being constrained by them."[166] The Christian's understanding of this presence is in terms of word and sacrament in a way analogous to a person's verbal and physical presence. Therefore, the Church's identity as the community (or Body) of Christ is provided indirectly through word and sacrament—in a relatively permanent way in order to build and sustain the

Christian community. "Its existence is constituted by its history, following Christ at a distance as a collective disciple, imitating without approaching his pattern of exchange: serving and accepting the enrichment given by its neighbour, the human world."[167] As the members of that community focus on the identity of Jesus Christ, they

> discover one whose identity is inseparable from the identity of God, precisely as a history-like figure, who lends definition to all the ways in which he had been characterized in the story hitherto. Whether we can accept this historical claim, which . . . demands that we reorient our historical sensibilities around Jesus Christ, *is a matter of faith*.[168]

This is ultimately the position that Frei, and the development of the Christology in this work, comes to. His Christology does not demand a blind or uninformed leap of faith. Rather, it attempts to reveal a way of understanding unsubstitutable acts involving an unsubstitutable human being using language that is clearly contingent and contextual. And while its critics view this dependence on a literary approach to describing and understanding these narratives as problematic, therein also lies its power.

In other words, it is as a person encounters a community that is continually focusing on the identity and presence of Jesus Christ through the proclaimed word (scriptural texts) and the provision of the sacraments, allowing this experience to shape his or her entire life in its cultural context, that this person is invited to acknowledge the identity of Jesus Christ as portrayed in the biblical narratives and experienced in the life of that community. As one acknowledges this identity of Jesus Christ, one "sees" in this person both the divine savior and their own humanity, enabling them to lay hold of, or receive, their identity in Christ—which is the manifestation of the saving work of Christ. Jesus' disclosure of God's presence "makes possible the subjective dimension of people consciously participating in God's saving work by expressing in their own lives the same values of God's kingdom that Jesus expressed in his."[169]

Where does this Frei-inspired Christology fit within the traditional approaches to Christology? First of all, because it is not primarily concerned with ontological definitions, it is not easily classified into either of the two broad designations (following Moltmann[170]) for approaches to Christology: a therapeutic Christology (present knowledge of Christ as Savior) or an apologetic or theoretical Christology (which builds "an intellectual foundation for belief in Jesus as the divine Son of God"[171]). While this Christology clearly states that Jesus was manifested as the unsubstitutable, divine Son of God, it can't be classified as a cosmological Christology where a distinct, pre-existent *Logos* becomes incarnate as the human person, Jesus.[172] However, because of the undeniable divinity of Jesus, it does share something with these Christologies from above. Likewise, because this Christology does not have an anthropologically driven foundation that sets up Jesus as the exemplary human being, it cannot easily be classified as an anthropological Christology from below. However, it does share the same emphasis on the historical person of Jesus—his life and ministry—and, with its emphasis on disciples offering their lives to become congruent with Jesus, there is a kind of "Christopraxis" modeled on Jesus' earthly life, which is part of an anthropological approach to Christology.[173]

This Christology, with its understanding of God's history being the only real history, and the fact that God's revelation in the identity of Jesus Christ drives all of history toward its culmination in the eschaton, would have some affinity with Pannenberg's approach to Christian theology.

> All theological questions and answers have their meaning only within a framework of the history which God has with humanity, and through humanity with the whole creation, directed toward a future which is hidden to the world, but which has already been revealed in Jesus Christ.[174]

But two aspects of this "Frei-inspired" Christology that differentiate it from much of twentieth-century Christology are the fact that it is not apologetically driven—it is not trying to make the Christian faith reasonable within a larger, general frame of reference—and, while it clearly has a soteriological outcome, it does not begin with soteriology.

"Why is this approach to Christology powerful in a 21st century post-modern context?"

First, this approach recognizes the constantly evolving nature of language and texts and views them as part of what makes up a particular local community or culture.

> The descriptive context, then, for the *sensus literalis* is the religion of which it is a part, understood at once as a determinate code in which beliefs, ritual, and behaviour patterns, ethos, as well as narrative, come together as a common semiotic system, and also as the community which is that system in use.[175]

Second, it calls us back to reconsider a *figural* approach to examining scripture and history. At first, this can appear to be an attempt to return to a prior era of scriptural interpretation. Conversely, it can also free us to examine our present history in the light of scripture without being necessarily encumbered by an externally prescribed general frame of reference.

The figural vision believes that each particular awaits its fulfillment in concrete relationship to God in Christ—and that *there is no more general way of fixing the truth or meaning of any particular.* This results in a commitment to an unending *learning* of the world which does not know in advance what it will find, and which is not simply recalling or confirming general truths already known.[176]

It invites us beyond the grand meta-narrative of modernity into a kind of indefinite meta-narrative—one which we cannot know in advance and yet one in which we intimately participate.

Thirdly, because the *sensus literalis* of the narrative texts upon which the identity of Jesus is based is constantly evolving and being transformed as the culture of the community that counts it as authoritative continues its journey as disciples of Jesus Christ, the resultant Christologies will always be in a reflexive relationship with the culture of the community that has constructed them. At the same time, because of the local community's willingness to constantly allow itself to be examined by the ongoing revelation of Jesus Christ through the objectivity of the texts in its contemporary cultural context, it remains open to a transformative engagement with the local culture (Niebuhr's Type Five) rather than acquiescing into a more passive relationship (Niebuhr's Type Two) of over-identification with its own culture.

Finally, given the understanding that these (ultimately variable) texts express the identity of Jesus in ways that enable one to position one's own life within the life of the biblical narrative and thereby come to know this identity of Jesus, the Eucharistic Prayer—that great prayer which brings together Word and Sacrament—becomes, potentially, a superb occasion when this "coincidence of the recital of one's own story with the recital of the 'disclosive' or 'reinterpretive' moment"[177] can take place. The Eucharistic Prayer is (ideally) shaped by the cultural community that uses it, so that it becomes a deep and authentic expression of thanksgiving to God, and an anamnesis and prolepsis of the gift of Jesus Christ whose identity continues to inform and transform that community and, through its witness, the world at large.

In the next chapter, the importance of creating inculturated liturgical texts in order to bring the worshiper's personal and the community's collective narratives into relationship with the biblical narrative of Christ will be discussed, and twentieth century examples of the evolution of this challenge (particularly from the Anglican Communion) will be explored.

NOTES

1. Roger Haight, *Jesus: Symbol of God* (Maryknoll, NY: Orbis Books, 1999), 141.

2. David Ford and Rachel Meurs, eds., *The Modern Theologians*, 3rd ed. (Oxford: Blackwell Publishing Ltd., 2005), 234.

3. Hans W. Frei, *Theology and Narrative: Selected Essays*, ed. George Hunsinger and William C. Placher (New York: Oxford University Press, 1993), 5, 6.

4. Ibid., 170.

5. For example, take the approach of Friedrich Schleiermacher in the nineteenth century and Paul Tillich in the twentieth century. Both theologians built their Christocentric theologies by way of soteriology. See Colin J. D. Greene, *Christology in Cultural Perspective* (Grand Rapids, MI: Eerdmans Publishing, 2004), 107–108; 122–125.

6. Hans W. Frei, *The Identity of Jesus Christ: The Hermeneutical Bases of Dogmatic Theology* (Philadelphia: Fortress Press, 1975), 61–62.

7. *Theology and Narrative: Selected Essays*, 174.

8. Mike Higton, *Christ, Providence and History* (London: T & T Clark International, 2004), 32.

9. Ibid., 33.

10. Ibid., 34.

11. Ibid., 34–35.

12. Ibid., 47–8.

13. Ibid., 54.

14. This approach to Christology only accounts for the divine nature of Christ as being operative in salvation—as opposed to viewing the wholeness of the divine and human natures of Christ together—playing an active role.

15. Higton, 56. However, Higton acknowledges that in later work Barth more clearly expresses, in positive terms, the particularity of human reality—including the person of Jesus of Nazareth (p. 55). For a particular example of this, see Karl Barth, The Humanity of God, trans. J. N. Thomas and T. Weiser (Richmond, VA: John Knox Press, 1966, c1960), 47–50.

16. Hans W. Frei, *Types of Christian Theology*, ed. George Hunsinger and William C. Placher (New Haven, CT: Yale University Press, 1992), 144.

17. *H. Richard Niebuhr on History, Church and Nation* (Minneapolis, MN: Augsburg Fortress, 1981), 7.

18. *Theology and Narrative: Selected Essays*, 169.

19. Eric Auerbach, *Scenes from the Drama of European Literature* (New York: Meridian Books, Inc., 1959), 29.

20. Ibid., 30.

21. Ibid., 34.

22. Hans W. Frei, *The Eclipse of Biblical Narrative* (London: Yale University Press, 1974), 19–20.

23. Ibid., 33.

24. *Theology and Narrative: Selected Essays*, 21. See footnote #10 where Placher refers to Frei's appreciation (from Auerbach) of

> the originality of serious narratives of the lives of ordinary people in the biblical texts, the relation of doctrine and story in these texts so that, as Frei liked to put it, the story is the meaning of the doctrine, not the doctrine the meaning of the story.

25. Ibid., 7.
26. Ibid., 10.
27. Ibid., 11.
28. Ibid., 174.
29. John F. Woolverton, "Hans W. Frei in Context: A Theological and Historical Memoir," *Anglican Theological Review* 79, no. 3 Sum (1997): 383–4.
30. Frei, *The Identity of Jesus Christ: The Hermeneutical Bases of Dogmatic Theology*, xi.
31. *Types of Christian Theology*, 2. For a discussion of this cultural-linguistic approach see George Lindbeck, *The Nature of Doctrine: Religion and Theology in a Postliberal Age* (Louisville, KY: Westminster John Knox Press, 2009), 18–27.
32. Higton, 196.
33. Frei, *Types of Christian Theology*, 2.
34. Ibid., 3.
35. Ibid.
36. Ibid., 3–4.
37. Ibid., 4.
38. Higton, 200.
39. Frei, *The Identity of Jesus Christ: The Hermeneutical Bases of Dogmatic Theology*, xvi.
40. Ibid., 89.
41. Ibid., xv.
42. *Types of Christian Theology*, 110.
43. *The Eclipse of Biblical Narrative*, 10.
44. *Theology and Narrative: Selected Essays*, 34.
45. Ibid., 35.
46. *The Identity of Jesus Christ: The Hermeneutical Bases of Dogmatic Theology*, 87.
47. Ibid., 88–9.
48. Ibid., 89. Frei makes the point that the approach of modern theologians Paul Tillich and Rudolph Bultmann are examples of this latter approach.
49. Ibid., 92.
50. Ibid., 94.
51. Ibid., 99. Frei refers in particular to Hegel, the early work of Heidegger, Kierkegaard, Bultmann, and Tillich as examples. (p. 98).
52. Ibid., 101.
53. Auerbach, 53.
54. *Mimesis: The Representation of Reality in Western Literature*, trans. Willard R. Trask (Princeton, NJ: Princeton University Press, 1953), 156. [Italics mine]
55. Ibid. The example that Auerbach uses is from the Christmas play Mystere d'Adam in which Adam, though lamenting his sin, is already aware of the "Son who will come from Mary."
56. Ibid., 157–8.
57. Frei, *The Eclipse of Biblical Narrative*, 5.

58. Higton, 139. Frei understood providence to be "an ordering of the history of public intentional action, characters, and circumstances, cumulative sequences of events, credible people, ordinary and extraordinary events, historical forces."

59. Ibid., 140.

60. See 1 Peter 3.20–21, in which a figural relationship is made between Noah's experience of water in the flood and the rite of baptism in New Testament times.

61. Gerard Loughlin, *Telling God's Story: Bible, Church and Narrative Theology* (Cambridge: Cambridge University Press, 1996), 43. Emphasis mine.

62. Ibid., 42, footnote 45.

63. Higton, 141.

64. Frei, *Theology and Narrative: Selected Essays*, 100.

65. Brevard S. Childs, "The Sensus Literalis of Scripture: An Ancient and Modern Problem," *Beiträge zur alttestamentlichen Theologie: Festschrift fur Walter Zimmerli* 70 (1977). Childs provides a helpful discussion of the history of "sensus literalis" in the Jewish and Christian communities and agrees with Frei's emphasis on the authoritative use of the text by the community. "The biblical text must be studied in closest connection with the community of faith which treasured it." (p. 92)

66. Frei, *Theology and Narrative: Selected Essays*, 103.

67. Ibid., 103.

68. Ibid., 104–5.

69. Ibid., 110.

70. Ibid., 111.

71. Kevin J. Vanhoozer, *Biblical Narrative in the Philosophy of Paul Ricoeur* (Cambridge: Cambridge University Press, 1990). In particular, see Chapter 5, pp. 86–118, which discusses Ricoeur's approach to narrative.

72. Frei, *Theology and Narrative: Selected Essays*, 112.

73. Ibid., 114.

74. *Types of Christian Theology*, 15.

75. Ibid., 16.

76. Ibid.

77. Higton, 203.

78. Frei, *Theology and Narrative: Selected Essays*, 118. This is a statement made by the editors, Hunsinger and Placher, in the introduction to Frei's essay.

79. James A. Smith, *Who's Afraid of Postmodernism?: Taking Derrida, Lyotard, and Foucault to Church* (Grand Rapids, MI: Baker Academic, 2006), 38.

80. Ibid., 56.

81. Frei, *Theology and Narrative: Selected Essays*, 32.

82. Higton, 203.

83. Ibid., 204.

84. Ibid., 205.

85. Ibid., 206.

86. Ibid., 139.

87. Ibid., 140.

88. Ibid.

89. Ibid., 141.

90. Frei, *The Eclipse of Biblical Narrative*, 3.
91. Ibid., 5.
92. Ibid., 6.
93. Ibid., 43.
94. Ibid., 46.
95. Ibid., 50.
96. Ibid., 228.
97. Ibid., 233.
98. Ibid., 234–5.
99. Ibid., 236.
100. Ibid., 271–2.
101. Ibid., 272.
102. Ibid., 248.
103. Ibid., 270.
104. Ibid., 271.
105. Ibid., 279.
106. *Types of Christian Theology*, 108.
107. Ibid., 109.
108. *The Identity of Jesus Christ: The Hermeneutical Bases of Dogmatic Theology*, 4.
109. Ibid., 6.
110. Ibid., 14.
111. Ibid., 61.
112. Ibid., 15.
113. Higton, 68.
114. Frei, *The Identity of Jesus Christ: The Hermeneutical Bases of Dogmatic Theology*, 37–8.
115. Ibid., 44.
116. "Theological Reflections on the Accounts of Jesus' Death and Resurrection," in *Theology and Narrative: Selected Essays*, ed. George Hunsinger and William C. Placher (New York: Oxford University Press, 1993), 60.
117. *The Identity of Jesus Christ: The Hermeneutical Bases of Dogmatic Theology*, 107.
118. Ibid., 108.
119. *Theology and Narrative: Selected Essays*, 50–1.
120. Higton, 73.
121. Frei, *The Identity of Jesus Christ: The Hermeneutical Bases of Dogmatic Theology*, 118.
122. Higton, 74.
123. Ibid., 75.
124. See Frei, *The Identity of Jesus Christ: The Hermeneutical Bases of Dogmatic Theology*, 58, 69, 111.
125. *Theology and Narrative: Selected Essays*, 248.
126. Ibid., 249.

127. Ibid., 250. Hunsinger then points out the incongruity between the high view of Christ's work and the low view of Christ's person—suggesting that this raises further questions about the status of Frei's method.

128. "Theological Reflections on the Accounts of Jesus' Death and Resurrection," 49.

129. Ibid., 50.

130. Ibid., 51.

131. Ibid., 57.

132. Ibid., 63. Frei outlines how a transition takes place between identity-action description, which is foremost in the passion narratives through what is done to Jesus and his response, to ascriptive-subject description, which is foremost in the resurrection narratives where Jesus is manifest as who he is as the Son of God. See pages 73–74.

133. *The Identity of Jesus Christ: The Hermeneutical Bases of Dogmatic Theology*, 148. Frei explores the Gospel narratives of the resurrection to assert Jesus' "aliveness"—in terms that it would be inconceivable to think of him as anything but living.

134. "Theological Reflections on the Accounts of Jesus' Death and Resurrection," 76.

135. Ibid., 58.

136. Luke 24: 38, 39a. New Revised Standard Version Bible. See also Jesus' resurrection appearance with the disciples and with Thomas in John 20:20 and 20:26, 27.

137. Matthew 28: 5b–7. New Revised Standard Version Bible. See also the analogous verse in Mark 16: 6–7.

138. Frei, "Theological Reflections on the Accounts of Jesus' Death and Resurrection," 75.

139. It is true, however, that there does seem to be a concern to show that the risen Christ is truly an embodied person and not merely a ghost. (See Matthew 28:9 where the women encounter Jesus and take hold of his feet and worship him; Luke 24:39b where Jesus invites the disciples to touch him and see that he has "flesh and bones" which, if he were merely a ghost, he would not have; and John's account of Jesus and the disciples' breakfast on the beach, John 21:9–13)

140. Hans W. Frei, "How It All Began: On the Resurrection of Christ," *Anglican and Episcopal History* 58, no. 2 (1989): 141, 141.

141. "Theological Reflections on the Accounts of Jesus' Death and Resurrection," 81.

142. Ibid., 82.

143. Ibid., 83.

144. "'Narrative' in Christian and Modern Reading," in *Theology and Dialogue: Essays in Conversation with George Lindbeck*, ed. Bruce D. Marshall (Notre Dame, IN: Univeristy of Notre Dame Press, 1990), 152.

145. Ibid., 155.

146. Ben Fulford, *Divine Eloquence and Human Transformation: Rethinking Scripture and History through Gregory of Nazianzus and Hans Frei* (Minneapolis, MN: Fortress Press, 2013), 11.

147. Brevard S. Childs, *Biblical Theology of the Old and New Testaments* (Minneapolis, MN: Fortress Press, 1992), 19.

148. Ibid., 20.

149. Frei, *The Eclipse of Biblical Narrative*, 315.

150. Mark I. Wallace, *The Second Naiveté: Barth, Ricoeur and the New Yale Theology* (Macon, GA: Mercer University Press, 1990), 104.

151. Ibid., 105.

152. Ibid., 107.

153. Francis Watson, *Text, Church and World: Biblical Interpretation in Theological Perspective* (Grand Rapids, MI: Eerdmans Publishing, 1994), 21.

154. Ibid., 23.

155. Ibid., 24.

156. Ibid., 28.

157. Fulford, 199.

158. Higton, 89.

159. Ibid., 93–4.

160. George Hunsinger, "What Can Evangelicals and Postliberals Learn from Each Other? The Carl Henry/Hans Frei Exchange Reconsidered," *Pro Ecclesia* 5, no. 2 (1996): 165.

161. Ibid., 169.

162. Ibid., 171–2.

163. Loughlin, 156.

164. "Following to the Letter: The Literal Use of Scripture," *Literature and Theology* 9, no. 4 (1995): 380.

165. Fulford, 219.

166. Ibid., 221.

167. Ibid., 222.

168. Ibid., 263–4.

169. Don Schweitzer, *Contemporary Christologies: A Fortress Introduction* (Minneapolis, MN: Fortress Press, 2010), 26.

170. J. Moltmann, *The Way of Jesus Christ: Christology in Messianic Dimensions* (London: SCM Press, 1990), 44.

171. Colin J. D. Greene, *Christology in Cultural Perspective: Marking out the Horizons* (Grand Rapids, MI: Wm. B. Eerdmans Pub., 2004), 20.

172. Ibid., 32–43.

173. Ibid., 51–60.

174. W. Pannenberg, *Basic Questions in Theology*, trans. George H. Kehm and R.A. Wilson, vol. 1 (London: SCM Press, 1959), 15.

175. Hans W. Frei, "Biblical Narrative in the Christian Tradition: Does It Stretch or Will It Break?," in *The Bible and the Narrative Tradition*, ed. Frank McConnell (New York: Oxford University Press, 1986), 70–71.

176. Higton, 166.

177. Frei, "Biblical Narrative in the Christian Tradition: Does It Stretch or Will It Break?," 161.

Chapter 6

Transformative Potential of Inculturated Texts in the Liturgy

LOCAL CULTURE AND CONTEMPORARY EUCHARISTIC TEXTS

In working toward the incorporation of a narrative Christology in the Eucharistic liturgy, this chapter explores some of the challenges and opportunities of creating a Eucharistic liturgy for a local community's culture, including a discussion of some early examples of this type of liturgical inculturation. This will be followed by an examination of some of the impacts of Vatican II on Eucharistic liturgies and, in particular, Anglican Eucharistic prayer revision. Several Eucharistic prayers from around the Anglican Communion will be examined for evidence of inculturation to their local context, concluding with the most recently authorized Eucharistic Prayers of the Anglican Church of Canada.

Narrative Texts and the Liturgical Act

In the previous chapter, a narrative-based Christology was developed based on the work of Hans Frei. It was shown how this approach to Christology is particularly well suited to a postmodern context because of its ability to respond to the contingency of culture and language. Narrative interpretation is not relevant only to the interpretation of written texts. Rather, narrative is an essential component of self-understanding.[1] Each of us continually works with our own self-narrative. Our narrative is shaped by our experiences, our understanding of those experiences, and our own self-reflection. Juliette Day, in her chapter on narrative texts in liturgy, states it this way: "This narrative is not just a device by which I organize my sense of self, but it is the only means by which I can know myself."[2] When one participates in a community with a collective narrative, there is the opportunity to engage the community's narrative with one's personal narrative. This opportunity presents itself when the Christian community gathers in liturgical worship and rehearses (or retells) the narrative about God's saving work in the person of Jesus Christ. Participation invites one to embed their personal narrative in the larger narrative of the community. "An embedded narrative is "a story within a story"—participation in the liturgy permits me to embed my narrative in the narrative of salvation."[3] This narrative of salvation is not only made up of past events. As discussed in chapter 5, when the Christian community focuses on the identity and presence of Jesus Christ through word and sacrament, the encounter of personal narrative and the narrative of salvation happens in the present.

Therefore, manifesting the identity of Jesus Christ takes place in the context of the history of a community whose members work at conforming their lives to the pattern of Jesus' identity. This work of patterning their identity after that of Jesus takes place, in part, from their own intentional actions—including both worship involving the proclamation of the Word and the celebration of the Eucharist, as well as the formation for, and practice of, Christian discipleship. And this identity patterning takes place by the grace received from the presence of the risen Christ in the community—referred to as the Holy Spirit. Therefore, the church's identity as derived from the identity of Christ is supplied by the indirect presence of Christ through word and sacrament.[4] Each time one's personal narrative, situated in its own cultural context, encounters the presence of Christ, there is the possibility of transformation (Niebuhr's Type 5). As Day outlines, "Each new experience needs to be integrated into our self-understanding in order to maintain coherence in our sense of ourselves."[5] Sometimes these experiences will involve a challenge to one's previous self-understanding and behavior (Niebuhr's Type 1, Christ against culture). Sometimes they may involve a deeper affirmation of some portion of one's self-understanding and behavior (Niebuhr's Type 2, Christ of culture).

As discussed in the previous chapter, it is a particular context/community/culture that provides the interpretive frame (or semiotic system) for this to take place. This community is part of the indefinite meta-narrative described in the previous chapter—being in a continual state of learning of the world—not knowing in advance and yet fully participating in its fulfillment.[6]

And therefore, the community is constantly creating and recreating the application of the *sensus literalis* of the narrative texts of the identity of Jesus Christ—continually in a reflexive relationship with local culture. This interpretive role of the community enables a person not only to position his or her life within the biblical narrative and, by doing so, to grasp the identity of Jesus Christ, but also to recognize his or her own humanity in the person of Jesus as described in the narratives, and the ways in which the objective identity of Jesus Christ addresses humanity and its cultural assumptions.

The telling of the biblical narratives in the context of liturgy and worship does not simply call to mind historical events of the past. The sacred story or narrative of the Christian liturgical tradition involves *anamnesis* of past God-events, as well as *prolepsis*—the looking toward the eschatological culmination of God's purposes for human history.

> The liturgical *anamnesis* is never simply history or chronology, but story and recollection. Its effects are illumination and transformation rather than simply knowledge, by the making present of a past reality and its effects together with anticipated eschatological hope of our salvation [*prolepsis*] in the life-giving ongoing encounter with the Triune God, culminating in the paschal mystery.[7]

Anamnesis and *prolepsis* are at the heart of the church's Eucharistic Prayer. It is in this prayer that the community rehearses (retells) the story of God's salvation of the world, particularly in the Gospel of Jesus Christ. As Gibaut states, the telling of this story

> grants us communion with Christ in the present and fulfilled in the future. . . . Here, narrative is a dynamic process: neither a subjective nor didactic calling to mind of what is past and of its significance, but rather the Church's *effective* proclamation of God's mighty acts and promise.[8]

However, the challenge in contemporary, postmodern Western cultures is whether this enabling of *anamnesis* of the salvific events, and the looking forward with eschatological hope, is even possible. This question was posed in the Roman Catholic context by Romano Guardini writing in response to Vatican II's *Constitution on the Liturgy*. He identifies the problem in twentieth-century culture, observing that, rather than members of the congregation gathering as a focused community, their approach was a private, inward-looking one surrounded by outward ceremonial.[9] But Guardini goes even further toward the end of his letter and questions whether contemporary human beings are even capable of the liturgical act based on historical forms.

> Is not the liturgical act and, with it, all that goes under the name of "liturgy" so bound up with historical background—antique or medieval or baroque—that it would be more honest to give it up all together? Would it not be better to admit that man in this industrial and scientific age, with its new sociological structure, is no longer capable of a liturgical act?[10]

In making a response to Guardini's challenge, David Stosur acknowledges the difficulty of recognizing that there are "a large number of people who are already in this position of seeing liturgy as irrelevant and therefore impossible."[11]

Hence, Stosur proposes a postmodern understanding of liturgy and its authority—recognizing that now individuals see themselves as sufficiently autonomous that they will decide whether to engage in worship and liturgical texts, and interpret them in the way they choose. "In any event, the liturgy means different things to different persons, and its power to signify is an illusion if our notion of signification assumes any stability in the reality signified."[12] In other words, it is simply not possible to assume that a uniform liturgical text will carry the same meaning and be experienced in the same way within a given worshiping community. Stosur continues by restating Guardini's question, focusing it in particular on his own denomination's traditional liturgy, and asking, "Would it not be better to admit that the individual in this advanced technological and scientific age . . . is no longer capable of the liturgical act presupposed by the Roman Rite?"[13]

In response, Stosur proposes a narrative approach which values each individual's identity and story and the various communal stories it incorporates—including the history and tradition of the liturgical assembly. Rather than annihilating individuality, this approach encourages and affirms each individual's place in the corporate story and action that is taking place. Stosur even suggests that the diversity within a given community actually aids and strengthens the effectiveness of the liturgical act. Drawing on the work of Paul Ricoeur, Stosur emphasizes the mediating role of others in helping us acquire and own our own uniqueness. "Our hospitable responsiveness to the faces of others gathered, faces that embody their stories, help mutually to secure our own identity and the identity of the entire body."[14]

In a manner congruent with Frei's narrative approach to Christology, Stosur draws on Ricoeur's notion of the "semantic innovation" of narrative—which takes place when the narrative plot of the liturgical action itself interacts dynamically with the narratives of the worshipers themselves.[15] And Stosur strongly affirms the need for the individual to be able to locate their identity and story in the larger identity and story of the community and ultimately God's story. "We will continue to find in the liturgical here-and-now the Author of our life, if only we have the courage honestly to narrate and implicate ourselves in the Story through which we discover our living and true identity."[16] While Stosur does not use the word "inculturation," his narrative approach to liturgical texts brings about exactly that effect. The word does not appear in his vocabulary because its typical usage is in more overtly ethnic cross-cultural contexts. However, the thrust of this work shows that all liturgy needs to be locally inculturated in order to be an effective source of realizing the identity, and therefore presence, of Jesus Christ.

120   Chapter 6

Stosur's narrative response is encouraging and certainly is in the spirit of the reforms that emerged at the end of Vatican II intended to empower afresh the worship life of the church.[17] However, one of the challenges in traditional liturgical communities is that the written liturgical texts are already prescribed (though in contemporary liturgies often with considerable flexibility as to their use) and the community is expected to follow these uniform texts in their worship. Therefore, it is important that those creating and revising liturgical forms be sensitive to what F. W. Dillstone refers to as the speech community, which

> is helping to create the liturgical form and for whose more vital worship the form is intended. This implies that there is a constant dialectic within a speech community, a dialectic in which the members create communication and are at the same time created by the communication.[18]

Therefore, the process of creating and revising narrative liturgical texts needs to be in a reflexive relationship with the culture of the community using those texts.

Can inculturation of liturgical texts happen accidentally or unintentionally? As new or revised liturgies are created, their shape and content may both intentionally and unintentionally reflect the culture of the local community. While those compiling the liturgies may (or may not) intentionally be attempting to incorporate scriptural texts, images, attitudes, and values that are meaningful in their local culture, the mere fact that members of that cultural community are the architects of the liturgical text means that some of their cultural signs may also be unconsciously incorporated into these new liturgical forms. This will be explored further in the section dealing with the Eucharistic Prayers of the Canadian *Book of Alternative Services* (1985).

Having examined some of the challenges and opportunities of creating effective, inculturated liturgical texts, the discussion now moves to exploring some examples of Anglican Eucharistic prayer texts from the last half of the twentieth century.

Early Examples of "Inculturation" of Liturgical Texts (Eucharistic Prayers)

The dependence of the proclamation of the Gospel on the local culture became most obviously apparent as Western Christian societies sought to "Christianize" the members of local cultures in "foreign lands." In addition to the need to translate texts into the local language, it also became apparent that the living out of the Gospel needed to be immersed in the local culture—members of that community needed to be able to experience living in response to the Gospel in their own local context. Hence the notion of the "inculturation" of the Gospel emerged, and for the purposes of this work—specifically, inculturation of liturgical texts.

In the last decade of the twentieth century, the Lutheran World Federation (LWF) held three international consultations on worship and culture. The first, in 1993, focused on the biblical and historical foundations of the relationship between worship and culture and produced the "Cartigny Statement on Worship and Culture."[19] The second consultation in 1994 took place in Hong Kong and investigated the issues and questions involved in the relationships between contemporary world cultures and Christian liturgy, music, church architecture, and art. The papers of these two consultations were published as *Worship and Culture in Dialogue*.[20] The third consultation, which took place in Nairobi, resulted in the "Nairobi Statement on Worship and Culture."[21]

While not making a direct reference to Niebuhr's typology, the statement attempted to address some of the same challenges of the interaction of theology (in this case, as expressed in Christian worship) and culture. The consultation determined four ways in which Christian worship "relates dynamically to culture."[22] These were: worship as transcultural, worship as contextual, worship as counter-cultural, and worship as cross-cultural. While the report's description of the first principle (worship as transcultural) may assume more commonality of liturgical pieces across various cultures than is warranted, it does affirm that the resurrected Christ transcends—is beyond—all cultures. This claim is congruent with Niebuhr's affirmation about Christ and culture(s).

One of the important contributions of the report to the process of inculturation under the second aspect (worship as contextual) is the application of processes of "dynamic equivalence" and "creative assimilation."[23] Dynamic equivalence is a process by which the primary aspects of Christian worship and their purpose for expressing the identity of Christ and the meaning of the Gospel in one culture are submitted to a study of the other culture in an attempt to derive comparable signs (text, ritual, etc.) that evoke the same identity and meaning in that other culture. This is an ongoing process which requires continual reflection on the spiritual and pastoral benefits of the effects in both cultures. Creative assimilation is addition to the worship practices of one culture of certain local cultural elements to enrich the received tradition in the new culture.[24] Creative assimilation would be an example of a critical approach to employing Niebuhr's second type: Christ of culture.

The third aspect (worship as counter-cultural) is realizing that "the contextualization of Christian faith and worship necessarily involves challenging of all types of oppression and social injustice wherever they exist in earthly cultures."[25] This represents an application of Niebuhr's first type: Christ against culture.

The fourth aspect (worship as cross-cultural) affirms that the treasures of all cultures are welcomed by Christ as Savior of all people and encourages the sharing of these cross-culturally and ecumenically.[26] This is an excellent summary application of Niebuhr's fifth type: Christ the transformer of culture. It continues to affirm that all cultures are in need of transformation, but it also affirms that Christ can and is continuing to work through all cultures and can use the wisdom and practice of one culture to enhance (transform) another.

As will be obvious from the examples below, much of the early interest in inculturation arose from the desire of churches that had received the proclamation of the Gospel and their foundational church practices from cultures outside of their own, and who were now working to make their church more indigenous. The first example below, the Church of South India (CSI), initially focused on achieving a successful amalgam of the worship practices of the four denominations that came together to form this uniting church, but eventually the CSI also found itself grappling with the need to be more authentically indigenous (Indian) in its liturgical life.

The Church of South India

The CSI formed in 1947 as a union of Congregationalist, Presbyterian, Methodist, and Anglican Churches.[27] The creation of a new church afforded the opportunity to compile a new Eucharistic liturgy at a time when the emerging liturgical landscape was rich with opportunity. The emerging principles and aims of the Liturgical Movement, coupled with the relative freedom from the expected traditions of any one of CSI's founding denominations, afforded a rare opportunity to create something new and responsive to the needs of its contemporary worshipers. The result was not only of benefit to the CSI but to other churches around the world. The Church of South India "was willing to take the risk of re-ordering its worshipping practice in line with the discoveries and aims of the Liturgical Movement, and so to act as a model or trail-blazer for other Churches."[28]

However, what resulted, as progressive as it was for its time in the middle of the twentieth century, might be appropriately described as a kind of "church inculturation." There was little evidence of concern for reflecting the contemporary local culture—a process that might be termed indigenization. Even though the topic had surfaced in discussions of the International Missionary Council, concern for indigenization was barely recognized in liturgical revision at that time.[29]

These liturgical texts were a helpful and enriching expression of the multi-denominational nature and current liturgical thinking of the church. This new liturgy was first used at the CSI Synod in 1950 and from there it spread throughout India and beyond, helping to influence Eucharistic liturgical revision around the globe. But perhaps its transportability was also evidence of an inherent weakness or incompleteness. Fenwick and Spinks make this observation: "As the years passed, however, some of the strongest criticisms of the CSI rites have come from India itself. Their ready acceptance elsewhere is perhaps a pointer to their lack of specifically Indian character."[30]

Even as early as 1958, there was a growing awareness that the liturgical forms "are for the most part imported from the West, and that even those elements in them which have had their birth in India show marked signs of Western influence."[31]

The example of CSI and its place in contemporary Indian culture is worth exploring more deeply. There are several complex dynamics that influence the place and understanding of Christianity in India, which are of particular interest to this work dealing with contemporary postmodern culture. "The context of southern India is a pluralist society, which in different but parallel ways echoes the pluralism of the Western world today."[32]

In his introductory essay to the compilation of eight inter-cultural liturgies at the United Theological College in Bangalore, Eric Lott discusses some of the challenges of inculturating Christian liturgies in India. Even though there have been over three thousand years of various Hindu traditions in India, "it would be manifestly *mistaken* to suppose that there is only *one* homogenous—even if inclusive—Indian cultural tradition. Cultural styles, values and goals are greatly diversified even within Hindu traditions."[33] Even though the classical Sanskrit traditions are often seen as normative of Indian culture, it would be more accurate to describe them as the dominant classical culture.[34]

The Christian church in India traces its roots back to the first century and shortly thereafter to the East Syrian (Persian) Church.[35] These were known as the St. Thomas Christians. However, this Nestorian tradition is non-Chalcedonian, with the consequence that when Roman Catholic Portuguese colonists arrived in the late fifteenth and sixteenth centuries, they regarded the indigenous Christianity as inferior to their own.[36] In addition, based on some of the prohibitions introduced at the Synod of Diamper in 1599, it is suggested that, "to some extent the St. Thomas Christians lived and worshipped according to indigenous norms, rather than those current among East Syrian Rite Christians elsewhere."[37] It has even been suggested that "prior to the sixteenth century the St. Thomas Christians were as one "Hindu" caste among others."[38]

The Roman Catholic missionaries established a new Christian tradition apart from the pre-existing Syrian Church. However, they did so against the backdrop of the caste system of the dominant Hindu culture. Those who were at the bottom of the caste social hierarchy were deemed to be outcaste or tribal and labeled with the collective term of "Dalit"—a Sanskrit word meaning "crushed or downtrodden."[39] From the sixteenth century onward, many Dalits entered the Roman Catholic Church in the hope of a better life;

they tried to leave behind their "indigenous Christian lifestyle congenial with orthodox Hindu culture."[40]

Against the backdrop of these intercultural tensions, a British military and bureaucratic presence grew in the eighteenth and nineteenth centuries. However, during this time, there was a growing frustration at the occupation of India by foreigners. "This frustration related in part to the growing realization that the Christian churches, which had been produced by the efforts of Western missionaries in India, looked like a foreign import."[41]

This diverse cultural and religious background has left the Church of South India with complex inculturation challenges both inside and beyond the church. The CSI is attempting to overcome the perception of Christianity as the white man's religion. Sundar Clarke, in a provocative book entitled *Let the Indian Church be Indian* describes this problem: "Jesus Christ is avowedly a westerner's God, and as for the place of worship, the music and the other patterns they are so much the relics of our Missionary Fathers."[42] But the challenge then becomes trying to determine what is truly an Indian culture. Clarke identifies the problem in this way: "Many of us confuse indigenization with Hinduisation."[43] Within the church, the adoption of symbols, rituals, and texts that appear to be of Hindu culture causes additional problems. The majority of Christians are in fact Dalits.[44] The incorporation of pieces of liturgy that appear to be Hindu is received by the Dalit as a reinforcement of the (Hindu) caste system that has oppressed them for generations. And even though a greater equality is proclaimed in Indian Christianity, there is still discrimination against Dalits within the church.[45] The Christian Dalits are twice alienated—by the dominant Hindu culture as well as much of the Christian church. This inequality is perpetuated in the theological education of Christian leaders. Upper castes are over-represented, and the Dalits and tribals are under-represented at the higher levels of theological education, and lower castes and Dalits constitute a disproportionately small percentage of all theological teachers.[46] "The theological conceptions of the Christians are obviously not the same as those of the dominant sections, but in their effect these Christian abstractions have not greatly helped the Dalit and tribal aspirations."[47] Even the Christianity that Dalits have adopted has been alienating too, "with its Western moorings, i.e., worship and thought patterns, institutional services, and a faith-practice of inward looking, other-world-centered pietism, passivity and uninvolvement in social action and individual seeking for salvation."[48] This has resulted recently in the emergence of a Dalit Theology movement—-a liberation movement that shows some parallels to the liberation of black people in the United States—sharing the common need to rid themselves of feelings of inferiority—or a slave mentality.[49] This division and alienation within the church results in an even greater inculturation challenge.

Against these challenges, the CSI has worked on liturgical revision, beginning in 1985, "to relate the eucharist more appropriately to Indian cultural ways."[50] The CSI is an example of a church that has employed both textual and non-textual approaches to inculturation. A few examples of this include an offering of a tray of flowers at the time of the offertory, signifying God's goodness in creation, as well as the text of a prayer over the gifts which begins, "Glory to God, source of all bounty and beauty whose fullness and fragrance can transform us within and without."[51] In Eucharistic Prayer B of CSI's *Book of Common Worship* (2006), the *Sursum Corda* (which doesn't use the words "Lift up your hearts") is Trinitarian but an entirely new composition, and the people have a common response to all three sentences: *Saranam, saranam, saranam* which means "I take refuge."[52] There are also vivid phrases that resonate with the local culture in the narrative supplicatory section following the *anamnesis* in Prayer B—"Restore the broken life of your creation; heal the disfigured body of your world; draw all creatures unto yourself" and in the opening thanksgiving section in Prayer C, referring to Jesus' coming into the world: "He met us as a refugee, a threatened child."[53]

Even so, the analysis of the task of inculturation is much more than a question of whether or not to borrow certain religious/cultural practices. It goes to the heart of the issue of what kind of relationship is possible among different faith systems and communities.[54] The intercultural challenges in India have some parallels to the intercultural challenges in Canada between Indigenous and non-Indigenous people. These will be highlighted in chapter 8.

The Anglican Church of Kenya

After working with a modern English translation of the 1662 Church of England Prayer Book in the 1970s, the Provincial Board of Theological Education prompted the production of the Kenyan Service of Holy Communion. "They produced in June 1987 an almost completely new service, written in English, but without any inbuilt dependence upon western models."[55] Like the rite from South India, this liturgy was also circulated worldwide, and it was published in England as an example of African inculturation.[56] Much of the structure is traditional, but there is an imaginative use of text to reflect local culture. The opening dialogue of the Eucharistic Prayer (*Sursum Corda*) is preceded by a Trinitarian text in the interrogative:

Is the Father with us?	*He is.*
Is Christ among us?	*He is.*
Is the Spirit here?	*He is.*
This is our God.	*Father, Son and Holy Spirit.*
We are his people.	*We are redeemed.*
Lift up your hearts[57]	

Like the South India liturgy, the Eucharistic Prayer contains some vivid phrases in the opening thanksgiving section—"From a wandering nomad you created your family; for a burdened people you raised up a leader; for a confused nation you chose a king; for a rebellious crowd you sent your prophets."[58] This language is particularly appropriate for Kenya because of its nomadic history.[59]

Response in the Anglican Communion

By the closing decades of the twentieth century, the spread of local liturgies in places like Church of South India, Kenya, and Uganda, along with other African Provinces, brought the discussion on inculturation to the forefront.

The 1988 Lambeth Conference of bishops from across the Anglican Communion passed Resolution 22 on Christ and Culture:

This Conference

a. Recognizes that culture is the context in which people find their identity
b. Affirms that God's love extends to people of every culture and that the Gospel judges every culture according to the Gospel's own criteria of truth, challenging some aspects of culture while endorsing others for the benefit of the church and the society
c. Urges the church everywhere to work at expressing the unchanging Gospel of Christ in words, actions, names, customs, and liturgies, which communicate relevantly in each contemporary society.[60]

In the year following the 1988 Lambeth Conference, the Third International Anglican Liturgical Consultation was held in New York, UK. Its theme was "liturgical inculturation" and it issued a statement entitled "Down to Earth Worship."[61] Of particular interest in the statement are Sections Three, Five, and Six. In Section Three, entitled First Principles, the following statement is made about revelation and culture: "The incarnation is God's self-inculturation in this world, in a particular cultural context."[62] Section Five cites Anglicanism's lack of inculturation, which has alienated some Christians and caused others to try to live in two different cultures—one for their religion and the other for their daily lives.[63] Section Six describes the approach one must take to engage inculturation in the liturgical setting: "True inculturation implies a willingness in worship to listen to culture, to incorporate what is good and to challenge what is alien to the truth of God."[64] These insights into the practice of inculturation, which speak strongly about the interdependent, reflexive relationship between liturgy and culture, will be helpful in exploring contemporary Eucharistic texts later in this chapter.

In 1993, the Kanamai Consultation (on African Culture and Anglican Liturgy) was convened by Bishop David Gitari (Kenya) and gathered under the aegis of the Council of Anglican Provinces in Africa (CAPA).[65] The Consultation issued The Kanamai Statement, and in the first section dealing with principles of inculturation, the statement outlined the importance of beginning, not with a text, but with a structure from the inherited liturgical tradition. It proposed this structure:

1. Gathering together
2. Telling the Christian story with intercessory prayer
3. The meal with thanksgiving
4. Sending out

Each part will have its own sub-culture. It is important for people to discover the structure of the Eucharistic Prayer, and compose their own within that framework, rather than translate from English language sources.[66]

As with the Lambeth statement above, this simple structure for the Eucharist will be helpful in constructing a Eucharistic prayer for the Anglican Church of Canada in its present culture.

Vatican II and Examples of Its Impact on Liturgical Revision in Anglicanism

For those who currently experience Eucharistic liturgies in the Anglican and Reformed traditions, it is difficult to realize that from the fourth century until Vatican II in the 1960s, the Roman Rite (or Canon) was the only Eucharistic Prayer authorized for use around the Roman Catholic world. While the Canon underwent various revisions over those more than 1600 years, there was still only one prayer that was to be used everywhere.[67] As a result of the liturgical revisions of Vatican II, there are four regular Eucharistic prayers: two intended for Masses of Reconciliation and four additional prayers for various needs and occasions.

These prayers are based on several ancient western and eastern Eucharistic texts that came to light earlier in the twentieth century as part of the work of the Liturgical Movement. What was the primary thrust behind the revisions?

> The overriding consideration was . . . not an archeological reconstruction of the past. In the thinking of those who framed the Constitution [on the Sacred Liturgy], a return to the classical Roman tradition could bring out more clearly the meaning and purpose of the Eucharistic celebration and at the same time enhance devout and active participation of the faithful.[68]

This is particularly the case in Eucharistic Prayer Three, which is a modern presentation of the Roman Canon but includes aspects of the ancient Mozarabic and Gallican traditions that helped form the original prayer. It is interesting to note that this is the Eucharistic Prayer most often used in the contemporary church.[69] While these prayers contain a broader and more flexible approach to some of the classic Roman Eucharistic themes, such as sacrifice, the paschal mystery being about both Jesus' crucifixion and resurrection, and the inclusion of a "first epiclesis" (prior to the words of institution), they still are framed by the theology of the Roman Canon itself. However, they do contain more narrative about Jesus' earthly ministry and thereby more effectively enable the identification of our humanity with his. The new prayers "contain affirmations about his person and, increasingly with the most recent prayers, about his life and ministry."[70] This is particularly the case in the prayers for children and various needs. "Here Jesus' life is evoked in more concrete and human terms. One senses something of his actual ministry and of the relation between it and his final act of self-giving that led to the cross."[71]

As much as the greater variety allows for the representation of more themes from the story of God's salvation as well as our own experience of humanity, Anscar Chupungco raises an interesting challenge to the centralized nature of the liturgical life of the Roman Catholic Church. When looking at the ten Eucharistic prayers available in Pope Paul VI's Roman Missal, Chupungco asks, "Do these ten Eucharistic prayers correspond to any people's established patterns of praising and thanking God for God's gifts, particularly for food and drink? Are these prayers evocative of the institutions, traditions, and life experience of any given community?"[72] Chupungco is questioning whether any centralized liturgical form, unless it is flexible enough to allow for considerable local adaptation and input, can actually serve as a fully inculturated liturgy. His question illustrates the value of every local church having "a particular Eucharistic prayer that expresses the richness and variety of culture and traditions."[73]

Church of England

The Church of England had attempted liturgical revision in the form of a proposed Prayer Book in 1927–1928, which was designed to replace the 1662 Prayer Book currently in use. It was not successful—largely on traditional theological grounds between different theological parties in the Church of England.[74] However, by the mid-1960s, liturgists in the Church of England were calling for a fresh start to liturgical revision rather than simply carrying out minor revisions to the forms in the 1662 Prayer Book and the proposed Prayer Book of 1928. There were two movements throughout the twentieth century that helped to promote this desire for liturgical revision—the

Liturgical Movement and the Parish Communion Movement, which brought many parishes into a pattern of weekly Holy Communion. It was recognized that the current 1662 Eucharistic liturgy was not conducive to this new situation. "The Prayer Book liturgy . . . was a poor vehicle for a participatory, corporate, all-age understanding of the Eucharist."[75] During the 1970s, experimental liturgies (Series Two and Three) were authorized for trial use. From this work, and particularly the Series Three Rite (a revised version appears in the final book), *The Alternative Services Book 1980* (ASB) was produced and authorized for use.[76]

Following the example of the Vatican II revisions, there was a multiplicity of Eucharistic prayers in the ASB (four plus the Prayer Book text in Rite A, and two more prayers in Rite B), and in keeping with other contemporary rites of the same era, there was a definite desire to express the full diversity of the ancient anaphoras with a strong dependence on the Prayer of Hippolytus as well as the Prayer of Consecration in the 1549 *Book of Common Prayer*.[77] This return to the approach of the 1549 Prayer Book is in keeping with Vatican II's return to the approach of the ancient Roman Rite. In both cases, there was a desire to reclaim the Eucharistic liturgical roots of their respective churches.

The Preface of the ASB states the intended purpose behind its production. "Rapid social and intellectual changes, however, together with a world-wide reawakening of interest in liturgy, have made it desirable that new understandings of worship should find expression in new forms and styles"[78] The real challenge that faced liturgical revision of the Eucharistic Prayer in the Church of England was how to treat the anamnesis and the epiclesis.[79] Here, the earlier liturgical revisions in Anglicanism—particularly the liturgy of the Church of South India (1950)—were helpful. These contemporary examples provided "a certain studied ambiguity in the theology expressed in the Eucharistic Prayer, a form of words capable of differing theological slants."[80] Employing this contemporary wording helped to overcome old divides around theological concerns and avoid the hard-line objections of various theological positions,[81] which had resulted in the rejection of the proposed 1928 Book.

It appears that the Eucharistic Prayers of the ASB were more of a response to the church culture than to the local societal culture. While there is clearly a desire to provide a greater variety of themes pertinent to the context (season of the year, focus of the liturgy—for example, ministry to the sick, inclusion of children), the primary attention was being paid to theological concerns—attempting to reflect the greater variety of ancient anaphoras and to use language that was acceptable to a wide range of theological sympathies. The focus was very much on the plurality of theological persuasions within the Church of England and producing a faithful liturgy that would find wide acceptance across the church.

Anglican Church of Canada

At approximately the same time as the new Roman Rite (with its multiple Eucharistic prayers) was being shared within and beyond the Roman Catholic Church, the Anglican Church of Canada was also involved in liturgical revision. In 1971, the General Synod of the Anglican Church of Canada directed its National Executive Council

> to initiate a process of revision of Church Services without delay, which will produce alternatives to services now offered by the 1959 Canadian *Book of Common Prayer*; and which will provide guidelines for their use throughout the Anglican Church of Canada.[82]

The next decade saw the distribution and experimental use of the Canadian Anglican Liturgical Series, "The Holy Eucharist" (CALS 4) in 1974 and "The Holy Eucharist: Third Canadian Order" in 1981. Learning from reflection on and evaluation of these rites, the Canadian church eventually produced and authorized a new Eucharistic rite in its *Book of Alternative Services* published in 1985.

What was the driving force behind the development of these contemporary Anglican Eucharistic rites? William Crockett chaired the Eucharistic Task Force (part of the Doctrine and Worship Committee of the General Synod) that prepared the texts. When reflecting on the mind of the Task Force, he comments,

> What was important was to recover a sense of the fullness of the catholic tradition in terms of Eucharistic praying; and of the biblical tradition, and to try to have sufficient scope in the Eucharistic prayers so that could be reflected.[83]

Crockett continued to explain the driving force behind this work:

> Of course, Rome had already brought out the four Eucharistic prayers so there was already precedent for a number of Eucharistic prayers. I think if Rome had not done that, we might not have thought in terms of a range. . . . So I think that Rome really opened up the whole possibility of multiple Eucharistic prayers and, of course, that caught on with Lutherans and ecumenically. . . . So we were on that wave, and I also think we were on the wave of the whole liturgical movement which was already shaping Anglicans; and the liturgical reforms of

the Second Vatican Council. All of that process of liturgical change was sort of the ethos.[84]

Crockett continued to refer to the importance of Vatican II's emphasis by referring to the emerging emphasis on the Church being the whole people of God and, therefore, the sense of the liturgy being the work of the whole church—not just the presider. In addition, the fact that liturgical scholars from many denominations were working together on revision resulted in a strong ecumenical thrust to the work.

As discussed above in chapter 4, while there is evidence in the Eucharistic prayers of a growing openness to the issues emerging in late twentieth-century Western culture as experienced in Canada, it is probably more accurate statement to attribute the Eucharistic prayer texts of the BAS as a response to the Church culture more than the local societal culture, as was the case with the ASB in the Church of England. Any evidence of the inclusion of the society's local culture might be deemed as being "unintentional"—occurring simply because members of that culture were creating the texts. Instead, the priority was to take advantage of the richness of both the biblical and theological tradition of the Church and to express that in contemporary language so that it might enrich the worshipers in the local churches. At the same time, it is clear that the Anglican Church of Canada's *Book of Alternative Services* Eucharistic liturgy pays increased attention to the society in which the Church is situated. Boyd Morgan describes this connection as discussed in Crockett's work on the Eucharist: "William Crockett established the connection between those who celebrate this communal meal and justice for all God's creation. Eucharist, [Crockett] maintained, in itself has social implications."[85] "When the meal is celebrated in thanksgiving for the gifts of creation, the community that celebrates it cannot fail to seek justice for all God's creation."[86]

Emerging "Inculturation"—Recent Liturgical Forms

Church of the Province of New Zealand

While the initial impetus for liturgical revision in the Anglican Church in New Zealand began at the same time, and in a similar way, to its counterparts in England and Canada, the resultant delay in producing authorized texts gave the New Zealand Church the opportunity to work more aggressively with the notion of inculturation. The initial commissioning for Prayer Book revision took place in 1964, but it was not until 1989 that the Church produced *A New Zealand Prayer Book, He Karakia Mihinare o Aotearoa*. The introduction to the Prayer Book explains the great changes that took place in New Zealand society during that time:

> In the last twenty-five years the fabric of New Zealand society has changed. We live in a different, and to many, a strange world. There has been an increasing awareness of the delicate ecological balance within our country, interdependent with others. New Zealand has adopted an anti-nuclear stance. The basis of our economy has radically changed. The re-emergence of a sense of identity within the Maori people has seen the Maori language approved as an official language of the nation.[87]

The introduction goes on to identify other key issues such as the ordination of women, the importance of gender-inclusive language, and an emphasis on the ministry of all the baptized.[88] While some of these concerns might be identified as church culture, clearly there are several that pertain to the culture of New Zealand as a whole—evidence of an attempt to engage the local culture in the liturgical texts.

Most traditional Prayer Books of the Anglican Churches simply begin with pages that explain how they came to be compiled, by what authority they have been produced for use, and perhaps some suggestions about appropriate ways to use the texts themselves. *A New Zealand Prayer Book* begins with a welcoming page that does not assume that the book's user is necessarily a regular worshiper, or even a member of that church. The text begins,

> Welcome to you as you come to worship. Worship is the highest activity of the human spirit. In this book you will find the means to express all the hopes and vision, common purpose and emerging love of which we are capable.[89]

The text continues by describing something of the purpose, intent, and hope of Christian worship. This is a good example of reaching out to include all members of the local culture and not simply those already identified with the Anglican Church.

Like the Canadian BAS, there are introductory instructional pages that precede the Eucharist liturgy. While the BAS has some good pedagogical material on the various parts of the liturgy, the New Zealand book gives a powerful contextualization of the celebration of the Eucharist. It begins, "Christ comes to us bringing good news of God's grace and generosity. Christ has inaugurated for us a sacral meal, and summoned us to have communion with him."[90] The explanatory note continues by explaining the purpose behind presenting a variety of texts: "You will find several forms of the Eucharist which are deliberately quite different from each other. This is to provide richness in our worship and to cater to the variety in the church community."[91]

As mentioned above, the Maori language is an official language of New Zealand. Hence, many of the texts in *A New Zealand Prayer Book* appear in both Maori and English. The Anglican Church of New Zealand is actually comprised of three partners (*tikanga*): *Tikanga Pakeha* (English-speaking), *Tikanga*

Maori, and *Tikanga Pacefika* (Polynesia—including Fiji, Tonga, Samoa, and the Cook Islands).[92] Consequently, in addition to the two official languages, there is also a Great Thanksgiving in both Fijian and Tongan languages. As with other contemporary liturgies, there are a number of optional Prefaces and other insertions to reflect the seasons of the liturgical year as well as pastoral themes (i.e., baptism, marriage, burial). But there are also texts that reflect the needs and hopes of the world. In a separate Eucharistic liturgy entitled *Thanksgiving for Creation and Redemption,* an opening canticle entitled *Benedicite Aotearoa* praises God for the elements of creation common to the local culture: "All mountains and valleys, grassland and scree, glacier, avalanche, mist and snow. . . . You kauri and pine, rata and kowhai, mosses and ferns . . . Dolphins and kahawai, sealion and crab, coral, anemone, pipi and shrimp."[93]

It is clear that the liturgical texts of *A New Zealand Prayer Book* move beyond a mere consciousness of the local "church culture" and intentionally attempt to engage the wider local culture of New Zealand society in all its diversity.

Signs of "Inculturation" in a Postmodern Culture

Church of England

While the New Zealand liturgies afford a powerful example of inculturation—they have emerged from a somewhat unique cultural context—one in which the state officially recognized more than the one dominant culture. The church then responded to this phenomenon in a way that demonstrated its willingness to place its liturgical texts in a reflexive relationship with the local cultures.

With the emergence of postmodern cultures in Western societies in general, it is appropriate to include some examples of recent Anglican Eucharistic texts in these contexts, and to explore these texts for signs of "inculturation." In these Western societies, the perspective is not of an externally imposed culture attempting to adapt the texts of its culture to the local indigenous culture, but from the perspective of new postmodern cultures emerging in the midst of the late modern culture characteristic of the West. From the discussions in chapters 4 and 5, liturgical texts that are narrative in form—providing a description of the identity of the person of Jesus; that are intentionally inclusive (races, genders, ages, etc.); that respect the autonomy of the individual; and demonstrate an awareness of, and concern for, those on the margins of society as well as for the creation, are texts that are congruent with these emerging cultures.

The Anglican Church in the United Kingdom (The Church of England) is a helpful example because it is from this church that the Anglican Church of

Canada emerged at the beginning of the twentieth century and whose contemporary Eucharistic texts will be examined in more detail below.

The Church of England produced its *Alternative Services Book* (1980) in a similar period to the Canadian Church's *Book of Alternative Services*. And in slightly over a decade, further liturgical revision was attempted, though it failed to be authorized.[94] Within two decades of publishing the ASB, the Church of England engaged in further liturgical revision, and *Common Worship: Services and Prayers for the Church of England* was published in 2000.[95] In a manner somewhat similar to the New Zealand Prayer Book, this volume attempts to reach out to the worshiper without any assumptions about their membership in, or familiarity with, the Church of England. A section of the Preface reads:

> The services provided here are rich and varied. This reflects the multiplicity of contexts in which worship is offered today. They encourage an imaginative engagement in worship, opening the way for people in the varied circumstances of their lives to experience the love of God in Jesus Christ in the life and power of the Holy Spirit. In the worship of God, the full meaning and beauty of our humanity is consummated and our lives are opened to the promise God makes for all creation—to transform and renew it in love and goodness. . . . Worship not only strengthens Christians for witness and service, but *is itself a forum in which Christ is made known*. Worship is for the whole people of God . . . and those who attend services are all at different stages of that journey.[96]

This introduction clearly shows a concern for contemporary cultures and, in particular, is sensitive to the narrative Christology at work in worship, particularly in the Eucharist—stating overtly the expectation that individuals will be able to receive the identity of Jesus Christ.

Common Worship offers eight Eucharistic Prayers. Some of these texts show evidence of attempting to embrace contemporary cultures in their narratives. The opening Thanksgiving of Prayer D uses personal language to connect the worshiper directly with God:

> Almighty God, good Father of us all, your face is turned towards your world. In love you gave us Jesus your Son to rescue us from sin and death. Your Word goes out to call us home to the city where angels sing your praise.[97]

After the *Sanctus,* there is a narrative description of Jesus' ministry.

> With signs of faith and words of hope he touched untouchables with love and washed the guilty clean. . . . The crowds came out to see your Son, yet at the end they turned on him. On the night he was betrayed he came to table with his friends to celebrate the freedom of your people.[98]

This narrative description resonates with contemporary human experience—much of it common to all—such as the seeming affirmation of people later turning to rejection and betrayal by friends.

Prayer F uses rich images and metaphors to refer to God as Creator and makes several references to God's (and our) desire for healing for the earth and for people—particularly the oppressed.[99]

Prayer G also contains rich and poetic language around God's act of creation and compares God's love for us to how "a mother tenderly gathers her children." Jesus is portrayed in intimate terms as one "in whom all our hungers are satisfied."[100]

Prayer H is more distinctive because of its structure than its language. The entire prayer is in a dialogue form between the presider and the congregation, and the prayer climaxes with the Sanctus at the end—as opposed to it being in its usual position after the opening thanksgiving. This structure shows an openness to changing the form of the liturgy so that there is much more engagement with the individual, and that the obvious climax of praise to God occurs at the end.

Therefore, it can be concluded that *Common Worship* Eucharistic texts do show modest signs of reaching out beyond the church culture to engage intentionally with contemporary postmodern culture.

Anglican Church of Canada

Within a decade of the publication of the BAS, the General Synod of the Anglican Church of Canada made an additional directive regarding liturgical texts. It "called for the creation of Eucharistic prayers reflecting a Reformed theological conscience and Eucharistic prayers inclusive in language and images."[101] This work was done in the latter part of the 1990s, at a time when inclusiveness (particularly around gender) had come to the fore. Professor Richard Leggett (Professor at the Vancouver School of Theology (VST) who became Professor Emeritus 2010) was a member of the Doctrine and Worship Committee in the triennium immediately preceding this work and taught Liturgics at VST. He commented on the needs that emerged from the work of the BAS Evaluation Commission and identified three specific things:

> The first thing that was noted in that triennium (1992–1995) was the need for a Eucharistic prayer with more inclusive language. And, in response to evangelical critique of the BAS, they wanted a Eucharistic prayer which reflected a Reformation Eucharistic theology. And then, . . . was this idea that our Eucharistic prayers are celebrations of the Resurrection for the most part—What kind of Eucharistic prayer do you use in times of lament, uncertainty, things like that?[102]

Leggett was then asked, "Do you believe there was any explicit desire to inculturate the prayers to the Canadian context?" He responded in the affirmative:

> The short answer is "yes." 1. It was an inculturation because it was asked for by the Church—the Canadian Church—and the Canadian Church adopted them. 2. Canadian culture has a different ear for inclusive language than our brothers and sisters in the United Kingdom and so there was Canadian culture particularly after the ordination of women that began to realize that things have to change. 3. It reflects Canadian culture in the *Sursum Corda* where there is, in some sectors of Canadian public, a dis-ease with the use of the word "Lord," and borrowing from some things in the UK and elsewhere, you get "May God be with you." That reflects Canadian culture. 4. It was a distinctly Canadian recognition re: Prayer S-2.[103] Where was the impetus for that? I think it was a brilliant response to come up with a prayer that can be used in these "other" circumstances.[104] But where did that come from? I think it may have come, in part, from a growing realization of the situation with aboriginal peoples in this country, and those kinds of things. And finally (5), It represented Canadian culture in that—Canadian culture tends to be what I call a both/and culture rather than an either/or culture. So you want a series of Eucharistic prayers which can be put in the pews . . . and everyone's happy.[105]

The two inclusive language Supplementary Prayers (S-1 and S-2) do exhibit signs of "inculturation" of emerging postmodern cultural concerns. Prayer S-1 uses rich images of God as Creator and refers to our lack of concern for our environment:

Holy God, Lover of creation,
we give you thanks and praise
for in the ocean of your steadfast love you bear us
and place the song of your Spirit in our hearts.
When we turn from your love and defile the earth,
you do not abandon us.[106]

In the post-*Sanctus* thanksgiving for the gift of Jesus, the prayer describes Jesus' mission to humanity in images that reflect contemporary human experience:

Through Jesus' life, death, and resurrection
you open the path from brokenness to health,
from fear to trust, from pride and conceit
to reverence for you.[107]

The Prayer also refers to Jesus being anointed by a woman prior to his celebrating the Last Supper, and in the *epiclesis* there is a petition, "that we may be signs of your love for all the world and ministers of your transforming purpose."[108]

Supplementary Prayer S-2 has been discussed above in the interview with Richard Leggett. In addition to the issues previously raised, there is the following narrative description of Jesus' earthly ministry—also relating to themes prevalent in a Western postmodern culture:

At the right time you sent your Anointed One
to stand with the poor,
the outcast, and the oppressed.
Jesus touched lepers, and the sick, and healed them.
He accepted water from a woman of Samaria
and offered her the water of new life.
Christ knew the desolation of the cross
and opened the way for all humanity
into the redemption of your reconciling love.[109]

These Supplementary Eucharistic Prayers do exhibit an awareness of postmodern culture, but their texts show only modest innovation in this respect. In the interview with Richard Leggett, the Indigenous or First Nations of Canada are referenced. While the General Synod's Faith, Worship and Ministry Committee has made liturgical resources available from time to time that reflect Indigenous cultures (particularly prayers for Indigenous justice),[110] there has been no formal compilation or authorization of Eucharistic rites. The Reverend Barbara Shoomski, a priest of the Diocese of Rupert's Land, Anglican Church of Canada, a person of Cree and Métis background, composed a Eucharistic Prayer as an assignment for a university liturgics course. It follows, approximately, an Antiochene shape and uses a traditional *Sursum Corda* and *Sanctus*. However, most of the imagery in the prayer comes from the local culture in which she was raised around Grand Rapids, Manitoba, Canada. Prophets and ancestors in the faith are referred to as "elders" and "memory keepers." At the Last Supper, Jesus takes "bannock" (a traditional bread of Indigenous peoples in Canada), blesses it, and shares it. Following the anamnestic text, there is a pneumatological thanksgiving for God's creation through the Spirit. The images of land and animals are all taken from the northern prairie context. Throughout the prayer, God is referred to as "Creator." It is one of few examples of a Eucharistic Prayer inculturated for contemporary Canadian Indigenous Peoples—in this case for the Cree people of western Canada. This lack of inclusion of Indigenous cultures in the Anglican Church of Canada's liturgical texts will be discussed further in chapter 8.

In this chapter, it has been shown that Eucharistic Prayer texts, and in particular those of the Anglican Church, show evidence of a growing awareness of liturgical inculturation—initially primarily to the cultural expectations of their church membership (at least those with decision-making power) and eventually engaging the wider culture in which their membership lives. In the next chapter, the Christology of the contemporary Eucharistic Prayers of the Canadian Church will be examined to explore whether the Christology expressed shows evidence of being in a reflexive relationship with the local contemporary culture.

NOTES

1. Juliette J. Day, *Reading the Liturgy: An Exploration of Texts in Christian Worship* (London: Bloomsbury T & T Clark, 2014), 61.
2. Ibid., 62.
3. Ibid., 63.
4. Fulford, 219, 21–22.
5. Day, 64.
6. Higton, 166.
7. John St. H. Gibaut, "The Narrative Nature of Liturgy," *Theoforum* 32, no. 3 (2001): 343.
8. Ibid., 365.
9. David A. Stosur, "Liturgy and (Post) Modernity: A Narrative Response to Guardini's Challenge," *Worship* 77, no. 1 (2003): 24.
10. Romano Guardini, "A Letter from Romano Guardini," *Herder Correspondence* 1, no. 8 (1964): 239.
11. Stosur, 27.
12. Ibid., 30.
13. Ibid., 30–31.
14. Ibid., 37.
15. Ibid., 39.
16. Ibid., 41.
17. Even though there was not an expectation of new Eucharistic prayers emerging from Vatican II, the new Roman Missal produced in 1970 contained three new Eucharistic prayers in addition to the Roman Canon. See Daniel Donovan, "Lex Orandi: The Christology of the Eucharistic Prayers of the Roman Rite," *Toronto Journal of Theology* 16, no. 1 (2000): 70.
18. F.W. Dillstone, "Liturgical Forms in Word and Act," in *Language and the Worship of the Church*, ed. David Jasper and R.C.D. Jasper (New York: St. Martin's Press, 1990), 18.
19. "Cartigny Statement on Worship and Culture: Biblical and Historical Foundations," in *Worship and Culture in Dialogue: Reports of International Consultations, Cartigny Switzerland, 1993, Hong Kong, 1994*, ed. S. Anita Stauffer (Geneva: Department for Theology and Studies, LWF, 1994).

20. S. Anita Stauffer, ed. *Worship and Culture in Dialogue: Reports of International Consultations, Cartigny Switzerland, 1993, Hong Kong, 1994* (Geneva: Lutheran World Federation, 1994).

21. World Council of Churches, "Nairobi Statement on Worship and Culture: Contemporary Challenges and Opportunities," *International Review of Mission* 85, no. 337 (1996): 184–88.

22. Ibid.

23. For a fuller presentation of creative assimilation and dynamic equivalence, see Anscar J. Chupungco, "Two Methods of Liturgical Inculturation," in *Christian Worship: Unity in Cultural Diversity*, ed. S. Anita Stauffer (Geneva: Lutheran World Federation, 1996).

24. World Council of Churches, 186.

25. Ibid., 187.

26. Ibid.

27. Colin Buchanan, ed. *Anglican Eucharistic Liturgies 1985–2010* (London: Canterbury Press Norwich, 2011), 195.

28. John Fenwick and Bryan Spinks, "South Indian Springboard," in *Worship in Transition* (New York: Continuum Publishing Company, 1995), 53.

29. Robert Gribben, "The Formation of the Liturgy of the Church of South India," *Studia Liturgica* 30, no. 2 (2000): 135.

30. Fenwick and Spinks, 58.

31. T.S. Garrett, *Worship in the Church of South India* (London: Lutterworth Press, 1958), 8–9.

32. Paul M. Collins, *Christian Inculturation in India* (Aldershot: Ashgate, 2007), 1.

33. Eric J. Lott, *Worship in an Indian Context: Eight Inter-Cultural Liturgies* (Bangalore: United Theological College, 1986), 5.

34. Ibid.

35. P.B. Ravi Prasad, "Dalit Theology: A Synpopsis," in *Towards a Dalit Theology*, ed. M.E. Prabhakar (Delhi: ISPCK, 1988), 183.

36. Collins, 16.

37. Ibid., 142.

38. Ibid., 143.

39. Ibid., 91.

40. Prasad, 184.

41. Collins, 13.

42. Sundar Clarke, *Let the Indian Church Be Indian* (Madras: The Christian Literature Society, 1980), 10–11.

43. Ibid., 18.

44. "Dalit Movement - Need for a Theology," in *Towards a Dalit Theology*, ed. M.E. Prabhakar (Delhi: ISPCK, 1988), 31.

45. Saral K. Chatterji, "Why Dalit Theology?," ibid., ed. M.E. Prabhakar, 14–15.

46. Ibid., 15.

47. Ibid., 16–17.

48. M.E. Prabhakar, "The Search for a Dalit Theology," ibid., ed. M.E. Prabhakar, 38.

49. Ibid., 45.

50. Buchanan, 195.

51. Ibid., 198.

52. Ibid., 200.

53. Ibid., 201.

54. Collins, 21.

55. Buchanan, 145.

56. Ibid.

57. Ibid., 149.

58. Ibid.

59. Phillip Tovey, *Inculturation of Christian Worship: Exploring the Eucharist* (Aldershot: Ashgate, 2004), 141.

60. "The Truth Shall Make You Free: The Reports, Resolutions & Pastoral Letters from the Bishops," (paper presented at the Lambeth Conference, London, 1988), 219.

61. Holeton, 5.

62. Ibid., 9.

63. Ibid.

64. Ibid., 10.

65. David Gitari, ed. *Anglican Liturgical Inculturation: The Kanamai Statement "African Culture and Anglican Liturgy"*, vol. 28, Alcuin/Grow Liturgical Study (Bramcote: Grove Books Ltd., 1994), 33.

66. Ibid., 38.

67. Anscar J. Chupungco, *Worship: Progress and Tradition* (Beltsville, MD: The Pastoral Press, 1995), 89.

68. Ibid., 91.

69. Enrico Mazza, *The Eucharistic Prayers of the Roman Rite*, trans. Matthew J. O'Connell (New York: Pueblo Publishers, 1986), 123–24.

70. Donovan, 78.

71. Ibid., 79.

72. Chupungco, *Worship: Progress and Tradition*, 95–96.

73. Ibid., 97.

74. R.C.D. Jasper and Paul F. Bradshaw, *A Companion to the Alternative Services Book* (London: SPCK, 1986), 171.

75. David J. Kennedy, "A Kind of Liturgical Arcic? The Ecumenical Potential of the Four Eucharistic Prayers of Rite a in *the Alternative Services Book 1980*," *Scottish Journal of Theology* 44, no. 1 (1991): 58.

76. Jasper and Bradshaw, 175.

77. Ibid., 229–31.

78. *The Alternative Services Book 1980* (Colchester: Clowes, 1980), 9.

79. Kennedy, "A Kind of Liturgical Arcic? The Ecumenical Potential of the Four Eucharistic Prayers of Rite a in *the Alternative Services Book 1980*," 58.

80. Ibid., 59.

81. Ibid. Kennedy presents specific examples for the wording of the anamnesis (pp. 63–64) and the epiclesis (pp. 68–70) in the ASB Eucharistic prayers.

82. *The Book of Alternative Services of the Anglican Church of Canada,* (Toronto: Anglican Book Centre, 1985), 7.

83. Interview with William Crockett.

84. Interview with William Crockett.

85. Morgan, 248.

86. Crockett, *Eucharist: Symbol of Transformation,* 262.

87. *A New Zealand Prayer Book, He Karakia Mihinare O Aotearoa* (Auckland: William Collins Publishers Ltd., 1989), x.

88. Ibid., x–xi.

89. Ibid., xv.

90. Ibid., 403.

91. Ibid.

92. "Anglican Church in Aoteroa, New Zealand and Polynesia," http://www.anglican.org.nz/.

93. *A New Zealand Prayer Book, He Karakia Mihinare O Aotearoa,* 457.

94. The Liturgical Commission and the Revision Committee proposed six Eucharistic Prayers to the 1996 meeting of the General Synod. They received the necessary majority from the bishops and the clergy but failed to receive the necessary number of votes from the Laity to be approved. They subsequently became starting material for the prayers in Common Worship. They have been published separately. Colin Buchanan and Trevor Lloyd, *Six Eucharistic Prayers as Proposed in 1996* (Cambridge, UK: Grove Books Limited, 1996).

95. *Common Worship: Services and Prayers for the Church of England* (London: Church House Publishing).

96. Ibid., ix–x. Emphasis mine.

97. Ibid., 94.

98. Ibid.

99. Ibid., 200.

100. Ibid., 201.

101. *Eucharistic Prayers, Services of the Word, and Night Prayer: Supplementary to the Book of Alternative Services* (Toronto: ABC Publishing, 2001), 5.

102. Interview with Richard Leggett.

103. The reference refers to the Second Supplementary Eucharistic Prayer. In the introduction to the publication, the following is stated about the three Eucharistic Prayers: "One reflects the Reformed theological conscience, and two distinct inclusive prayers reflect different points of view of which the Committee became aware." [*Eucharistic Prayers, Services of the Word, and Night Prayer: Supplementary to the Book of Alternative Services,* 5–6.

104. The "other circumstances" refer back to Leggett's earlier comment about requesting a prayer for use in time of lament and uncertainty. The pre-*Sanctus* thanksgiving narrative makes references to experiences of betrayal, injury, and brokenness:

> When those we trust betray us, unfailingly you remain with us. When we injure others, you confront us in your love and call us to the paths of righteousness. You stand with the weak, and those, broken and alone, whom you have always welcomed home, making the first last, and the last first. [ibid., 17.]

The post-*Sanctus* narrative about God's salvation highlights motifs of deliverance of Israel.

105. Interview with Richard Leggett.
106. *Eucharistic Prayers, Services of the Word, and Night Prayer: Supplementary to the Book of Alternative Services*, 15.
107. Ibid.
108. Ibid., 16.
109. Ibid., 18.
110. "Indigenous Ministries Anglican Church of Canada," http://www.anglican.ca/im/.

Chapter 7

Examining the Christology of Canadian Anglican Contemporary Eucharistic Prayers for Cultural Reflexivity

CHRISTOLOGIES IN CONTEMPORARY CANADIAN ANGLICAN LITURGIES

In chapter 6, various Anglican Eucharistic texts from 1950 to 2000 were examined for their engagement with the local cultures in which they were used. In most cases, these prayers showed a gradual evolution from representing the "church culture" of their time to increasingly representing some of the values and concerns of the larger societal culture. In this chapter, the Christologies of the Eucharistic prayers of *The Book of Alternative Services,* as well as the three Supplementary Prayers of the Anglican Church of Canada, will be explored, in preparation for, in the final chapter, the construction of new inculturated Eucharistic Prayer texts that demonstrate a narrative Christology.

Paul Gibson, retired Liturgical Officer for the Anglican Church of Canada, sent a communiqué to me during the research phase of this work reflecting on the Christology at work in the (Canadian) Book of Alternative Services Eucharistic Prayers.[1] In that piece he makes the observation that "We cannot separate Christological theology from atonement theology. As St. Paul put it in 2 Corinthians 5:19, 'In Christ God was reconciling the world to himself.' The purpose of the incarnation is the restoration of the relationship of humanity and God."[2] Gibson then makes the point that Christianity has never adopted only one atonement theory. Therefore, how should one evaluate a particular Christology? Gibson draws on the work of Roger Haight and suggests three criteria that could be used:

- faithfulness to the tradition,
- intelligibility in today's world, and
- empowerment of the Christian life.[3]

Gibson then uses these criteria to show how (particularly) Eucharistic Prayer 1 in the BAS effectively fulfills them. He calls attention to the second paragraph of the prayer, a thanksgiving for the reconciling work of Jesus Christ, which expresses atonement simply as "In the fullness of time, you sent your Son, Jesus Christ, . . . to reconcile us to you,"[4], and then describes that reconciliation in terms of Jesus' actions:

> He healed the sick and ate and drank with outcasts and sinners; he opened the eyes of the blind and proclaimed the good news of your kingdom to the poor and to those in need. In all things he fulfilled your gracious will.[5]

"We are at-one with God as we are drawn into the agenda of the Christ."[6]

Gibson's closing remarks capture well the essence of Haight's three criteria as well as the need for Eucharistic texts to engage the cultural world of the worshiper and empower them to reflect Christ's identity in their world.

> I suggest that a Eucharistic Christology today needs terms of reference which are specific rather than general and more this-worldly than cosmic. It is important for a Eucharistic prayer to honour the tradition but it is equally important that it speak in terms that are intelligible to those whose thinking is shaped by contemporary ideas and that it empower Eucharistic participants in a ministry which is potentially as practical as that of Jesus . . . A Eucharistic Christology must in some measure paraphrase and even begin to answer Bonhoeffer's question, "Who is Christ for us today?"[7]

In chapters 4 and 5, the interaction of the Christian Gospel with contemporary culture has been explored using Niebuhr's "Christ and Culture" typology; and a narrative Christology that honors a semiotic and reflexive approach with its linguistic (Christian) community has been developed using the work of Hans Frei. Early examples of inculturation were explored in chapter 6. What follows will be an exploration of Canadian Eucharistic Prayers using Haight's criteria for evaluating Christologies as a frame, and Niebuhr's typology and the "Frei-inspired" Christology to fill in that frame.

Faithfulness to the Tradition

Even though it has been shown that the Eucharistic Prayers of the Canadian *Book of Alternative Services* are concerned primarily with the local "church culture," and show only very generalized sensitivity to the values of postmodern cultures emerging in Western societies, there still are considerable strengths in both the Christology and structure of these prayers.

First, the Christology itself is congruent, in several ways, with the Christology developed in this work based on Frei's work. In the BAS Eucharistic Prayers, the death and resurrection are kept together—both being part of the saving work of Jesus Christ.[8] "The saving work of Christ is not presented as a forensic transaction whereby the guilty are granted 'full and free pardon' because of Jesus' bloody execution in their stead. It is presented as a transformative event"[9] Salvation is based on the entire work of God in Jesus Christ—

> from his taking flesh of a virgin through his sharing the human lot, his ministry and passion to his resurrection and ascension . . . It is not envisaged as forensic acquittal but rather as the restoration of full humanness with the purposes of God.[10]

And this salvation is made real to the worshiper through the presence of Christ. This presence is not limited only to the symbols of the consecrated bread and wine of the Eucharist. As Stephen Reynolds remarks of the underlying assumptions in the BAS Eucharistic rites: "The presence of Christ is an event which happens, and which happens principally *in the community*, not only or even primarily to the bread and wine."[11] This is also the intention of the "Frei-inspired" Christology of this work, in which the worshiper is engaged by, and engages, the identity of Jesus Christ through the whole worship experience and is specifically aided by the narrative texts of the Eucharistic Prayer.

William Crockett who, as previously mentioned, was instrumental in the compilation of the Eucharistic Prayers in the BAS, states that the Eucharistic rite in the BAS focused on three (Christological) images in particular:

1. Jesus' death as an act of vicarious suffering on behalf of the people (cf. the suffering servant of Isaiah 53)
2. Jesus' death as a sin offering (cf. expiatory sacrifices offered in the Temple), and
3. Jesus' death and resurrection as an act of divine deliverance from the power of sin and death[12]

Each of the above images is an example of figural relationships in scripture. As stated above, Jesus' death as vicarious suffering is in a figural relationship with the suffering servant image of Isaiah 53. The notion of Jesus's death as a sin offering is in a figural relationship with the Hebrew Scriptural accounts of expiatory sacrifices offered in the Temple (or Tabernacle). And Jesus' death and resurrection as an act of divine deliverance is in a figural relationship with the accounts of the Exodus from Egypt in the book of Exodus. Also, each of these motifs is a faithful presentation of the identity of Jesus Christ as a unique human being whose salvific actions were expressions of his total obedience to God. Therefore, they are congruent with some of the key pieces of the "Frei-inspired" Christology.

Examples of these Christologies will now be illustrated from the six Eucharistic prayers of the BAS, and a similar analysis will be carried out on the three Supplementary Prayers.

Eucharistic Prayer 1

This prayer,[13] while a new composition, is inspired by the prayer text of the fourth-century *Apostolic Constitutions* Book 8.[14] It provides a fulsome account of creation and the history of salvation with references to humanity being created in God's image, the covenant with Israel, the exodus deliverance, and the challenge of the prophets. The layout of the narrative invites a figural interpretation of the providence of God, who acts continuously through history to create and then restore humanity, with the incarnation of Jesus "in the fullness of time" as the climactic act.

After the Sanctus, there is a statement about Jesus' incarnation which underlines his unsubstitutability, remaining faithful to his identity as portrayed in the Gospel narrative.

In the fullness of time, you sent your Son Jesus Christ,
to share our human nature, to live and die as one of us,[15]

This is followed by a full narrative expressing Jesus' ministry and teaching about the kingdom of God.

He healed the sick and ate and drank with outcasts and sinners;
he opened the eyes of the blind and proclaimed the good news
   of your kingdom to the poor and to those in need.[16]

Jesus' death is presented as a "perfect sacrifice [which] destroys the power of sin and death." And it is closely linked to his resurrection through which God "give(s) us life for evermore."[17] Clearly Jesus' life is offered as both an eradication of sin and a deliverance from its power, but there is no attempt to explain how that is accomplished. In the epiclesis, there is a sense that the worshiping community is being offered to God through Christ as "a living sacrifice in Jesus Christ, our Lord." This prayer incorporates the Christological images of #2 (sin offering) and #3 (divine deliverance) above. One of the strengths of this prayer, and what would make it particularly appealing to contemporary Canadian culture, is its rich narrative about the life and ministry of Jesus and, in the epiclesis, the call to unity in the human community. This strong emphasis on Jesus' humanity should, perhaps, not come as a surprise given the Arian leanings of its likely source. "The editor is shown to have had Arian leanings by the best manuscript (Vatican gr 1506), which contains passages which have been omitted from all other manuscripts."[18] It is interesting to note that, in spite of its less-than-orthodox roots, the *Apostolic Constitutions* provides a helpful foundation for contemporary Eucharistic prayers.

The several references throughout the prayer to our need for transformation are congruent with Niebuhr's Type 5 (Christ, the transformer of culture). In the opening preface, it is not only humanity in the past that sinned but also we in the present. "When we turned away from you in sin, you did not cease to care for us."[19] In the concluding epiclesis, there is a prayer "that all who eat and drink at this table may be one body and one holy people, a living sacrifice in Jesus Christ, our Lord."[20] This introduces the notion of "objectivity" characteristic of Frei's Christolog—in that the worshiping community is submitting itself to the presence of Christ. There is also an invitation to view our present experiences of "being at table' to be in a figural relationship with Jesus' gathering with his disciples at the table of the Last Supper.

Eucharistic Prayer 2

This prayer is a Canadian adaptation of the *Apostolic Tradition of Hippolytus*. This prayer uses a *Logos* Christology, bringing together the deliverance image of Jesus as Savior and Redeemer with the Johannine image of Christ as the living Word of God[21]—reaffirming the unsubstitutable identity of Jesus as portrayed in the Gospel narratives. There is a corporate sense to salvation in the text: "he stretched out his hands in suffering, to bring release to those who place their hope in you; and so he won for you a holy people." The sense of vicarious suffering continues with a direct reference to Isaiah 53 in the words, "he chose to bear our griefs and sorrows"—inviting a figural interpretation to these events. The effect of the crucifixion and resurrection is the creation of a new people.[22] Even though the salvific actions of Jesus' bearing "our griefs and sorrows" are events in the past, the concluding line of this section brings the contemporary worshiper into God's presence in this act of worship: "By his resurrection he brings us into the light of your presence."[23] While the epiclesis begins with a reference to offering, "send your Holy Spirit upon the offering of your holy Church," it does not necessarily refer only to the Eucharistic elements but to the Eucharistic worship as a whole.[24] This prayer is a good example of Christological images #1 (vicarious suffering) and #3 (divine deliverance) above. Its strength lies in the fact that it is clearly an ancient prayer, though perhaps not the model prayer of a single local community of the third century as it has been thought to be.[25]

Other than a general reference in the closing supplicatory epiclesis ("Gather into one all who share in these sacred mysteries, filling them with the Holy Spirit"[26]) there is no direct evidence of interaction with culture that could be described in Niebuhrian terms.

Eucharistic Prayer 3

This prayer, adapted from the contemporary American Episcopal Prayer B, is also modeled after Hippolytus but shows greater latitude in its vocabulary.[27] It, too, uses a *Logos* Christology, but now the "Word" emphasis is more on the Word spoken through the prophets and the Word made flesh than the Word in creation. Again, it exemplifies the uniqueness of Jesus Christ as one sent by God. It also invites a figural interpretation supporting the ongoing providence of God as it recalls salvation history from creation through to incarnation. This prayer has less of the suffering servant motif and a more fully expounded deliverance soteriology—Christological image #3 above. After a reference to God in Christ delivering us from evil, the theme is further developed in the text, "you have brought us out of error into truth, out of sin into righteousness, out of death into life." The sense of offering in this prayer is on elements of God's creation (bread and wine)—modeled after the Jewish offering of first fruits.[28] A strength of this prayer is its powerful eschatological emphasis: "In the fullness of time, reconcile all things in Christ, and make them new, and bring us to that city of light where you dwell with all your sons and daughters."[29] It creates in the worshiping community a sense of expectation—that God's redeeming work continues and that God's will is for a better world than that in which they currently dwell. Again, it invites a providential view of history (and figural relationships) where God is continuing to work in the present community as God has done with God's people throughout history. This could be considered an example of Niebuhr's Type 5 (Christ, the transformer of culture) as there is an expectation that the world is continuing to be transformed through Christ. The prayer also calls for the use of a variable Preface, which enables the inclusion of rich narrative material focused around particular themes of God's salvation and our experience of it.

Eucharistic Prayer 4

This is a contemporary prayer based on the American Episcopal Prayer C.[30] The prayer carries a strong creation theme throughout and includes a narrative of Old Testament salvation history. One of the strengths of this prayer is the re-narration of creation using contemporary, more scientific vocabulary. "At your command all things came to be: the vast expanse of interstellar space, galaxies, suns, the planets in their courses, and this fragile earth, our island home."[31] Like Prayer 1, the soteriological emphasis is on vicarious suffering, "He was wounded for our transgressions and bruised for our iniquities."[32] Other than this figural relationship between the suffering servant in Isaiah and Jesus Christ, this prayer does not invite, particularly, a figural interpretation of history to the same extent as the previous prayers.

Redemption is expressed as the creation of "a new people by water and the Spirit," which is particularly appropriate given the strong creation emphasis throughout the prayer. Like Prayer 3 there is a close association between the offering and the epiclesis,[33]

> We . . . now bring you these gifts. Send your Holy Spirit upon us and upon this offering of your Church, that we who eat and drink at this holy table may share in the divine life of Christ our Lord.[34]

Christological image #1 (vicarious suffering) is the primary reference in this prayer. One of its strengths is the closing epiclesis, which makes reference to the Spirit being poured "upon the whole earth" to make it new, and the coming together of all people, "of every language, race, and nation [to] . . . share in the banquet you have promised."[35] Along with the identification of God's kingdom being a place "where peace and justice are revealed," this text emphasizes the continuing re-creation of the world and its movement toward the eschatological future. In this sense, one could deduce a "Christ, the transformer of culture (Niebuhr Type 5)" approach, though the reference is quite general.

Eucharistic Prayer 5

This prayer represents a re-worked version of a Roman Catholic prayer prepared for masses with children. It begins by expounding on the wonder of creation and then tells of a "divine love story in which the power of sin and death are broken and God's family is re-united."[36] There is a richness in the narrative describing the various ways in which evil is manifested in the world, including human rebellion, but it is cast in easily accessible language. Jesus is portrayed as the great healer who exemplifies God's love triumphing over evil and calling humanity to unity and wholeness. "In Jesus, your Son, you bring healing to our world and gather us into one great family."[37] There is only a simple offering reference—referring to the worshipers' self-offering in Christ.

Like Prayer 1, there is a rich narrative section before the Sanctus that describes Jesus' earthly ministry. "He cares for the poor and the hungry.

He suffers with the sick and the rejected. Betrayed and forsaken, he did not strike back but overcame hatred with love."[38] While the reference is indirect, one could reach the conclusion that the present-day members of the Christian community should follow the same pattern. With that understanding, one could attribute to the above a retelling of the Gospel narratives in such a way as to provide an objective critique and call to transformation in the lives of the worshipers—exemplifying a key part of Frei's *sensus literalis* of Christian, in this case, liturgical texts. This call to transformation is echoed in the closing doxology as mentioned below. In terms of a Niebuhrian analysis, while the narrative portions reveal Jesus of Nazareth as taking an "over against" stance toward aspects of his first-century culture (Type 1—Christ against culture), there is not a strong reference to contemporary culture in this prayer.

This prayer is an example of Christological image #3—divine deliverance. A particular strength of this prayer is its concluding petition/doxology, which views the worshipers as now being given both power and responsibility to be agents of God's eschatological kingdom. "Father, you call us to be your servants; fill us with the courage and love of Jesus, that all the world may gather in joy at the table of your kingdom."[39]

Eucharistic Prayer 6

This prayer stands out from the other five in that its source (Basil of Caesarea) is eastern. Typical of that heritage is the fact that it portrays a cosmic vision of redemption using Johannine themes. God dwells in eternal light and creates all things to share in this divine light. The (earthly) Eucharistic community's praise joins that of the angelic, heavenly realm.[40] Given the strong Logos Christology of this prayer, the portrayal of Jesus as being unsubstitutable comes through with force. There is an equally strong sense of Jesus being one whose life was entirely an obedient response to God. "He lived as one of us, yet without sin . . . To fulfil your purpose he gave himself up to death"[41] The Prayer expresses a full and rich narrative of God's creation and of God's salvation history. The Christological narrative spans the full scope of the life and work of Jesus Christ—incarnation, earthly life and ministry, death, and resurrection. "Through Christ's death and resurrection death is destroyed (the victory motif) and the whole creation is made new."[42] However, there is no attempt to explain how this takes place. Rather, the prayer simply reads, "To fulfill your purpose he gave himself up to death, and, rising from the grave, destroyed death and made the whole creation new." This is a particularly helpful way of presenting the soteriology (Christological image #3—divine deliverance) because the outcome of salvation is the focus rather than hypotheses of how it might have been accomplished.

Reflecting its eastern roots, the prayer moves on to a reference of the work of the Spirit in the story of salvation and introduces the institution narrative in the Johannine context: "When the hour had come for him to be glorified by you, his heavenly Father, having loved his own who were in the world, he loved them to the end."[43] Another strength of this prayer is the engaging nature of the epiclesis, which employs participles in describing the work of the Spirit: "sanctifying" and "showing." The inclusion of a series of petitions at the end of the prayer not only represents an ancient Eucharistic tradition; it also gives the worshiping community the sense that the finished work of Christ and the grace of this Eucharistic experience are for *this life*—here and now.

Because of the continuing emphasis of the providential love of God for humanity and all of creation, there is an invitation to a figural approach to history, but there are no obvious figural relationships exemplified in the prayer. Like Prayer 1, there is a narrative section which yields a faithful, Gospel-based, objective re-narration of the person of Jesus—again presenting this aspect of Frei's Christology. However, with the prayer's strongly transcendent character, there is little obvious interaction with contemporary culture—other than the supplicatory section in the final part of the prayer.

Crockett concludes his study of the six BAS Prayers in this way:

> The new Eucharistic prayers in the *BAS* are an attempt to recover for Canadian Anglicans the full riches of the biblical and traditional vision of salvation. Drawing upon scripture and the liturgical and theological traditions of both east and west, they attempt to mediate a truly catholic heritage while remaining evangelical in their proclamation of the fullness of the Gospel of salvation.[44]

This is an interestingly revealing quote. Clearly, the Prayers in the BAS afforded Anglicans a much richer Eucharistic diet than they had previously had access to. However, as with our analysis of the engagement of these prayers with culture (chapter 4), the Prayers primarily respond to the culture of the Anglican Church of Canada. While the prayers do represent a wider interpretation of God's salvation in Jesus Christ (beyond merely the substitutionary atonement of the Eucharistic Prayer in the Cranmerian-style Prayer Books), they still focus entirely on three understandings of the life and work of Jesus Christ and contain little direct missiological emphasis—reaching out to those beyond the church and interpreting to them why the Christian faith and the work of Christ should matter to them. It has been shown that the prayers are congruent with the aspects of a figural approach to God and history as well as a faithful narration of the uniqueness of Jesus Christ. Because of the prayers' weak interaction with the wider culture, there are not many references to challenge the Christian community to transformative change, but there is a clear and objective presentation of Jesus Christ and at least an invitation to his disciples to model themselves after him—thereby opening themselves to the transformation that Niebuhr had in mind in Type 5. (Christ, the transformer of culture.)

Supplementary Prayers (S-1, S-2, and S-3) Anglican Church of Canada

The background to these texts, which were presented to the 1998 meeting of General Synod, has been discussed toward the end of chapter 4.[45] They were produced in order to respond to an expressed need for Eucharistic Prayers that were more inclusive (particularly of gender: S-1 and S-2) as well as providing a contemporary-language text reflecting a more Reformed theology (S-3). The Christologies of these prayers will now be examined in a manner analogous to the BAS Prayers.

Eucharistic Prayer S-1

The fixed Preface (before the Sanctus) of this prayer contains only a very brief reference to salvation history but intentionally names a female prophet from the Old Testament. "Your Spirit speaks through Huldah[46] and Micah, through prophets, sages, and saints in every age, to confront our sin and reveal the vision of your new creation."[47] However, the "ongoing" sense of God's love for us in this Preface does engage the worshiper and focus the prayer on the present day. "Holy God . . . for in the ocean of your steadfast love you bear us and place the song of your Spirit in our hearts."[48] While the pre-Sanctus preface does not contain material that would be considered foreign to scripture, this prayer is weaker in its recounting of salvation history. Other than portraying God as one whose love for us never ends, a sense of the providential ordering of history and/or a figural interpretation is not really present.

The Christological section following the Sanctus is *Logos*-like, (affirming the unsubstitutability of Christ), though the title, Son, is not used explicitly. In the text, "In the fullness of time you sent Jesus the Christ to share our fragile humanity," there is the sense of the pre-existent *Logos* being incarnated. However, the narrative section presenting Jesus from the Gospels is weaker than in the six prayers from the BAS. Jesus' life, death, and resurrection are described as opening "the path from brokenness to health, from fear to trust, from pride and conceit to reverence to you."[49] These three dialectics are reminiscent of BAS Prayer 3 where error-truth, sin-righteousness, and death-life are used. Likewise, the dominant Christological image is that of deliverance from sin and death, though more contemporary language is used. Interestingly, the transition to the Last Supper and Institution narrative employs the Johannine language as did BAS Prayer 6. "Rejected by a world that could not bear the Gospel of life, Jesus knew death was near. His head anointed for burial by an unknown woman, Jesus gathered together those who love him."[50] Like BAS Prayer 2 (Hippolytus), the epiclesis involves more than a focus on the bread and cup but also includes an emphasized reference to the worshipers themselves. "Breathe your Holy Spirit . . . this bread, this cup, ourselves, our souls and bodies."[51] This prayer has strengths in responding to contemporary culture, but its Christology is not noticeably different from the BAS Eucharistic Prayers of fifteen years earlier. While the epiclesis includes a petition that the worshipers would become "signs of your love for all the world and ministers of your transforming purpose,"[52] this is the only reference to contemporary culture—again exemplifying Niebuhr's Type 5 (Christ, the transformer of culture).

Eucharistic Prayer S-2

Like Prayer S-1, the fixed Preface begins with a contemporary expression of God's love for us. It intentionally reaches out to the worshiper in an "existential" identification with sin, by rehearsing the many ways that we hurt, or are hurt by, others and over and against these affirms God's faithful love. "When those we trust betray us, unfailingly you remain with us. When we injure others, you confront us in your love and call us to paths of righteousness."[53] The prayer continues by stating some of the ethics of God's kingdom—preference for the poor and broken, the last being first. The interesting thing about putting these texts at this point in the prayer is that they bring God and Christ very close together in the mind of the worshiper. The prayer is addressed to "Eternal God, Source of all being," but the empathetic stance of God is often associated with the ministry of Jesus. While the images portrayed are not direct references from the Gospels, they are examples in contemporary terms of the ministry and teaching of Jesus. In that sense, the prayer provides the objective stance required by Frei's understanding of the *sensus literalis* and the importance of the Christian community being open to challenge by the text.

Following the Sanctus, the history of God's deliverance is recited, intentionally including the female figure of Hagar. Unlike Prayer S-1, this piece does present a providential view of history and invites a figural connection between the various instances of God's deliverance of God's people.

Though there is clearly a Logos-based Christology which supports the unsubstitutability of Christ ("At the right time you sent your Anointed One"), it is not as clear a Christological image in Prayer S-2 as there is in Prayer S-1. In addition to the narrative piece on Jesus' earthly ministry, there is only an indirect reference to vicarious suffering. "Christ knew the desolation of the cross and opened the way for all humanity into the redemption of your reconciling love."[54] This corresponds to Christological image #1 above—but it is a brief and more subtle reference to this soteriology.

The Prayer does have an eschatologically oriented epiclesis. At the end of the anamnesis, the following offering prayer and petition appears: "we offer you these gifts, longing for the bread of tomorrow and the wine of the new age to come."[55] Also, the epiclesis concludes with a petition that the Spirit, through the Eucharistic gifts will "sustain us in our hunger for peace," after which there is a brief petition for others and for ourselves. Like Prayer S-1, while the prayer uses images from contemporary culture and makes vague references to Christ continuing to transform the world (Niebuhr Type 5), there is little interaction with the wider culture. Also similar to Prayer S-1, this prayer is strong in empathizing with contemporary culture, but does not introduce any new Christological images and, if anything, is weak in its soteriology.

Eucharistic Prayer S-3

As stated in the introduction to the three Supplementary Prayers, Prayer S-3 was compiled to offer a more "Reformed"-style prayer. Consequently, it is more "Cranmerian" in its structure. The Preface is entirely focused on praising and thanking God for God's goodness. Other than a reference to God being "faithful to your people in every generation," there is no recounting of salvation history and hence no clear invitation to a providential ordering of history or to figural interpretation.

As would be expected from a Cranmer-style prayer, it is strong in its Logos Christology ("you gave the world your only Son, in order that the world might be saved through him"[56]) and, therefore, this prayer does present the unsubstitutability of Jesus Christ.

Unlike the typical Eucharistic Prayers in the (Cranmer) Prayer Book, there is mention of Jesus' earthly ministry. "He made you known by taking the form of a servant, healing the sick, liberating the oppressed, reaching out to the lost."[57] In graphic language, Jesus' "work" in his crucifixion is portrayed as being both a sacrifice for sin as well as a deliverance from evil. (Christological images #2 and #3 above.) While the language is very close to the Prayer Book prayers and implies substitutionary atonement, the emphasis is on Jesus' work more than on humanity's sin. In the epiclesis at the end of the prayer, there is a self-offering, but it is presented as a *response* to the grace of the Holy Spirit, as would be expected in a Reformed theology.

In a manner similar to the other Supplementary Prayers, there is a call for the Christian community to become involved in the ongoing transformational ministry of Christ (Niebuhr Type 5): "May we be renewed in his risen life, filled with love, and strengthened in our will to serve others."[58] However, there is little interaction with the wider culture. While this prayer is presented in accessible, contemporary language, it still follows a traditional pattern, including its soteriology.

The exploration of these nine contemporary Canadian Anglican Eucharistic Prayers, using Gibson's approach to Haight's three criteria to evaluate the Christologies of Eucharistic Prayers, produces several examples of how contemporary texts can help us respond to Bonhoeffer's question "Who is Christ for us today." This analysis helps us prepare for constructing, in the next chapter, new Eucharistic Prayer texts that are faithful to the tradition and intelligible in today's world.

NOTES

1. Paul Gibson, April 23, 2009.
2. Ibid., 1.
3. Haight, 47.
4. Canada, 194.
5. Ibid.
6. Gibson.
7. Ibid.
8. Reynolds, 43.
9. Ibid., 44.
10. John Webster, "Bas and Bcp: Some Thoughts on a Theological Shift," ibid. (Anglican Book Centre), 87–88.
11. Stephen Reynolds, "Bas Evaluation: Some Theological Questions Responses'," ibid. (The Anglican Church of Canada), 47.
12. Crockett, "The Theology of the Eucharistic Prayers in the Book of Alternative Services of the Anglican Church of Canada," 102.
13. The reader may wish to refer to the full text of each of the BAS Eucharistic Prayers in Appendix 3.
14. Crockett, "The Theology of the Eucharistic Prayers in the Book of Alternative Services of the Anglican Church of Canada," 102.
15. Canada, 194.
16. Ibid.
17. Crockett, "The Theology of the Eucharistic Prayers in the Book of Alternative Services of the Anglican Church of Canada," 103.
18. R. C. D. Jasper and G. J. Cuming, *Prayers of the Eucharist: Early and Reformed*, 3rd ed. (New York: Pueblo Publishing Co., 1987), 100. See also W. E. Pitt, "The Anamneses and Institution Narrative in the Apostolic Constitutions Book Viii," *The Journal of Ecclesiastical History* 9, no. 1 (1958): 4.
19. Canada, 193.

20. Ibid., 195.

21. Crockett, "The Theology of the Eucharistic Prayers in the Book of Alternative Services of the Anglican Church of Canada," 103.

22. Ibid., 104.

23. Canada, 196.

24. Paul F. Bradshaw, Maxwell E. Johnson, and L. Edward Phillips, *The Apostolic Tradition: A Commentary* (Minneapolis, MN: Augsburg Fortress, 2002), 104.

25. Ibid., 13–14.

26. Canada, 197.

27. Crockett, "The Theology of the Eucharistic Prayers in the Book of Alternative Services of the Anglican Church of Canada," 105.

28. Ibid., 106.

29. Canada, 200.

30. Crockett, "The Theology of the Eucharistic Prayers in the Book of Alternative Services of the Anglican Church of Canada," 106.

31. Canada, 201.

32. Ibid.

33. Crockett, "The Theology of the Eucharistic Prayers in the Book of Alternative Services of the Anglican Church of Canada," 106.

34. Canada, 203.

35. Ibid.

36. Crockett, "The Theology of the Eucharistic Prayers in the Book of Alternative Services of the Anglican Church of Canada," 107.

37. Canada, 204.

38. Ibid., 205.

39. Ibid., 206.

40. Crockett, "The Theology of the Eucharistic Prayers in the Book of Alternative Services of the Anglican Church of Canada," 107.

41. Canada, 208.

42. Crockett, "The Theology of the Eucharistic Prayers in the Book of Alternative Services of the Anglican Church of Canada," 107.

43. Ibid., 108.

44. Ibid.

45. The reader may wish to refer to the full text of each of the Supplementary Eucharistic Prayers in Appendix 3.

46. Huldah appears towards the end of the Second Book of Kings, in connection with the reforms of King Josiah. In 2 Kings 22:14, she is identified as a prophetess and the wife of Shalum, keeper of the wardrobe. She is sought out and consulted by Hilkiah the priest, with various royal officials, at Josiah's command. She proclaims God's judgement upon the nation, calling Israel from the worship of other gods to the one true God. She is also the first person recorded in the Bible to have made a judgement about the canon of Scripture, with the result that the books discovered by Josiahthe "books of the covenant"—are proclaimed in solemn assembly, and continue to be proclaimed in Jewish and Christian worship to this day. (*Eucharistic Prayers, Services of the Word, and Night Prayer: Supplementary to the Book of Alternative Services*, 5.)

47. Ibid., 15.
48. Ibid.
49. Ibid., 16.
50. Ibid.
51. Ibid.
52. Ibid.
53. Ibid., 17.
54. Ibid., 18.
55. Ibid., 19.
56. Ibid., 20.
57. Ibid.
58. Ibid., 21.

Chapter 8

Bringing Together Culture and Christology in Proposed Eucharistic Prayer Texts

INITIAL CONSIDERATIONS

As in the Canadian *Book of Alternative Services*, this new proposed Eucharistic prayer will maintain much of the structure that is typical of the contemporary Antiochene (West Syrian)style Eucharistic prayers. Reynolds is critical of the BAS on this point—that it still reflects a model of aiming at liturgical consensus (what the majority in the church might prefer) rather than offering a true diversity. He notes that all of the Eucharistic Prayers in the BAS follow the West Syrian pattern and goes on to suggest that "it may be one of the tasks of *liturgical* renewal within 'the Canadian context of our theology' to help create in our own church an atmosphere where real alternatives are possible."[1]—suggesting that it would be helpful to use other prayer structures—either from other historic models or from contemporary innovations. However, in this work, the primary reason for using the Antiochene structure in forming a new prayer, while providing some assurance about "faithfulness to the tradition," is the fact that this structure offers the opportunity for rich narrative descriptions—about God's loving purposes for all of the created order—and particularly about the person and work of Jesus Christ. The emphasis on using the Antiochene anaphoral structure in contemporary Eucharistic prayers, with its accent on narrative, emerged out of an ecumenical consensus. "While the Antiochene anaphoral structure is far from normative, its accent on the place of narrative certainly is."[2] It is precisely these narrative pieces, which encourage identity descriptions, that make the Eucharistic Prayer an ideal vehicle for encountering the saving presence of Christ.

These narrative descriptions will be drawn from scripture or from traditional theological statements based on scripture narratives in order to be congruent with the first point of Haight's three criteria for evaluating

Christologies—"faithfulness to tradition." As shown in chapters 4 and 5, it is important that the narrative descriptions are faithful and objective representations of the identity of Jesus Christ, as in Frei's presentation of employing the *sensus literalis* in the interpretive (sociolinguistic) Christian community, and not merely the community's "preferred presentations" of Christ. In order to faithfully present a Christology rooted in a providential understanding of history, these prayer texts should invite a figural interpretation of God at work in history. Of primary importance in constructing the Eucharistic prayer texts is the choice of narratives that speak effectively about the identity of Jesus Christ in terms that are rooted in the local culture—in this case, Canadian culture(s),[3] which responds to the "intelligibility in today's world" portion of Haight's three criteria. This will satisfy the thrust of this work that a local community's theology and culture are in a reflexive relationship, and that an objective presentation of Jesus Christ is made accessible to the members of that community through their local culture and in a way that invites transformational change in accordance with Niebuhr's Type 5 interaction—Christ, the transformer of culture.

Intelligibility in Today's World

Earlier in the examination of recent Eucharistic prayer texts, it was noted that the intention of the compilers was probably better described as engaging local "church culture" rather than attempting to embrace the wider societal culture. The revisions in the New Zealand liturgies (1989) and the Church of England's liturgies (2000) showed modest signs of attempting this wider inculturation so as to be more "intelligible in today's world."

As has been discussed previously, the challenge, particularly in a large and regionalized country like Canada, is the fact that there are many cultures and subcultures which make up Canadian society. In order to create a Eucharistic prayer for the Anglican Church of Canada that will be "intelligible in today's world," one needs to be able to bring together, in a reflexive relationship, a Christology that is faithful to tradition and express it in a local Canadian culture.

To create this reflexive relationship between the local culture and the Christology inherent in contemporary Eucharistic Prayers, the relevant characteristics or social values of that culture have to be determined. This is more difficult than it may at first appear because, as has been discussed in a previous chapter, local cultures can only be described and not objectively assessed. And even in the act of description, the culture will still be compared and contrasted with other local cultures. Hence, there can be no "absolute" measure of the values of a particular culture. Rather, any distinctive characteristics stand out only in a relative sense when described with reference to other comparable cultures.

Given the relatively small population of Canada, coupled with its relatively recent formation as a federal state (1867), there has been little work published on Canadian social values—especially attempts at expressing current, contemporary values. There has been some descriptive work generated, but even that is not particularly helpful in trying to generate a Canada-wide description of the nation's culture.[4] Much of what has been published highlights the *diversity* which is so much a part of Canadian culture.[5] However, this descriptor only underlines the difficulty in arriving at helpful, overarching characteristics of this culture. This diversity emerges not only in the studies by sociologists but also in literature and the arts. In 1945, Hugh MacLennan published a novel depicting the separation and difference between Francophone and Anglophone cultures in Canada.[6] Alluding to that work, Jamie Scott reflects on the expanding diversity of Canadian literature toward the close of the twentieth century: "Instead of the two solitudes of English and French we now have 2,000."[7] Scott also quotes Canadian poet, novelist, and critic Tom Marshall in reflecting on how this diversity impacts and informs the Canadian poetic idiom.[8] Marshall describes it as

> the complex search for harmony in continuing diversity, communion and community among people and between land and people; and related to this, our northern mysticism, a longing for unity with the world that leads to a greater and greater openness to and acceptance of the beautiful and terrifying universe in flux.[9]

Attempting to appeal to religion to construct an overarching description of Canadian culture does not bear much fruit either. Paul Bramadat published the results of a study of religion and ethnicity in Canada in the early years of the twenty-first century and concluded that one of the key shifts that has contributed to the decline of the influence of the Christian churches in Canada was a move of society to become more liberal and multicultural.

> As Canadian society moved during the past 30 years to become more liberal and multicultural, the public sphere could not appear to favour *any* particular religion . . . the Canadian state itself has also increasingly distanced itself from a simple endorsement of Christian values and beliefs.[10]

Since it is impossible to ascertain a concise description of "a Canadian culture," and the fact that the reflexive relationship between theological statements and local culture has to be relevant across Canada because the liturgical texts are to be used throughout the country, it was decided to explore using social values to indicate a kind of consensus "distillation" of the characteristics of Canadian culture. "Values, or deep dispositions, are important because they guide decisions about right and wrong and because they underpin a whole array of social, economic, and political preferences. They are also important because they are foundations for action."[11] The use of social values is not without its critics. In a review of Neil Nevitte's book, Harry Hiller makes the point that Nevitte is "measuring opinion and behaviour which is then wrapped together and labelled as 'values.'"[12] The problem is sometimes stated in terms of desired values versus actual behavior. However, for the purposes of this work, it is actually helpful to be able to ascertain ideal values that the majority of Canadians hold in high esteem. These will reflect the nature of the local culture as they would like it to be. If one begins at this point to bring these values into a relationship with the Christology of the Gospel, it is akin to beginning with Niebuhr's Type 3 (Synthesis of Christ and Culture) and moving toward Type 5 (Christ the transformer of culture).

This work draws on two social value studies in particular—the first, by Michael Adams,[13] one of the founders of the research firm, *Environics*, based in Toronto, and the second by Neil Nevitte,[14] Professor of Political Studies at the University of Toronto. Though the two studies use different instruments, both are designed to measure social values.

Michael Adams's study uses a tool that he brought to Canada from France called the 3SC Social Values Monitor. It was developed by CROP (le Centre de Recherche sur l'Opinion Publique) to measure the dynamics of social change. "The 3SC Social Values Monitor tracks trends in the underlying social values of Canadians, Americans and Europeans. '3SC' stands for *Système Cofremca de Suivi des Courants Socio-Culturels.*"[15] The introduction to Adams's work closes with these words, "What follows is my view of Canada's evolution from an industrial nation-state to a post-industrial, post-modern community."[16] A thorough discussion of Adams's work is beyond the scope of this work. Rather, his basic findings, along with some significant critiques of his work, will be presented.

Instead of trying to categorize the Canadian population by demographics, Adams took the responses to the 3SC Values Monitor and, through a social value analysis, determined distinctive groups or "tribes" that shared a common cluster of social values. He did initially subdivide his sample set into three age demographics—those born before 1947, those born between 1947 and 1962 (baby boomers), and those born after 1962 (post-boomers). Of particular interest is his determination that the data from the group born before 1947 generated three groups or "tribes"; the "boomers" generated four groups; and the "post-boomers" generated five groups. Adams uses this result to support the notion that Canadian society has fragmented more in the past 50 years as illustrated by the fact that the most recent "post-boomer" demographic divides into more (social value) groups than their predecessors.[17]

One of the first observations Adams makes of the "post-boomer" or "Generation X" demographic is that they have moved beyond the kind of individualism that characterized Canadian (and American) society earlier in the twentieth century. This most current generation of his study "is now blazing trails from individualism to a sort of post-individualism in which experience-seeking connections are more important than the mere assertion of autonomy and personal control."[18] Adams defines this post-individualism as "a progression to communities of choice based on mutual interest, affinity, and need."[19]

This notion of "communities of choice" is congruent with Adam's (and others') observations that since the 1960s there has been a widespread questioning of institutional authority that has become part of civic life in much of the Western world. With this shift away from loyalty to institutions, people are determining for themselves how, and in what ways, they will engage communally. However, he notes the rapid evolution of this characteristic in Canadian society and cites it as even being considered a "revolution" by the journalist Peter C. Newman.[20]

Adams also comments on the priority and importance of multiculturalism as a contemporary value in Canadian society. He makes the important observation that this positive attitude toward multiculturalism is not rooted in persons' pasts, but rather in a recognition of differences that exist in the present.[21] This is of particular interest to the local context of this author (Winnipeg, Canada), whose city hosts the largest and longest-running multicultural festival (Folklorama) of its kind in the world, as determined by the International Organizations of Folklore Festivals and Folk Arts.[22]

However, Adam's work has come under some criticism. This particular text, *Sex in the Snow*, provides very little in terms of statistical data or examples of the 3SC Social Values Monitor that was used. There are questions about the arbitrary nature of the "12 tribes" (groups) that Adams generates to categorize different types of Canadians across the three generations that he has studied.[23] There is concern expressed about the lack of attention paid to matters of class and economic circumstances.[24] But the focus of these criticisms is primarily on the conclusions that Adams draws about how and why contemporary Canadian values have emerged as they have at the beginning of the twenty-first century, rather than a challenge to the observed values themselves.

About the same time that Adams published his work, Neil Nevitte published *The Decline of Deference*. Nevitte begins his work by classifying Canada as an "advanced industrial state"—making reference to the notion of late industrialism and its various names: postindustrialism, technetronic society, post-welfarism, postbourgeois, post-materialist, and identifying two important themes of this type of state. The first of these is the fact that these states have crossed several important thresholds: affluence, economies driven by the tertiary sector, expansion of educational opportunities, "information revolution," and growth in communications-related technologies. The second is that "these structural transformations are linked to fundamental shifts in the value systems of publics."[25] As stated above, social values are important because they guide the decisions that are made and become a foundation for a wide range of social, economic, and political preferences. Therefore, these values should help determine the relationship between a contemporary local culture and the relevance of the Christological narrative in the liturgical texts being employed.

Nevitte used the World Values Survey, which directly asks questions about people's values. The survey was used in 1981 (for twenty-one countries) and again in 1990 (for over forty countries)—both times including Canada. Nevitte is careful to make the point that "the only way to know if, and how, Canadian values have changed is by making cross-time comparisons."[26] Nevitte observed the same move away from institutional bureaucracies (governmental and non-governmental) that Adams noted. Nevitte commented, in particular, on what he termed "bureaucratic hierarchies," in which he included the church. He noted that "confidence in the Church" dropped quite sharply between 1981 and 1990 in almost all of the countries surveyed— including Canada.[27] He also made the observation that progressive secularization is common in the societies of advanced industrialism and that "as religious values lose their social force world views become more pluralized and fragmented."[28]

Though the influence of institutionally based religion on society has declined in Canada, Nevitte makes the point that, though an individual's well-being may be less dependent on the institution of the church,

> it does not follow that religious values have changed very quickly or become irrelevant. Life may now be less risky, [a characteristic of advanced industrialism] but people still face fundamental questions about the meaning of human existence, about life and death.[29]

Nevitte also observed, between 1981 and 1990, a sharp increase in support for the environment and women's rights in Canada. "Canadian support for the environment and women's rights is among the highest anywhere."[30] He also noted that support for the general principles of tolerance increased significantly in Canada between 1981 and 1990 and was reflected in Canada moving from seventh to third out of twelve countries identified as being "advanced industrial."[31]

As with Adam's work, Nevitte's has also come under criticism—but of a different sort. It has been noted that Nevitte anchors his work in a framework established by Ronald Inglehart, which has limitations inherent in its design. Of particular note in this case is the fact that Nevitte's conclusions about changes in values are measured over only two points in time and only nine years apart. In spite of this and other methodological limitations, the reviewer states that Nevitte's "depictions of family and workplace values are particularly novel, revealing, and important."[32] Other questions have been raised about Nevitte's lack of definition of the term "deference,"[33] as well as the fact that these types of surveys measure opinion and not necessarily actual behavior.[34] As with the critique of Adam's work, however, these concerns have minimal impact on the actual values observed and described and are more directed at arguments of causation as well as indications of future evolution and development.

In attempting to determine a range of social values as overarching characteristics of Canadian culture, the goal is not so much a compilation of every possible social value (which would be a very complex and difficult task) but rather a distillation of the key values that appear to have wide applicability in the dominant culture(s) across the country. The resulting list will not be indicative of all possible descriptions but rather produce a list of values in whose applicability one can be relatively confident. A definite limitation of this approach is the fact that only two such studies have been conducted in recent history, and one of those, whose basis is longitudinal, has only two points of measurement separated by only nine years. However, in support of these studies' inclusion is the fact that, though the two studies are completely independent of one another and use different assessment tools, they have yielded much the same result.

To summarize this exploration of contemporary Canadian social values, the following values will be considered in the interaction with a local Christology and its liturgical presentation in Eucharistic prayers:

- Personal autonomy—particularly as expressed in the freedom to choose communities, associations, and commitments
- Inclusion—particularly as it pertains to women in society
- Tolerance (a natural outcome of personal autonomy and inclusiveness)
- Democratic processes (a natural necessity with personal autonomy and inclusiveness)
- Concern for the environment

These contemporary Canadian social values were also validated in a more recent survey by Nanos Research.[35] This survey, conducted in 2016, asked the question, "If you were to describe the top three Canadian values to someone who was not Canadian in only a few words, what would they be?" The top seven responses were:

- Rights and freedoms
- Respect for others

- Kindness/compassion
- Multiculturalism/diversity/bilingualism
- Social values (education, healthcare, opportunities)
- Equality, equity and social justice
- Tolerance/acceptance

These results appear to support the findings of earlier studies in the 1990s.

In chapter 3, the congruency between the local culture of the members of the Anglican Church of Canada and that of the dominant Canadian culture was affirmed. While some of the above values also appear (to some degree) in the priorities of the culture of the Anglican Church of Canada as expressed in the last part of the twentieth century, there are three additional priorities or values that were expressed as being characteristic of the Anglican Church of Canada, in particular. These are:

- Poverty
- Racism (may be related to inclusion and tolerance)
- War and peace

Therefore, these three values will be included so that eight values will be employed in describing the characteristics of the local culture of the Anglican Church of Canada and its cultural context in Canada at the beginning of the twenty-first century.

While it is not possible within the scope of this work to begin to explore their applicability to various parts of Canada and, in particular, Canada's "cultural patchwork," further work could be done with these eight values to ascertain regional emphases and to determine if there are additional values or cultural characteristics in these smaller cultural units. Initially, one could consider exploring the cultures of the ten provinces and three territories that make up the nation of Canada. But the problem with this choice is that provincial boundaries are somewhat arbitrary—being determined by different geographic, economic, and historical factors that have been important from time to time throughout Canada's history of nationhood. In some cases, natural physical barriers such as rivers or mountain ranges that would have been significant cultural boundaries at one time have ceased to be so with the prevalence of rail, road, and air travel. Given the interest in this work in the Anglican Church of Canada, a more fruitful approach would be to consider the local cultures inherent in each of the thirty dioceses of the Anglican Church of Canada. These are smaller geographical units than the civil provinces and territories and also are able to yield more cultural information. Just as the work of the national (General) Synod of the Anglican Church of Canada was explored to determine programmatic and ministry priorities at different times in the church's history, the same kind of comparisons could be made at the level of diocesan synod. The Journals and Acts of Synod (resolutions) of meetings of the various diocesan synods could be investigated to determine if the eight social values identified for Canada as a whole were also priorities in the region of the dioceses or if other value priorities have emerged. This investigation is not within the scope of this work because the resultant discoveries, while interesting, could not easily be incorporated into Eucharistic liturgies since these texts are compiled and authorized at the national level of the church.

What about the cultural values of indigenous cultures and any resulting liturgical texts in a reflexive relationship with those cultures? In chapter 6, an example of a Eucharistic prayer written in the cultural context of the Cree people of western Canada was discussed. However, two troubling questions emerge concerning Indigenous cultures in Canada. Are these cultures fairly and adequately represented in the Canadian social values data such that liturgical texts constructed using those social values will be effective in presenting the identity of Jesus Christ in an objective way—using the *sensus literalis* approach in those cultural communities? Second, since there does not appear to be any attempt in the authorized Canadian Eucharistic liturgies to offer texts that are inculturated for these distinct cultures, why is this the case?

In response to the first question above, the answer is "no." Even though it is becoming an increasingly accepted fact that the dominant, apparently European-based, culture of Canada is actually a hybrid of several non-Indigenous cultures with the Indigenous cultures of this land,[36] the distinctiveness of these Indigenous cultures is submerged in the social values analysis of the dominant culture. This submersion is largely a function of the Canadian government's policy of assimilation of Indigenous peoples into the mainstream of Canadian society, which began in earnest with the Indian Residential School system and the policies that undergirded it in the nineteenth century.[37] The *Indian Act*, which came into effect in 1876 "brought together all of Canada's legislation governing Indian people. The act both defined who Indians were under Canadian law and set out the process by which people would cease to be Indians."[38] It is only in the last few decades that Indigenous cultures and people are being seen as legitimate in Canadian society.

In response to the second question about the lack of inculturated liturgical texts for Indigenous peoples in the Anglican Church of Canada, the legacy of assimilation and the Indian Residential School system is also behind this issue.[39] The nineteenth century missionaries believed that it was important to convert Indigenous peoples to Christianity in an effort to "save their souls." "This belief provided justification for undermining traditional spiritual leaders (who were treated as agents of the devil), banning sacred cultural practices, and attempting to impose a new moral code on Aboriginal people."[40]

For better or for worse, the Indigenous persons who did embrace the Christian faith in the Anglican Church carried with them the view that their traditional cultural practices were antithetical to (European) Christianity and, hence, have been very reluctant to allow the re-introduction of some of the traditional practices of the local cultures.

The situation that Indigenous members of the Anglican Church of Canada find themselves in has some similarity to the Dalit members of the Church of South India. On the one hand, Canadian Indigenous persons are trying to reclaim something of their original local cultures and bring those cultures into a (reflexive) relationship with their Christian community. But with that comes a struggle, both for them and for the non-Indigenous members of their church, to overcome prior ill-conceived meanings that have been attached to some of those cultural practices.

In recent years, a section for liturgical resources for Indigenous ministries has appeared on the website of the Anglican Church of Canada.[41] Encouragingly, Indigenous ministries across Canada are beginning to work on generating more appropriately-inculturated liturgical texts such as the example referred to in chapter 6.

"Faithful and Intelligible"

As Richard Niebuhr illustrated in his model of five types of interaction between Christ and culture—not all cultural values are congruent with the Christian Gospel and the person of Jesus Christ. Therefore, how can a determination be made on which of the above values are reflections of the revelation of Jesus Christ in contemporary Canadian culture? Given the fact that both the values and the language used to express them are contingent on their cultural context, one must employ the same kind of special hermeneutic that Frei used in describing the *sensus literalis* of biblical texts and their interpretation. Ultimately, the values that a given local community determine as being faithful to the revelation or identity of Jesus Christ will be brought into engagement with the values of their local culture and will interact with that culture in one or more of the Niebuhrian types described above—revealing which are congruent (Type 2, Christ of culture), which are in opposition (Type 1, Christ against culture), and which are open to transformation (Types 5, Christ the transformer of culture). An initial criterion would be that if the commonly accepted interpretation of a biblical text supports or illustrates a particular cultural value, that value will be taken as being congruent with the Christian Gospel and the identity of Jesus Christ, and therefore be counted as "faithful." However, further criteria are needed. As discussed in chapter 3, in considering whether one might be able to identify a distinct "Christian culture," it was shown that it is not the cultural elements themselves that distinguish their identity to a particular culture (i.e., Christian culture), but rather how those elements are used that would help to identify the identity of the Christian community. This point will be illustrated below using a few examples from the identified social values in question.

Personal Autonomy

A person's free ability to be in control of their own destiny, to make their own decisions governing their life, would not necessarily be a value that is congruent with the Gospel or the identity of Jesus Christ. *How* that autonomy is used is a critical factor. If the value of personal autonomy in a local culture was practiced as one using their personal power to gain status and power over others, Christ would be in a Niebuhrian Type 1 (Christ against culture) relationship with this particular expression of the cultural value. A faithful portrayal of the identity of Jesus Christ would include Jesus' words as recorded in Mark 10:43b, 44, "whoever wishes to be become great among you must be your servant, and whoever wishes to be first among you must be slave of all." This same attitude of using one's personal autonomy for the good of others is explained by St. Paul in the context of the Christian community in 1 Corinthians 12:7, "To each is given the manifestation of the Spirit for the common good." This additional scriptural narrative outlining *how* one is to use personal autonomy would be an example of the priority in the "Frei—inspired" Christology of the community being open to being challenged by an objective portrayal of the identity of Jesus Christ. Therefore, it will be important that Eucharistic prayer texts not only include narratives that highlight the value of personal autonomy but that also accurately reveal *how* Jesus, or the Christian community in the New Testament, use that attribute in a manner congruent with the *sensus literalis* of the Gospel texts.

Inclusion

If members of a local culture exhibited an attitude of radical hospitality—reaching to include and care for those traditionally considered to be "outside" of that culture, then Christ would be in a Niebuhrian Type 2 (Christ of culture) relationship. There are many examples in the Gospels of Jesus exhibiting this attitude. One example is in Lk. 19:1–10 which is the story of Jesus engaging the Jewish tax collector Zacchaeus, who would have been regarded as a traitor by the Jewish community because of his role in extricating taxes for Rome. At the same time, there are examples in the New Testament letters of the Christian community being instructed to exclude a certain person because of a grievous sin until they have repented and changed their behavior.[42] Obviously, in this context, the interaction of the cultural value of *inclusion* with Christ would be Niebuhrian Type 1 (Christ against culture). Again, these two narratives are capable of expressing an objective portrayal of Christ and the community that Christ calls into being. As above, in the discussion on personal autonomy, Eucharistic prayer texts would need to portray the attribute of inclusion in a way that is congruent with the *sensus literalis* of the Gospel texts. In both of the above illustrations, the Eucharistic prayer texts might affirm an understanding that is congruent with the identity of Jesus Christ, challenge an understanding that is not congruent, or both.

Empowerment of the Christian Life

It is beyond the scope of this work to explore the third criterion (empowerment of the Christian life) that Haight proposes for the evaluation of a contemporary Christology. This can only be determined by studying a particular community over time and attempting to discover if a given Christology (in Eucharistic prayers or in other authoritative teaching) is resulting in a growth in the Christian life of that community and its positive expression of the Gospel of Jesus Christ, and therefore a deeper discernment of the identity of Jesus Christ in their local context. However, liturgical texts that summon or even challenge the community to transformative action in their lives would at least have the potential for the empowerment of the Christian life.

In summary, the desired Eucharistic prayer texts will exemplify the *sensus literalis* of the community—a faithful and objective presentation of the identity of Jesus Christ employing the commonly held authoritative understanding of the biblical narratives. They will communicate this understanding of the identity of Jesus Christ using language and imagery that is meaningful and intelligible within the contemporary culture of the community. These two pieces stand in a direct and self-refining relationship. If the description of the identity of Jesus Christ becomes such that it corresponds only to Niebuhr's Type 2 (Christ of culture), thereby eliminating any sense of the ongoing transformation of that culture by Christ (Type 5), then the insistence on a full and objective presentation of the identity of Christ in the biblical narratives will correct this imbalance. Likewise, if the description of the identity of Jesus Christ becomes such that it is completely foreign and incomprehensible in a particular cultural context, suggesting that Christ is entirely absent from or against that culture (Niebuhr's Type 1), and hence the culture is not able to be transformed into greater Christ-likeness, then the presentation of Christ using language and imagery from the local culture will correct this imbalance and encourage the members of that culture in their expectation that Christ is indeed present in their culture and continuing to transform it (Niebuhr's Type 5) into greater Christ-likeness.

BUILDING A NEW EUCHARISTIC PRAYER FOR THE ANGLICAN CHURCH OF CANADA

The "Kanamai Statement" (1993),[43] proposing a strategy for building an inculturated Eucharistic liturgy, begins not with particular texts, but with a simple structure:

1. Gathering together
2. Telling the Christian story with intercessory prayer
3. The meal with thanksgiving
4. Sending out

The third section ("meal with thanksgiving") pertains most directly to the Eucharistic prayer. In the proposed Antiochene structure for this prayer (as discussed in chapter 6), there are two primary sections of thanksgiving. The first is the initial section of praise and thanksgiving to God for creation and redemption, which might be either a fixed or variable Preface (or a combination of both) prior to the Sanctus. The second is the section of thanksgiving for the life, ministry, death, and resurrection of Jesus Christ as the mediator of God's salvation, which follows the Sanctus and leads into the institution narrative. These two sections of the Antiochene prayer structure, and particularly the latter section describing Jesus Christ, are the primary places to employ narrative pieces from the tradition that resonate with cultural values of the local community. In addition, in the supplicatory section following the anamnesis and leading into, or forming a part of, the epiclesis, there is the opportunity to employ petitions that look forward to the fullness of God's reign and challenge the worshipers to offer themselves to the transforming power of Christ—particularly referring to the hopes expressed in the community's cultural values.

The prayer will be structured in a dialogical response pattern between the presider and the other participants. This structure exemplifies the cultural value of inclusion and seems congruent with the desire for democratic processes and a less-hierarchical approach.

Thanksgiving for Creation and Redemption

Given the expressed cultural value of "concern for the environment," a rich description of creation based on the opening chapters of Genesis[44] would be appropriate such as:

Creator of the universe, you formed this world and everything in it as your
    Garden;

calling it good, and giving this created order to the humanity you formed in your image.
You charged us with caring for this fertile gift.

"Inclusion" is another cultural value, along with tolerance, and both of these reflect the scriptural picture of God as one who cares, and calls Israel to care for all—including the alien in its midst.[45] This can be expressed in this way:

> You made a covenant with Israel; and through them called the peoples of all nations[46] to live in peace, justice and righteousness with all of humanity.

Both of the above petitions might be concluded with the presider's invitation and participants' response [*italics*] such as:

> We give you thanks:
> *For we are gifted with your likeness, O God.*

This could be followed by a statement about the need for redemption and a thanksgiving for God's faithfulness.

> But we have abused the responsibility and freedom you gave us, and used the gifts you provided to injure your creation, each other, and ourselves. Still you called us back to yourself with the gift of the Law and the testimony of the prophets.

This can be followed by another section emphasizing God's faithfulness even in spite of our faithlessness.

> Though we break faith with you, the one true God, and make other things the gods of our lives[47] you refuse to abandon us and continue to seek us out as a lover does their beloved.[48]

Both of the above petitions could also be concluded with an invitation/response such as:

> We give you thanks:
> *For your unfailing, redeeming love for us, O God.*

The entire Preface would read:

> Creator of the universe, you formed this world and everything in it as your Garden;
> calling it good, and giving this created order to the humanity you formed in your image.
> You charged us with caring for this fertile gift. We give you thanks:
> *For we are gifted with your likeness, O God.*
> You made a covenant with Israel; and through them called the peoples of all nations to live in peace, justice and righteousness with all of humanity. We give you thanks:
> *For we are gifted with your likeness, O God.*
> But we have abused the responsibility and freedom you gave us, and used the gifts you provided to injure your creation, each other, and ourselves. Still you called us back to yourself with the gift of the Law and the testimony of the Prophets. We give you thanks:
> *For your unfailing, redeeming love for us, O God.*
> Though we break faith with the one true God and make other things the gods of our lives, you refuse to abandon us and continue to seek us out as a lover does their beloved. We give you thanks:
> *For your unfailing, redeeming love for us, O God.*

This Preface would be followed by a traditional introduction to, and recitation of, the Sanctus. This Preface is designed to portray God as one who has been and continues to be intimately involved in creation and with humanity in particular. While it does not specifically identify figural relationships in that history, it clearly presents a providential view of history by linking together God's loving actions in ancient history with God's actions and expectations of people in the contemporary world. In an objective way, the statements concerning contemporary humanity's misuse of creation and substitution of other things for God offer a critique to the local culture. In this Preface, there is affirmation of the God-given nature of creation and human life, which is analogous to Niebuhr's Type 2 (Christ of culture), but there is also a challenge to that culture for the ways in which it does not display God's purposes—Niebuhr's Type 1 (Christ against culture). While the Preface uses generalized terms (abuse of responsibility, injury of creation, etc.), it is not difficult to make connections to the contemporary culture for specific evidence of these attitudes and actions.

Thanksgiving for the Life, Ministry, Death, and Resurrection of Jesus Christ

In this section, images and descriptions of the ministry of Jesus are chosen to exemplify concern for the created order, inclusiveness and tolerance, a concern for those on the margins of society, a more egalitarian community, and a concern for personal autonomy.[49] This portion of the prayer is intentionally addressed to the risen Christ in order to bring the worshipers into a direct "dialogue" with Christ. The traditional Sanctus and Benedictus conclude with the words, "Blessed is the One who comes in the name of the Lord." The post-Sanctus section continues:

> Living Christ, you indeed are blessed and worthy of all thanks and praise. As the ultimate gift of your love for the whole creation, you came into our midst as one of us.
>
> As the whole of creation groaned for our restoration as your stewards of this world,[50] you were born to your mother named Mary.[51]
>
> Having lived as a child, you welcomed children in your ministry and blessed them.[52] You reached out to those who were forgotten or ignored, moving beyond acceptable boundaries to heal a foreign woman,[53] to call a society outcast to become one of your colleagues,[54] and to reach out to and receive the support and fellowship of women.[55]
>
> You initiated the politics of God's Kingdom where every person who receives God's truth is free;[56] where all who respond to the call to love are named your friends,[57] and where the great ones are those who serve.[58]
>
> To begin the final act of your transforming love for us, you gathered together your disciples as their Lord, and washed their feet, commanding all of your followers to do the same.[59] As you prepared to offer the final gift of your life to death on a cross, for the sake of the whole world, you celebrated a meal with you friends. You took bread.

Each of these petitions could also be concluded with an invitation/response such as:

We give you thanks:
For your love and truth, O Christ.
The entire post-Sanctus thanksgiving would read:
Living Christ, you indeed are blessed and worthy of all thanks and praise.
  As the ultimate gift of your love for the whole creation, you came into our midst as one of us. As the whole of creation groaned for our restoration as your stewards of this world, you were born to your mother named Mary.
  We give you thanks:
For your love and truth, O Christ.

Having lived as a child, you welcomed children in your ministry and blessed them. You reached out to those who were forgotten or ignored, moving beyond acceptable boundaries to heal a foreign woman, to call a society outcast to become one of your colleagues, and to reach out to and receive the support and fellowship of women. We give you thanks:
For your love and truth, O Christ.
You initiated the politics of God's Kingdom where every person who receives God's truth is free; where all who respond to the call to love are named your friends, and where the great ones are those who serve. We give you thanks:
For your love and truth, O Christ.
To begin the final act of your transforming love for us, you gathered together your disciples as their Lord, and washed their feet, commanding all of your followers to do the same. As you prepared to offer the final gift of your life to death on a cross, for the sake of the whole world, you celebrated a meal with you friends. You took bread.

This section leads into the story of the institution of the Lord's Supper based on one of the Synoptic Gospels and/or the Pauline accounts. As mentioned above, the post-Sanctus thanksgiving is intentionally addressed directly to Christ. This form of address will heighten the sense of the identity and presence of Jesus Christ in the context of the worship. As expected in the "Frei-inspired" Christology, the uniqueness of Christ is affirmed in the first section by connecting Christ with the act of creation and affirming the incarnation as an act of that love. The next two sections provide strong narrative summaries of the ways in which Jesus was "counter-cultural" in his own local culture. These are clear expressions of Niebuhr's Type 1 (Christ against culture) and provide an objective standard by which contemporary worshipers can assess Christ's expectations of their culture. The references to women, children, outcasts, boundaries (meant to exclude), and the egalitarian nature of life with God are all easily accessible (and therefore, intelligible) to contemporary twenty-first-century cultures.

Anamnesis and Epiclesis

This would be followed by a statement of anamnesis leading into the epiclesis such as:

> God of everlasting love, with this bread and this cup we recall the transforming life of Jesus, the Christ; his ministry in our midst, his obedient love in revealing you to the world, and his final offering and vindication of humanity through his

death, resurrection and ascension. Pour out your Holy Spirit on these gifts and
upon us, uniting us to Christ as your children forever.[60]

This is now followed with supplications for the Christian community to exemplify the life of Christ and God's kingdom. To fill out an interesting Trinitarian approach, the supplicatory portion is addressed to the Holy Spirit. In order to emphasize the nature of these petitions as "prayers of the people," the petition is put into the voice of the participants, and its ratification is given to the presider.

Life-giving God, empower us to recognize the beauty and integrity of creation and to order our lives to be good stewards of its gifts.
Holy Spirit, open our eyes to see your truth.
Life-giving God, empower us to use our freedom to set people, institutions, and governments free to be sources of life and support for all people.
Holy Spirit, open our minds to receive your wisdom.
Life-giving God, empower us to witness to greatness by serving those around us, especially the poor and marginalized.
Holy Spirit, open our hearts to offer your love.
Life-giving God, empower us to entrust our lives to you, and to each other; making us a community of Jesus' disciples living in faith and hope.
Holy Spirit, open our lives to embrace your will.

The closing doxology could make reference to a gathering together of all people, and a reconciliation of all creation in the coming reign of God, which again is typical of many contemporary Eucharistic prayers.

The above prayer sections address most of the cultural values identified as being characteristic of contemporary Canadian society and extend them as requests for the Spirit's transformation of the worshipers and their cultural context. In an actual Eucharistic Prayer prepared for use in a community, portions of these sections might be omitted or transferred to another composition in order to keep the prayer at a reasonable length. Using these cultural values should make the prayer "intelligible" in the contemporary culture.

How do these texts exemplify the "Frei-inspired" Christology? With the use of contemporary language to describe the attributes of Christ and the continuing relevance of his attitudes and actions in our contemporary world, the Christology expressed is clearly in a reflexive relationship with the local (Canadian) culture as represented by the social values of Canada and the Anglican Church of Canada. The notion that receiving the identity of Jesus Christ results in giving identity to the worshiper in Christ is affirmed at the beginning of the epiclesis: "Pour out your Holy Spirit on these gifts and upon us, uniting us to Christ as your children forever." While specific examples of persons and their actions that are in a figural relationship are not presented, the ongoing providential nature of history is strongly affirmed. The God who created and who acted in ancient Israel is the God who came into the world in the person of Jesus and who continues to engage our lives in our contemporary world. The supplication section toward the end of the prayer encourages the worshipers to ask for and expect similar acts of God in and through them in their contemporary world. The final petition, with its reference to "living in faith and hope," is an example of prolepsis—a looking forward to the culmination of God's providential involvement in history. The strong narrative portions expressing God's salvation history and the ministry and teaching of Jesus Christ as found in the Gospels, expressed in the language and imagery of contemporary (Canadian) culture, provide the *sensus literalis* for this Christology in its local culture.

A Niebuhrian analysis of the pre- and post-Sanctus sections of the prayer is discussed above. It is the third section (epiclesis and supplication) which represents Christ as the transformer of culture (Niebuhr's Type 5). The strength of this section lies in the fact that it preserves Niebuhr's understanding that it is the ongoing activity of Christ acting in and through cultures that brings about the transformation of the world, as opposed to the interpretation of some of his critics who substitute the "Church" or "Christianity" for Christ in the engagement with culture. While the petitions in this section do carry with them an expectation that the transformation will take place, at least in part, through the community's Christ-like attitudes and actions, it is very clear that the ability to carry out this transformation will come entirely from the continuing presence of Christ as Holy Spirit.

As suggested above, when discussing Haight's third criterion in evaluating the Christology in Eucharistic prayers—empowerment of the Christian life—it is impossible to know the effectiveness of a particular text until it is prayed successively over time by a given local community. However, the suggested texts above do bring together, in an established Eucharistic prayer format, "faithful" scriptural images and "intelligible" cultural values in a Eucharistic prayer for the Anglican Church of Canada. The final supplication section certainly asks for, encourages, and expects the Christian community to be empowered in their life in the world.

The general shape of the prayer, as well as the flow of the contemporary language, has been kept in a form that is common to most contemporary Eucharistic prayers so as to not alienate the present worshiping community while attempting to make the prayer accessible to others beyond the church of the same cultural group.

This Eucharistic Prayer is designed to be effective with both the present membership of the Anglican Church of Canada, as well as with others who share the contemporary cultural values of the wider Canadian society.

NOTES

1. Reynolds, 58.
2. Gibaut, 360.
3. The plural, "cultures," is suggested because, as will be shown, Canada is best described as a mosaic of regional, local cultures.
4. See Graeme Chesters and Sally Jennings, *Culture Wise Canada: The Essential Guide to Culture, Customs and Business Etiquette* (London: Survival Books Limited, 2007), 29. In this section entitled "National & Regional Identity," the authors write, "Canada is an enormous, varied country, peopled by individuals from most corners of the world, as a result of which Canadians have struggled to develop a national identity and decide what it is exactly that makes them Canadian."
5. Michael Adams, *Sex in the Snow: Canadian Social Values at the End of the Millenium* (Toronto: Penguin Books, 1997), 5.
6. Hugh MacLennan, *Two Solitudes*, 1st ed. (Toronto: Collins, 1945). To give one an idea of its continuing influence, it has been printed a total of six times (the latest being in 2008) and was still a primary piece of Canadian literature in Canadian schools in the 1960s and beyond.
7. S. Jamie Scott, "Religion, Literature and Canadian Cultural Identities," *Literature and Theology* 16, no. 2 (2002): 117.
8. Ibid., 119.
9. T. Marshall, *Harsh and Lovely Land: The Major Canadian Poets and the Making of a Canadian Tradition* (Vancouver: University of British Columbia Press, 1979), xii.
10. Paul Bramadat, "Beyond Christian Canada: Religion and Ethnicity in a Multicultural Society," in *Religion and Ethnicity in Canada*, ed. Paul Bramadat and David Seljak (Toronto: Pearson Longman, 2005), 4.
11. Neil Nevitte, *The Decline of Deference: Canadian Value Change in Cross-National Perspective* (Peterborough: Broadview Press, 1996), 19.
12. Harry H. Hiller, review of *The Decline of Deference: Canadian Value Change in Cross-National Perspective* (Peterborough: Broadview Press, 1996), by Neil Nevitte, in *Canadian Public Policy* 23, no. 1 (1997): 103.
13. Adams, 34.
14. Nevitte.
15. Adams, 5.
16. Ibid., 19.
17. Ibid., 30.
18. Ibid., 34.
19. Ibid., 35.
20. Peter C. Newman, *The Canadian Revolution, 1985–1995: From Deference to Defiance* (Toronto: Viking, 1995).
21. Adams, 173.
22. "Folklorama," http://www.folklorama.ca/about (July 9, 2014).
23. Ian Coutts, "Books in Canada," in *Sex in the Snow: Canadian Social Values at the End of the Millenium*, ed. Michael Adams (Toronto: Penguin Books, 1997).

24. Jim Ward, "Community Action," ibid.
25. Nevitte, 11.
26. Ibid., 20.
27. Ibid., 59–60.
28. Ibid., 207.
29. Ibid., 209.
30. Ibid., 85.
31. Ibid., 238.
32. R. M. Merelman, "The American Review of Canadian Studies," in *The Decline of Deference: Canadian Value Change in Cross-National Perspective*, ed. Neil Nevitte (Peterborough: Broadview Press, 1999), 531.
33. Eric M. Uslaner, review of *The Decline of Deference: Canadian Value Change in Cross-National Perspective* (Peterborough: Broadview Press, 1996), by Neil Nevitte, in *Canadian Journal of Political Science* 30, no. 2 (1997): 372.
34. Hiller, 103.
35. Nanos Research, "Exploring Canadian Values—Values Survey Summary" (2016), 5.
36. See John Ralston Saul, *A Fair Country: Telling Truths About Canada* (Toronto: Viking Canada, 2008). The underlying thesis of this book is that contemporary Canadian culture is a hybrid of indigenous and non-indigenous cultures.
37. Truth and Reconciliation Commission of Canada, *They Came for the Children: Canada, Aboriginal Peoples, and Residential Schools* (Winnipeg: Truth and Reconciliation Commission of Canada, 2012).
38. Ibid., 11.
39. Ibid., 13–17.
40. Ibid., 13. See also John Webster Grant, *Moon of Wintertime: Missionaries and Indians of Canada in Encounter since 1534* (Toronto: University of Toronto Press, 1984). Jean Usher, *William Duncan of Metlakatla: A Victorian Missionary in British Columbia* (Ottawa: National Museums of Canada, 1974). See particularly the Introduction.
41. Anglican Church of Canada General Synod, "Resources for the Day of Prayer for Indigenous Justice (2013)," Anglican Church of Canada, http://www.anglican.ca/im/jan11/.
42. See 1 Corinthians 5:1–5 where Paul instructs that a member of the community who is in an inappropriate intimate relationship is to be expelled from the Christian community.
43. The full text of the proposed Eucharistic Prayer, including the Sursum Corda, Sanctus, and closing doxology can be found in Appendix 4.
44. Genesis 2:8–26 describes God's creation as being a garden over which humanity is given oversight—shown by the authority to "name" each of the animals in this account of creation, and by a direct commission to subdue and have dominion over creation (Gen. 1:28) in the first account of creation (Gen. 1:1–2:4).
45. Exodus 23:1–9 deals with the principle of justice for all—even one's enemy. Verse 9 reads: "You shall not oppress a resident alien; you know the heart of an alien, for you were aliens in the land of Egypt."

46. God speaks to Abram as recorded in Genesis 12:3, "I will bless those who bless you, and the one who curses you I will curse; and in you all the families of the earth shall be blessed." See also God speaking through the prophet to Israel in Isaiah 49.6, "It is too light a thing that you should be my servant to raise up the tribes of Jacob and to restore the survivors of Israel; I will give you as a light to the nations, that my salvation may reach to the end of the earth."

47. Paul describes this rebellion of humanity against God in this way: "they exchanged the truth about God for a lie and worshiped and served the creature rather than the Creator, who is blessed forever." Romans 1:25.

48. In the opening chapters of Hosea, Israel is cast as an unfaithful wife and God as her husband who refuses to give up on her. "And I will take you for my wife forever; I will take you for my wife in righteousness and in justice, in steadfast love, and in mercy." Hosea 3:19.

49. While being an egalitarian community does not necessarily involve democratic processes, it does involve relationships in which each individual matters to the whole, and whose autonomy is accepted and valued. This would be in keeping with the cultural values of personal autonomy and democratic processes.

50. Paul suggests that the disorder of creation is awaiting the manifestation of the children of God to be transformed and restored.

> For the creation waits with eager longing for the revealing of the children of God; . . . that the creation itself will be set free from its bondage to decay and will obtain the freedom of the glory of the children of God. We know that the whole of creation has been groaning in labour pains until now; (Rom. 8:20–22)

51. See Luke 8:1–3. See also Jesus' significant engagement with the woman of Samaria at the well. John 4:1–42.

52. "Jesus said, 'let the little children come to me, and do not stop them; for it is to such as these that the kingdom of heaven belongs'." Matthew 19:14. See also Mark 10.13–16 and Luke 18.15–17.

53. See Matthew 15.21–28 or Mark 7.24–30.

54. The "call of Matthew," Matthew 9.9–13 or the "call of Levi," Mark 2.13–17.

55. See Luke 8.1–3. See also Jesus' significant engagement with the woman of Samaria at the well. John 4.1–42.

56. "If you continue in my word, you are truly my disciples; and you will know the truth, and the truth will make you free." John 8.31b-32.

57. Jesus says, "You are my friends if you do what I command you," John 15.14, and "I give you a new commandment, that you love one another." John 13.34.

58. See Matthew 20.25–27 or Mark 10.42–44.

59. See John 13.14.

60. This initial section of the epiclesis is an original composition, but it is based on the traditional wording of the epiclesis of many contemporary Eucharistic Prayers, incorporating a reference to the Eucharistic gifts themselves as well as a uniting of the worshiping community with Christ. The notion of Christ's "sacrifice" is not alluded to directly since a sacrificial system is foreign to contemporary Western cultures.

Chapter 9

The Way Forward

This work began with a story about a conversation between a follower of the Christian faith and an inquisitive neighbor who asked about who Jesus is. This encounter exposed the huge deficit contemporary Christian disciples may have when it comes to employing an accessible vocabulary to speak about the person and work of Jesus Christ (Christology). It became obvious in the narrative encounter that the "insider" language which the Christian person used to respond to the question held little meaning for the inquirer. It revealed the need (and an urgent need for those who are concerned for the ongoing vitality of the Christian church) to develop a Christology that uses language familiar to a contemporary (postmodern) culture. As a response to how this Christology might be disseminated among congregational members, it was proposed that this narrative Christology be used in the appropriate sections of a Eucharistic Prayer. This would provide the opportunity for this vocabulary to be heard on a regular basis in Eucharistic worship.

CULTURE, REFLEXIVITY, AND INCULTURATION

The exploration of the development of the notion and understanding of culture over the last several centuries revealed that one can only *describe* another culture relative to one's own culture—there is no objective stance from which one can evaluate a culture. Because all aspects of life (meaningful symbols, signs, language, and the way in which these pieces combine) make up a local culture, a semiotic approach to describing a local culture was deemed most appropriate. And given that language is part of the sign system of a local culture, then Christian theology in that local culture will also be expressed as a local contextual theology. This is essential because of the Gospel's claim of universality. God's ongoing incarnation of Jesus must become real in each and every culture through the proclamation of the Gospel within and through the local context. Using the work of Robert Schreiter, two questions were posed to aid in expressing a local (contextual) theology, and five criteria were brought forward to help ensure that an emerging local theology was reflective of the gospel and faithful to the tradition. The importance of *reflexivity* was explored—particularly as it applied to the interaction of signs and symbols within a culture and between cultures, which led into a more in-depth discussion about *inculturation*. The important conclusion that emerged for the proclamation of the Gospel is the need for an ongoing dynamic relationship between the Gospel's proclamation in one culture and its subsequent emergence in another culture. This dynamic and reflexive interaction makes very real the sense that there is an ongoing incarnation of the person and work of Jesus Christ in each succeeding generation and each particular culture.

INTERACTION OF THEOLOGY (CHRISTOLOGY) AND LOCAL CULTURE

Richard Niebuhr's 5 typologies were discussed and used to describe the different approaches to Christ and culture—making clear that these types were mental constructs to help us understand more fully the issues that are part of the discussion. It became apparent that Niebuhr's fifth type (Christ, the Transformer of Culture) could serve as the overall principle at work in the interaction of Christ and culture.

The discussion then turned to the role of liturgical texts in both expressing a local community's understanding of the person and work of Jesus Christ, as well as being a source of experiencing the transforming power of Christ through their use in worship. The Anglican Church of Canada was chosen as a representative local church culture and that church's Eucharistic Prayers as being representative of its local theology (Christology). Eucharistic Prayer texts from three different periods in the twentieth century were examined for signs of a dynamic relationship between the local culture and the Christology expressed. Only the most recent of these Eucharistic Prayers (1985) began to show evidence of material that directly expressed the values of the local culture at the time.

CONTEXTUAL CHRISTOLOGY AND POSTMODERN CULTURE

The approach of the historical theologian, Hans Frei, in the later part of the twentieth century, was chosen to work on developing the new Christology.

Frei's approach represented a major shift from many other Christologies of the time because it was not apologetically driven and did not begin from a soteriological starting point. Instead, Frei believed that the Gospel texts should be treated as realistic narratives aimed at helping the reader come to know the identity of Jesus Christ. The key thrust of Frei's approach was to bring the focus of biblical interpretation on the person and work of Jesus Christ back to the narrative texts of the Gospels themselves. Frei insisted that the purpose and meaning of these texts were first and foremost *descriptive*—letting the text speak for itself and keeping it as independent as possible from apologetic concerns or truth claims. In addition to this hermeneutical approach, Frei employed three other key features—*figural interpretation* (linking together biblical and even extra-biblical events in our lives), giving primacy to the *sensus literalis* interpretation of those texts, and accepting a *providential view of history* in order to root the person and work of Jesus Christ in the history of the world. Of particular relevance to using this narrative material in worship is Frei's conviction that Christ's identity and presence are given to us together. One begins by focusing on the Gospels and the details of their portrayal of Jesus of Nazareth and asking the question: "What kind of Christology would fit with those texts?" To summarize Frei's approach: the primary concern of this Christology is to reveal the identity of Jesus Christ in the historical world of the text and to then invite the reader to locate the world with which they have become familiar within the historical world of the biblical text. In other words, it is as a person encounters a community that is continually focusing on the identity and presence of Jesus Christ through the proclaimed word (scripture texts) and provision of the sacraments, and allows the experience to shape his or her entire life in its cultural context, that this person is invited to acknowledge the identity of Jesus Christ as portrayed in the biblical narratives and experienced in the life of that community. As one acknowledges this identity of Jesus Christ, one "sees" in this person both the divine savior and their own humanity, enabling them to lay hold of, or receive, their identity in Christ. This approach is particularly effective in a twenty-first-century postmodern context because it recognizes the constantly evolving nature of language and texts and views them as part of what makes up a particular local community or culture. Therefore, the Eucharistic Prayer, especially when it is shaped by the cultural community that uses it, becomes a deep and authentic expression of thanksgiving to God, and an anamnesis and prolepsis of the gift of Jesus Christ whose identity continues to inform and transform that community and, through its witness, the world at large.

LOCAL CULTURE, NARRATIVE, AND EUCHARISTIC TEXTS

Consideration of the local worshiping community, the importance of narratives—of the biblical texts, the local community, and our own person—was explored. When one participates in a community with a collective narrative, there is the opportunity to engage the community's narrative with one's personal narrative. Therefore, in liturgical worship, participation invites one to embed their personal narrative in the larger narrative of the community. When the Christian community focuses on the identity and presence of Jesus Christ through word and sacrament, the encounter of personal narrative and the narrative of salvation happens in the present.

EXAMPLES OF LITURGICAL INCULTURATION IN ANGLICAN EUCHARISTIC TEXTS

Examples from around the Anglican Communion were discussed, beginning with, in particular, the Church of South India's work in the middle of the twentieth century, in addition to Kenya, the Church of England, the Anglican Church of Canada, and the Anglican Church in New Zealand. With the exception of the New Zealand work in the closing decade of the last century, most of the evidence of inculturation focused on making the liturgical texts more congruent with the breadth of local church cultures, as opposed to the local culture of the wider community.

The Christology of the contemporary Eucharistic Prayers of the Anglican Church of Canada was chosen to be examined for evidence of reflexivity with contemporary Canadian culture. The three criteria (from Roger Haight's work) of faithfulness to the tradition, intelligibility in today's world, and empowerment of the Christian life were used to explore the prayers. In addition, the three Christological images proposed by William Crockett (a primary architect of the prayers in the Canadian Book of Alternative Services)—Jesus' death as an act of vicarious suffering, Jesus' death as a sin offering, and Jesus's death and resurrection as an act of divine deliverance—were used to help describe the Christology present in the Prayers. It was noted that each of the above images is an example of a figural relationship in scripture. Because of the Prayers' weak interaction with the wider culture, there are not many references to challenge the Christian community to transformative change, but there is a clear and objective presentation of Jesus Christ and at least an invitation to his disciples to model themselves after him—thereby opening themselves to the transformation that Niebuhr had in mind in his Type 5—Christ, the transformer of culture.

CONSTRUCTING A CONTEMPORARY EUCHARISTIC PRAYER FOR A POSTMODERN CULTURE

In response to the "faithfulness to tradition criteria," narrative descriptions were drawn from scripture or from traditional theological statements based on scripture narratives. In order to create a Eucharistic Prayer that will be "intelligible in today's world," a Christology that is faithful to tradition was brought into a reflexive relationship with a local (Canadian) culture. The values of that culture were determined by exploring recent Canadian social values. Five values that emerged were combined with three additional values expressed as being characteristic of the contemporary Anglican Church of Canada. The commonly held authoritative understanding (*sensus literalis*) of biblical narratives was brought together in the language and imagery that is meaningful and intelligible in this contemporary culture to express the identity of Jesus Christ. These two pieces stand in a direct and self-refining relationship.

A traditional Antiochene anaphoral structure was chosen for this prayer because of the two potential narrative sections in this structure which encourage identity descriptions. These two sections of the Antiochene prayer structure, particularly the latter section describing Jesus Christ, are the primary places to employ narrative pieces from the tradition that resonate with the cultural values of the local community. In addition, in the supplicatory section following the anamnesis and leading into, or forming a part of, the epiclesis, there is the opportunity to employ petitions that look forward to the fullness of God's reign and challenge the worshipers to offer themselves to the transforming power of Christ—particularly referring to the hopes expressed in the community's cultural values.

The narrative texts above do bring together, in an established Eucharistic prayer format, "faithful" scriptural images and "intelligible" cultural values in a Eucharistic prayer for the Anglican Church of Canada. And the final supplication section certainly asks for, encourages, and expects the Christian community to be empowered in their life in the world.

In this work, the example of the Anglican Church of Canada and contemporary Canadian culture has been employed to generate a new Eucharistic Prayer. Is this work limited to the Canadian context? Not at all! The Canadian examples have been used simply because of the context in which the author lives and works. The same process can be used anywhere in the world where one is able to describe the local culture and construct, with some confidence, a set of values that fairly represent that local culture.

Will implementing this type of narrative Christology and exposing current church members to its descriptive vocabulary bring about a revitalization of our churches? There is no way to predetermine this. What can be said, with some degree of certainty, is that it will equip our church members with more effective ways to engage in "over the fence" conversations with their neighbors and provide more fruitful opportunities for the transforming power of the risen Christ to be experienced in our midst.

Appendix

A New Eucharistic Prayer

Presider	*Our God be with you.*
People	*And also with you.*
Presider	*Lift up your hearts.*
People	*We lift them to God.*
Presider	*Let us give thanks to the Lord our God.*
People	*It is right to give our thanks and praise.*

Creator of the universe, you formed this world and everything in it as your Garden; calling it good, and giving this created order to the humanity you formed in your image. You charged us with caring for this fertile gift. We give you thanks:

For we are gifted with your likeness, O God.

You made a covenant with Israel; and through them called the peoples of all nations to live in peace, justice and righteousness with all of humanity. We give you thanks:

For we are gifted with your likeness, O God.

But we have abused the responsibility and freedom you gave us, and used the gifts you provided to injure your creation, each other, and ourselves. Still you called us back to yourself with the gift of the Law and the testimony of the Prophets. We give you thanks:

For your unfailing, redeeming love for us, O God.

Though we break faith with you, the one true God, and make other things the gods of our lives, you refuse to abandon us and continue to seek us out as a lover does their beloved. We give you thanks:

For your unfailing, redeeming love for us, O God.

Therefore, with all of the beauty and wonder of your creation we lift our voices in praise to you:

Holy, holy, holy Lord, God of power and might, heaven and earth
  are full of your glory.
Hosanna in the highest.
Blessed is he who comes in the name of the Lord.
Hosanna in the highest.

Living Christ, you indeed are blessed and worthy of all thanks and praise. As the ultimate gift of your love for the whole creation, you came into our midst as one of us. As the whole of creation groaned for our restoration as your stewards of this world, you were born to your mother named Mary. We give you thanks:

For your love and truth, O Christ.

Having lived as a child, you welcomed children in your ministry and blessed them. You reached out to those who were forgotten or ignored, moving beyond acceptable boundaries to heal a foreign woman, to call a society outcast to become one of your colleagues, and to reach out to and receive the support and fellowship of women. We give you thanks:

For your love and truth, O Christ.

You initiated the politics of God's kKingdom where every person who receives God's truth is free; where all who respond to the call to love are named your friends, and where the great ones are those who serve. We give you thanks:

For your love and truth, O Christ.

To begin the final act of your transforming love for us, you gathered together your disciples as their Lord, and washed their feet, commanding all of your followers to do the same.

As you prepared to offer the final gift of your life to death on a cross, for the sake of the whole world, you celebrated a meal with your friends. You took bread, gave thanks, broke it, and gave it to your disciples saying, "Take, eat: this is my body which is given for you. Do this for the remembrance of me."

After supper you took the cup of wine; and after giving thanks, gave it to your disciples saying, "Drink this, all of you: this is my blood of the new covenant, which is shed for you and for many for the forgiveness of sin. Whenever you drink it, do this for the remembrance of me."

God of everlasting love, with this bread and this cup we recall the transforming life of Jesus, the Christ; his ministry in our midst, his obedient love in revealing you to the world, and his final offering and vindication of humanity through his death, resurrection and ascension. Pour out your Holy Spirit on these gifts and upon us, uniting us to Christ as your children forever.

Life-giving God, empower us to recognize the beauty and integrity of creation and to order our lives to be good stewards of its gifts.
Holy Spirit, open our eyes to see your truth.
Life-giving God, empower us to use our freedom to set people, institutions, and governments free to be sources of life and support for all people.
Holy Spirit, open our minds to receive your wisdom.
Life-giving God, empower us to witness to greatness by serving those around us, especially the poor and marginalized.
Holy Spirit, open our hearts to offer your love.
Life-giving God, empower us to entrust our lives to you, and to each other; making us a community of Jesus' disciples living in faith and hope.
Holy Spirit, open our lives to embrace your will.
O God, who fills all in all, knit us together as one in Jesus Christ,
to whom, with you and the Holy Spirit, be all honour and glory, now and forever.
Amen! Amen!

Eucharistic Prayer—The narrative sections are designed to describe the person and ministry of Jesus Christ as drawn from biblical references that resonate with the social values of Canadians in the twenty-first century. In the final section of Supplications, the *People* lead the prayer and the Presider confirms the petition.

Bibliography

Adams, Michael. *Sex in the Snow: Canadian Social Values at the End of the Millenium*. Toronto: Penguin Books, 1997.
The Alternative Services Book 1980. Colchester: Clowes, 1980.
"Anglican Church in Aoteroa, New Zealand and Polynesia." http://www.anglican.org.nz/.
Anglican Church of Canada. *The Book of Alternative Services of the Anglican Church of Canada*. Toronto: Anglican Book Centre, 1985.
———. *The Book of Common Prayer*. Cambridge: University Press, 1959.
———. "Number of Canadian Anglicans, Parishes and Congregations." http://www.anglican.ca/help/faq/number-of-anglicans/.
Anglican Church of Canada General Synod. "Resources for the Day of Prayer for Indigenous Justice (2013)." Anglican Church of Canada. http://www.anglican.ca/im/jan11/.
Ashcroft, Bill, Gareth Griffiths, and Helen Tiffin. *Post-Colonial Studies: The Key Concepts*. New York: Routledge, 2000.
Auerbach, Eric. *Mimesis: The Representation of Reality in Western Literature*. Translated by Willard R. Trask. Princeton, NJ: Princeton University Press, 1953.
———. *Scenes from the Drama of European Literature*. New York: Meridian Books, Inc., 1959.
Augustine, A., Bishop of Hippo. *City of God*. Translated by John Healey. Vol. 2, London: J. M. Dent, 1945.
Baby, Varghese. "Some Aspects of West Syrian Liturgical Theology." *Studia Liturgica* 31, no. 2 (2001): 171–78.
Benedict, Ruth. *Patterns of Culture*. Cambridge, MA: The Riverside Press, 1934.
Bergmann, Sigurd. *God in Context: A Survey of Contextual Theology*. Aldershot: Ashgate, 2003.
Berton, Pierre. *The Comfortable Pew*. Toronto: McLelland and Stewart Ltd., 1965.
Bevans, Stephen B. *Models of Contextual Theology*. Rev. ed. Maryknoll, NY: Orbis, 2002.

Beyer, Peter. "Modern Forms of the Religious Life: Denomination, Church, and Invisible Religion in Canada, the United States and Europe." In *Rethinking Church, State, and Modernity*, edited by David Lyon and Marguerite Van Die. Toronto: University of Toronto Press, 2000.

———. "Religious Vitality in Canada: The Complementarity of Religious Market and Secularization Perspectives." In *Religion and Canadian Society*, edited by Lori Beaman, 71–91. Toronto: Canadian Scholars Press, Inc., 2006.

Bibby, Reginald W. *Beyond the Gods and Back: Religion's Demise and Rise and Why It Matters*. Lethbridge, Alberta: Project Canada Books, 2011.

———. *Fragmented Gods: The Poverty and Potential of Religion in Canada*. Toronto: Irwin Publishing, 1987.

Bradshaw, Paul F., Maxwell E. Johnson, and L. Edward Phillips. *The Apostolic Tradition a Commentary*. Minneapolis, MN: Augsberg Fortress, 2002.

Bramadat, Paul. "Beyond Christian Canada: Religion and Ethnicity in a Multicultural Society." In *Religion and Ethnicity in Canada*, edited by Paul Bramadat and David Seljak, 1–29. Toronto: Pearnson Longman, 2005.

Buchanan, Colin, ed. *Anglican Eucharistic Liturgies 1985–2010*. London: Canterbury Press Norwich, 2011.

Buchanan, Colin, and Trevor Lloyd. *Six Eucharistic Prayers as Proposed in 1996*. Cambridge: Grove Books Limited, 1996.

"Cartigny Statement on Worship and Culture: Biblical and Historical Foundations." In *Worship and Culture in Dialogue: Reports of International Consultations, Cartigny Switzerland, 1993, Hong Kong, 1994,* edited by S. Anita Stauffer, 129–35. Geneva: Department for Theology and Studies, LWF, 1994.

Chatterji, Saral K. "Why Dalit Theology?" In *Towards a Dalit Theology*, edited by M.E. Prabhakar, 9–29. Delhi: ISPCK, 1988.

Chesters, Graeme, and Sally Jennings. *Culture Wise Canada: The Essential Guide to Culture, Customs and Business Etiquette*. London: Survival Books Limited, 2007.

Childs, Brevard S. *Biblical Theology of the Old and New Testaments*. Minneapolis, MN: Fortress Press, 1992.

———. "The Sensus Literalis of Scripture: An Ancient and Modern Problem." *Beiträge zur alttestamentlichen Theologie: Festschrift fur Walter Zimmerli* 70 (1977): 80–93.

Chupungco, Anscar J. "Two Methods of Liturgical Inculturation." In *Christian Worship: Unity in Cultural Diversity*, edited by S. Anita Stauffer, 77–94. Geneva: Lutheran World Federation, 1996.

———. *Worship: Progress and Tradition*. Beltsville, MD: The Pastoral Press, 1995.

Clarke, Brian. "Going, Going, Gone? Canadian Churches and the Rise of Non-Religion." In *Nonreligious Imaginaries of World Repairing*, edited by L.G. Beaman and T. Stacey, 43–57. Cha: Springer, 2021.

Clarke, Brian, and Stuart Macdonald. *Leaving Christianity : Changing Allegiances in Canada*. Montreal: McGill-Queens University Press, 2017.

Clarke, Sundar. "Dalit Movement – Need for a Theology." In *Towards a Dalit Theology*, edited by M.E. Prabhakar, 30–34. Delhi: ISPCK, 1988.

———. *Let the Indian Church Be Indian*. Madras: The Christian Literature Society, 1980.

Clement of, Alexandria. "The Instructor." Translated by Alexander Roberts and James Donaldson. In *The Ante-Nicene Fathers: Translations of the Writings of the Fathers Down to A.D. 325*, edited by Alexander Roberts and James Donaldson. Buffalo, NY: The Christian Literature Publishing Company, 1885.

Collins, Paul M. *Christian Inculturation in India*. Aldershot: Ashgate, 2007.

Common Worship: Services and Prayers for the Church of England. London: Church House Publishing, 2000.

Coutts, Ian. "Books in Canada." In *Sex in the Snow: Canadian Social Values at the End of the Millenium*, edited by Michael Adams, 24. Toronto: Penguin Books, 1997.

Crockett, William R. *Eucharist: Symbol of Transformation*. New York: Pueblo Publishing, 1989.

———. "The Theology of the Eucharistic Prayers in the Book of Alternative Services of the Anglican Church of Canada." *Toronto Journal of Theology* 3, no. 1 (1987): 100–09.

Day, Juliette J. *Reading the Liturgy: An Exploration of Texts in Christian Worship*. London: Bloomsbury T & T Clark, 2014.

Dillstone, F. W. "Liturgical Forms in Word and Act." In *Language and the Worship of the Church*, edited by David Jasper and R.C.D. Jasper. New York: St. Martin's Press, 1990.

Donovan, Daniel. "Lex Orandi: The Christology of the Eucharistic Prayers of the Roman Rite." *Toronto Journal of Theology* 16, no. 1 (2000): 69–89.

Eucharistic Prayers, Services of the Word, and Night Prayer: Supplementary to the Book of Alternative Services. Toronto: ABC Publishing, 2001.

Fenwick, John, and Bryan Spinks. "South Indian Springboard." In *Worship in Transition*. New York: Continuum Publishing Company, 1995.

Ford, David, and Rachel Meurs, eds. *The Modern Theologians*. 3rd ed. Oxford: Blackwell Publishing Ltd., 2005.

Frei, Hans W. "Biblical Narrative in the Christian Tradition: Does It Stretch or Will It Break?." In *The Bible and the Narrative Tradition*, edited by Frank McConnell. New York: Oxford University Press, 1986.

———. *The Eclipse of Biblical Narrative*. London: Yale University Press, 1974.

———, ed. *H. Richard Niebuhr on History, Church and Nation*. Edited by Ronald F. Thiemann. Minneapolis, MN: Augsburg Fortress, 1981.

———. "How It All Began: On the Resurrection of Christ." *Anglican and Episcopal History* 58, no. 2 (1989): 139–45.

———. *The Identity of Jesus Christ: The Hermeneutical Bases of Dogmatic Theology*. Philadelphia: Fortress Press, 1975.

———. "'Narrative' in Christian and Modern Reading." In *Theology and Dialogue: Essays in Conversation with George Lindbeck*, edited by Bruce D. Marshall, 149–63. Notre Dame, IN: Univeristy of Notre Dame Press, 1990.

———. "Theological Reflections on the Accounts of Jesus' Death and Resurrection." In *Theology and Narrative: Selected Essays*, edited by George Hunsinger and William C. Placher, 45–93. New York: Oxford University Press, 1993.

———. *Theology and Narrative: Selected Essays*. Edited by George Hunsinger and William C. Placher. New York: Oxford University Press, 1993.

———. *Types of Christian Theology*. Edited by George Hunsinger and William C. Placher. New Haven, CT: Yale University Press, 1992.

Fulford, Ben. *Divine Eloquence and Human Transformation: Rethinking Scripture and History through Gregory of Nazianzus and Hans Frei*. Minneapolis, MN: Fortress Press, 2013.

Garrett, T. S. *Worship in the Church of South India*. London: Lutterworth Press, 1958.

Geertz, Clifford. *The Interpretation of Cultures*. New York: Basic Books, Inc., 1973.

Gibaut, John St. H. "The Narrative Nature of Liturgy." *Theoforum* 32, no. 3 (2001): 341–65.

Gibson, Paul. 23 April 2009.

Gitari, David, ed. *Anglican Liturgical Inculturation: The Kanamai Statement 'African Culture and Anglican Liturgy'* Vol. 28, Alcuin/Grow Liturgical Study. Bramcote: Grove Books Ltd., 1994.

Grant, John Webster. *Moon of Wintertime: Missionaries and Indians of Canada in Encounter since 1534*. Toronto: University of Toronto Press, 1984.

Greene, Colin J. D. *Christology in Cultural Perspective: Marking Out the Horizons*. Grand Rapids, MI: Wm. B. Eerdmans Pub., 2004.

Gribben, Robert. "The Formation of the Liturgy of the Church of South India." *Studia Liturgica* 30, no. 2 (2000): 129–42.

Guardini, Romano. "A Letter from Romano Guardini." *Herder Correspondence* 1, no. 8 (1964): 237–39.

Haight, Roger. *Jesus: Symbol of God*. Maryknoll, New York: Orbis Books, 1999.

Harris, Marvin. *Theories of Culture in Postmodern Times*. Walnut Creek, CA: Altamira Press, 1999.

Hauerwas, Stanley. *Resident Aliens: Life in the Christian Colony*. Nashville, TN: Abingdon, 1989.

Hawley, George. *Demography, Culture, and the Decline of America's Christian Denominations*. Lanham, MD: Lexington Books, 2017.

Herder, Johann Gottfried. *Against Pure Reason: Writing on Religion, Language and History*. Translated by Marcia Bunge. Minneapolis, MN: Augsburg Fortress Press, 1992.

Higton, Mike. *Christ, Providence and History*. London: T & T Clark International, 2004.

Hiller, Harry H. Review of *The Decline of Deference: Canadian Value Change in Cross-National Perspective* (Peterborough, Canada: Broadview Press, 1996), by Neil Nevitte. *Canadian Public Policy* 23, no. 1 (1997): 102–04.

Holeton, David R., ed. *Liturgical Inculturation in the Anglican Communion Including the York Statement 'Down to Earth Worship'* Vol. 15, Acluin/Grow Liturgical Study. Bramcote: Grove Books Ltd., 1990.

Hunsinger, George. "What Can Evangelicals and Postliberals Learn from Each Other? The Carl Henry/Hans Frei Exchange Reconsidered." *Pro Ecclesia* 5, no. 2 (1996): 161–82.

"Indigenous Ministries Anglican Church of Canada." http://www.anglican.ca/im/.

Jasper, R.C.D., and Paul F. Bradshaw. *A Companion to the Alternative Services Book*. London: SPCK, 1986.

Jasper, R.C.D., and G.J. Cuming. *Prayers of the Eucharist: Early and Reformed*. 3rd ed. New York: Pueblo Publishing Co., 1987.

Kennedy, David J. *Eucharistic Sacramentality in an Ecumenical Context: The Anglican Epiclesis*. Aldershot: Ashgate, 2008.

———. "A Kind of Liturgical Arcic? The Ecumenical Potential of the Four Eucharistic Prayers of Rite a in *the Alternative Services Book 1980*." *Scottish Journal of Theology* 44, no. 1 (1991): 57–72.

Kroeber, A.L., and Clyde Kluckhohn. *Culture: A Critical Review of Concepts and Definitions*. New York: Vintage Books, 1952.

LaSelva, W. *The Moral Foundations of Canadian Federalism: Paradoxes, Achievements, and Tragedies of Nationhood*. Montreal: McGill - Queens University Press, 1996.

Lathrop, Gordon W. "Eucharist in the New Testament and Its Cultural Settings." In *Worship and Culture in Dialogue: Reports of International Consultations, Cartigny Switzerland, 1993, Hong Kong, 1994*, edited by S. Anita Stauffer, 67–82. Geneva: Department for Theology and Studies, LWF, 1994.

Long, D. Stephen. *Theology and Culture: A Guide to the Discussion*. Eugene, OR: Cascade Books, 2008.

Lott, Eric J. *Worship in an Indian Context: Eight Inter-Cultural Liturgies*. Bangalore: United Theological College, 1986.

Loughlin, Gerard. "Following to the Letter: The Literal Use of Scripture." *Literature and Theology* 9, no. 4 (9 Feb. 2010 1995): 370–82.

———. *Telling God's Story: Bible, Church and Narrative Theology*. Cambridge: Cambridge University Press, 1996.

Lyon, David. "Introduction." In *Rethinking Church, State, and Modernity*, edited by David Lyon and Marguerite Van Die. Toronto: University of Toronto Press, 2000.

MacLennan, Hugh. *Two Solitudes*. 1st ed. Toronto: Collins, 1945.

Marshall, Paul. "Overview of Christ and Culture." In *Church and Canadian Culture*, edited by Robert E. VanderVennen. Lanham, MD: University Press of America, 1991.

Marshall, T. *Harsh and Lovely Land: The Major Canadian Poets and the Making of a Canadian Tradition*. Vancouver: University of British Columbia Press, 1979.

Mazza, Enrico. *The Eucharistic Prayers of the Roman Rite*. Translated by Matthew J. O'Connell. New York: Pueblo Publishers, 1986.

Merelman, R.M. "The American Review of Canadian Studies." In *The Decline of Deference: Canadian Value Change in Cross-National Perspective*, edited by Neil Nevitte, 531. Peterborough: Broadview Press, 1999.

Meyers, Ruth A. "One Bread, One Body: Ritual, Language and Symbolism in the Eucharist." In *Our Thanks and Praise: The Eucharist in Anglicanism Today*, edited by David R. Holeton. Toronto: Anglican Book Centre, 1998.

Moir, John S. *The Americanization of Religion in Canada*. Christianity in Canada: Historical Essays. Edited by Paul Laverdure. Yorkton: Redeemer's Voice Press, 2002.

———. *Canadian Religious Historiography: An Overview*. Christianity in Canada: Historical Essays. Edited by Paul Laverdure. Yorkton: Redeemer's Voice Press, 2002.

———. "The Canadianization of the Protestant Churches." In *Christianity in Canada: Historical Essays*, edited by Paul Laverdure. Yorkton: Redeemer's Voice Press, 2002.

Moltmann, J. *The Way of Jesus Christ: Christology in Messianic Dimensions*. London: SCM Press, 1990.

Morgan, Boyd. "An Historical and Ecclesiological Study of the Book of Alternative Services (1985) of the Anglican Church of Canada." ThD. thesis, Boston University, 2001.

Nevitte, Neil. *The Decline of Deference: Canadian Value Change in Cross-National Perspective*. Peterborough: Broadview Press, 1996.

A New Zealand Prayer Book, He Karakia Mihinare O Aotearoa. Auckland: William Collins Publishers Ltd., 1989.

Newman, Peter C. *The Canadian Revolution, 1985–1995: From Deference to Defiance*. Toronto: Viking, 1995.

Niebuhr, H. Richard. *Christ and Culture*. New York: Harper & Row, 1951.

O'Toole, Roger. *Anglicanism in Canada: A Sociological Sketch*. Canadian Anglicanism at the Dawn of a New Century. Edited by M. Darol Bryant. Lewiston, NY: E. Mellen Press, 2001.

———. "Religion in Canada: Its Development and Contemporary Situation." In *Religion and Canadian Society*, edited by Lori G. Beaman, 7–21. Toronto: Canadian Scholars Press, Inc., 2006.

"Official Statements of the Anglican Church of Canada – General Synod Resolution Re: Cinola Gold Project." http://qumran.national.anglican.ca/ics-wpd/Textbases/search/official/search.aspx.

"Official Statements of the Anglican Church of Canada – General Synod Resolution Re: Human Rights." http://qumran.national.anglican.ca/ics-wpd/Textbases/search/official/search.aspx.

"Official Statements of the Anglican Church of Canada – General Synod Resolution Re: Pollution." http://qumran.national.anglican.ca/ics-wpd/Textbases/search/official/search.aspx.

"Official Statements of the Anglican Church of Canada – General Synod Resolution Re: Poverty in Canada." http://qumran.national.anglican.ca/ics-wpd/Textbases/search/official/search.aspx.

"Official Statements of the Anglican Church of Canada – General Synod Resolution Re: Social Action Concerns." http://qumran.national.anglican.ca/ics-wpd/Textbases/search/official/search.aspx.

Pannenberg, W. *Basic Questions in Theology*. Translated by George H. Kehm and R.A. Wilson. Vol. 1. London: SCM Press, 1959.

Pears, Angie. *Doing Contextual Theology*. Abingdon: Routledge, 2010.

Pitt, W.E. "The Anamneses and Institution Narrative in the Apostolic Constitutions Book Viii." *The Journal of Ecclesiastical History* 9, no. 1 (1958): 1–7.

Powles, Cyril. "The Anglican Church in Canadian Culture." In *Church and Canadian Culture*, edited by Robert E. VanderVennen. Lanham, MD: University Press of America, 1991.

Prabhakar, M.E. "The Search for a Dalit Theology." In *Towards a Dalit Theology*, edited by M.E. Prabhakar, 35–47. Delhi: ISPCK, 1988.

Prasad, P.B. Ravi. "Dalit Theology: A Synpopsis." In *Towards a Dalit Theology*, edited by M.E. Prabhakar, 183–85. Delhi: ISPCK, 1988.

Reimer, Samuel H. *A Look at Cultural Effects on Religiosity: A Comparison between the United States and Canada*. Religion and Canadian Society. Edited by Lori G. Beaman. Toronto: Canadian Scholars Press, Inc., 2006.

Research, Nanos. "Exploring Canadian Values – Values Survey Summary," 2016.

Reynolds, Stephen. "Bas Evaluation: Some Theological Questions Responses'." In *Thinking About the Book of Alternative Services: A Discussion Primer*, 39–61. Toronto: The Anglican Church of Canada, 1993.

Saul, John Ralston. *A Fair Country: Telling Truths About Canada*. Toronto: Viking Canada, 2008.

Schreiter, Robert J. *Constructing Local Theologies*. Maryknoll, NY: Orbis, 1985.

Schweitzer, Don. *Contemporary Christologies: A Fortress Introduction*. Minneapolis, MN: Fortress Press, 2010.

Scott, Jamie, S. "Religion, Literature and Canadian Cultural Identities." *Literature and Theology* 16, no. 2 (2002): 113–26.

Shorter, Aylward. *Toward a Theology of Inculturation*. Maryknoll, NY: Orbis Books, 1988.

Shriver, Donald W. Jr. *H. Richard Niebuhr*. Nashville, TN: Abingdon Press, 2009.

Smith, James A. *Who's Afraid of Postmodernism?: Taking Derrida, Lyotard, and Foucault to Church*. Grand Rapids, MI: Baker Academic, 2006.

Stackhouse, John G., Jr. *Making the Best of It: Following Christ in the Real World*. New York: Oxford University Press, 2008.

Stassen, Glen H. "Concrete Christological Norms for Transformation." In *Authentic Transformation: A New Vision of Christ and Culture*, edited by D.M. Yeager and John Howard Yoder Glen H. Stassen. Nashville, TN: Abingdon Press, 1996.

Stauffer, S. Anita, ed. *Worship and Culture in Dialogue: Reports of International Consultations, Cartigny Switzerland, 1993, Hong Kong, 1994*. Geneva: Lutheran World Federation, 1994.

Stocking, George W., Jr. *Race, Culture and Evolution*. New York: The Free Press, 1968.

Stosur, David A. "Liturgy and (Post) Modernity: A Narrative Response to Guardini's Challenge." *Worship* 77, no. 1 (2003): 22–41.

Tanner, Kathryn. *Theories of Culture: A New Agenda for Theology*. Minneapolis, MN: Fortress Press, 1997.

Taylor, Charles. *A Secular Age*. New York: Belknap Press, 2007.

Tertullian. "The Apology." Translated by Alexander Roberts and James Donaldson. In *The Ante-Nicene Fathers: Translations of the Writings of the Fathers Down to A.D. 325*, edited by Alexander Roberts and James Donaldson. Buffalo, NY: The Christian Literature Publishing Company, 1885.

Thomsen, Robert C., and Nanette L. Hale. "Exploring Environments." In *Canadian Environments: Essays in Culture, Politics and History*, edited by Robert C. Thomsen and Nanette L. Hale. New York : P.I.E.-Peter Lang, 2005.

Tovey, Phillip. *Inculturation of Christian Worship: Exploring the Eucharist*. Aldershot: Ashgate, 2004.

Truth and Reconciliation Commission of Canada. *They Came for the Children: Canada, Aboriginal Peoples, and Residential Schools*. Winnipeg: Truth and Reconciliation Commission of Canada, 2012.

"The Truth Shall Make You Free: The Reports, Resolutions & Pastoral Letters from the Bishops." Paper presented at the Lambeth Conference, London, 1988.

Usher, Jean. *William Duncan of Metlakatla: A Victorian Missionary in British Columbia*. Ottawa: National Museums of Canada, 1974.

Uslaner, Eric M. Review of *The Decline of Deference: Canadian Value Change in Cross-National Perspective* (Peterborough, Canada: Broadview Press, 1996), by Neil Nevitte. *Canadian Journal of Political Science* 30, no. 2 (1997): 371–73.

Vanhoozer, Kevin J. *Biblical Narrative in the Philosophy of Paul Ricoeur*. Cambridge: Cambridge University Press, 1990.

Wade, Christopher. "'To Reveal the Riches of Your Grace': Examining the Authorized Eucharistic Christologies of the Episcopal Church with Implications." Graduate Theological Union, 2009.

Wainwright, Geoffrey. *Doxology: The Praise of God in Worship, Doctrine and Life: A Systematic Theology*. New York: Oxford University Press, 1980.

Wallace, Mark I. *The Second Naiveté: Barth, Ricoeur and the New Yale Theology*. Macon, GA: Mercer University Press, 1990.

Ward, Graham. *Christ and Culture*. Oxford: Blackwell Publishing, 2005.

Ward, Jim. "Community Action." In *Sex in the Snow: Canadian Social Values at the End of the Millenium*, edited by Michael Adams, 7. Toronto: Penguin Books, 1997.

Watson, Francis. *Text, Church and World: Biblical Interpretation in Theological Perspective*. Grand Rapids, MI: Eerdmans Publishing, 1994.

Webster, John. "Bas and Bcp: Some Thoughts on a Theological Shift." In *Thinking About the Book of Alternative Services: A Discussion Primer*. Toronto: Anglican Book Centre, 1993.

Weil, Louis. "Proclamation of Faith in the Eucharist." In *Time and Community: In Honor of Thomas Julian Talley*, edited by J. Neil Alexander, 279–90. Washington, DC: The Pastoral Press, 1990.

Westhues, Kenneth. "Conrad Grebel Review." In *Fragmented Gods: The Poverty and Potential of Religion in Canada*, edited by Reginald W. Bibby, 85–87. Toronto: Irwin, 1988.

Woolverton, John F. "Hans W. Frei in Context: A Theological and Historical Memoir." *Anglican Theological Review* 79, no. 3 Sum (10 Feb. 2010 1997): 369–93.

World Council of Churches. "Nairobi Statement on Worship and Culture: Contemporary Challenges and Opportunities." *International Review of Mission* 85, no. 337 (1996): 184–88.

Yeager, D.M. "The View from Somewhere: The Meaning of Method in *Christ and Culture*." *Journal of the Society of Christian Ethics* 23, no. 1 (2003): 101–20.

Yoder, John Howard. "How H. Richard Niebuhr Reasoned: A Critique of *Christ and Culture*." In *Authentic Transformation: A New Vision of Christ and Culture*, edited by D. M. Yeager and John Howard Yoder Glen H. Stassen. Nashvill, TN: Abingdon Press, 1996.

Index

Adams, Michael–3SC Values Monitor, 161–62
Anglican Church of Canada, 2, 6, 8, 10–12, 15, 18n3, 28, 46, 57–69, 73–74, 77n82, 79n119, 80n130, 80n136, 116, 127, 130–31, 143, 151–55, 159, 165–67, 170, 175–76, 183–84; Eucharistic Prayers of, 63–73, 130–31, 135–37, 141n103, 143–55
Anglican Church of Kenya, 125–26
Anglican Communion, 15, 126, 183
Anglican liturgy post-Vatican II, 127–28; Anglican Church of Canada, 130–31; Church of England, 128–30; Church of the Province of New Zealand, 131–33
Antiochene structure, 12, 17, 64, 67, 137, 158, 170, 184
Auerbach, Erich, 13, 84, 89–90, 94, 104
Azevedo, M. de C., 43

Bibby, Reginald, 4
Burton, Pierre, 4, 5, 8

Canadian national census, 2
Christology, 2, 7–8, 12–14, 16, 18, 55, 58, 74, 81–83, 85–87, 97–100, 105–8, 116, 119, 134, 138, 143–54, 159, 161, 164, 168–69, 174–76, 180–84; in Canadian Anglican Eucharistic prayers, 143–55
Chupungco, Anscar, 10, 43, 128
Churches in Canada, 2, 4, 59, 160
Church of South India, 122–25
The Comfortable Pew, 4
Crockett, William, 16, 67, 130–31, 145, 151, 183
culture, Canadian, 4–6, 16–17, 43, 46–47, 53, 60–62, 66; concept of, 20–24; contemporary (postmodern), 159–65; local, 25–27; semiotic description of, 26–30; social values, 165–69

Diocese of Toronto, 5

emic, 9, 26–27, 38, 53
etic, 9, 27, 38, 53, 95
Eucharistic liturgies, 6, 116, 127, 166; Eucharistic Prayers of, 43, 47, 63–64, 66–73

figural, 13, 84, 87, 89–91, 94, 104, 108–09, 145–49, 151–54, 159, 172, 176, 182–83
Fragmented Gods: The Poverty and Potential of Religion in Canada, 4, 74n1
Frei, Hans, 12–14, 81–108; figural interpretation, 89–91; hermeneutical

201

principles, 85–87; providential ordering of history, 94–97; realistic narrative, 87–89; sensus literalis, 91–94; typology, 85–86
Frei-inspired Christology, 97–108

Geertz, Clifford, 9, 23, 29–30, 31n39, 40
General Social Survey, 3
Gibson, Paul, 143–44
Guardini, Romano, 118; David Stosur's response to, 118–19

Haight, Roger, 16, 143, 169
Haight's three criteria, 17, 144, 155, 159, 176, 183; Empowerment of the Christian life, 144, 169, 176; faithfulness to the tradition, 144–45; intelligibility in today's world, 16, 144, 159, 183
Hawley, George, 3
"history-like", 14, 88, 96–97, 104, 107
Hunsinger, George, 14, 99, 105
hybridity, 47

inculturation, 10–12, 15–17, 40–43, 63, 116, 119–27, 131, 133, 136–38, 159, 180–81, 183; liturgical postmodern inculturation, 133–38

Jesus Christ, 1–2, 7–9, 12–15, 17, 30, 35, 38–44, 48–53, 63, 73–74, 81–82, 86–89, 94, 97–100, 104–109, 117–19, 124, 134, 144–152, 154, 158–9, 166–70, 173–76, 180–84, 189

Kanamai statement, 127, 170
Karl Barth, 7, 12–13, 82–85, 89, 91, 94, 97, 103

Local culture, 6, 8, 10, 12, 16, 18, 20, 25–30, 38, 42, 46–48, 57–58, 61, 66, 73, 81, 109, 117, 120–22, 125, 131–33, 137, 159–61, 163, 165, 167–69, 172, 174, 176, 180–81, 183–84

narrative, 116–20
National Household Survey (NHS), 3
Nevitte, Neil–World Values Survey, 162–64
Niebuhr, H. Richard, 10–12, 46–56, 76n61, 82–84, 149, 152, 154–55, 167, 183; Niebuhr's typologies, 11, 15–16, 49–56
No religion, 3

Pew Research Center, 3
Powles, Cyril, 54, 60

Reflexive (reflexivity), 10, 12, 17, 28, 40–44, 57, 64, 73–74, 81, 109, 117, 120, 126, 133, 138, 144, 159–60, 166–67, 175, 181, 184
Ryle, Gilbert, 29, 85

Schreiter, Robert, 25–28, 34–39, 42, 181
semiotic(s), 9–10, 20, 25–30, 39, 57, 87, 93, 108, 180
Shorter, Aylard, 10, 41, 43
survey, 1980 *Project Canada*, 5

Tanner, Kathryn, 9, 24, 37
theology, contextual, 34–38, 40, 43

United States of America, 3–5, 33, 59–61, 124
unsubstitutable, 7, 12, 82, 87–88, 102–3, 107, 147

Vatican II, 15, 41, 43, 116, 120, 127, 129, 138n17

Yoder, John Howard, 53, 55, 76n61

About the Author

Bishop **Donald D. Phillips**, PhD, was born, raised, and educated in London, Ontario, Canada, obtaining an MSc in chemistry from Western University and an MDiv degree at Huron University College and commencing ordained ministry in the Anglican Church of Canada in 1981. In 2000, he was elected as the twelfth bishop of the Diocese of Rupert's Land centered in Winnipeg, Manitoba.

Having a keen interest in the development of new forms of local ministry, he has presented at workshops and conferences in Canada, the United States, and Great Britain. He completed a PhD from Durham University, UK, in contextual theology in 2016. Since retiring from full-time episcopal ministry in 2018, he has published a book review, presented two conference papers in Christology, and developed and taught university courses in liturgical theology and contextual theology.

He is married to Nancy Phillips, a retired occupational health nurse, spiritual director, and adult educator.

www.ingramcontent.com/pod-product-compliance
Lightning Source LLC
Chambersburg PA
CBHW030735100425
24897CB00002B/69